JFK Jr.—Marked For Death

'The Murder of America's Prince'

Damon Ise, Gary Fannin & Tim Brennan

JFK Jr.—Marked For Death may be purchased in bulk at special discounts for educational purposes. For conferences or guest speaking on this book or topic, please contact the authors at: jfkbooks1963@yahoo.com.

Visit our website at www.thejfkassassination.com.

Library of Congress Cataloging-in-Publication Data is available on file.
ISBN: 979-8-9883705-1-2

Printed by Square Publishing Coconut Creek, FL.

JFK Jr.—Marked For Death

'The Murder of America's Prince'

This book is lovingly dedicated to my biggest supporter.

My wife, Ann Marie.

And our children Zachary & Caroline.

May the truth, printed within this book,
come out in their lifetime by the U.S. Government

Gary Fannin—July 2023

This book is dedicated to people who have lived and died subjugated to oppressive governments throughout the history of the world. I may die someday still advocating my firm belief that the U.S. government was behind the killings of John F. Kennedy, his Brother Robert F. Kennedy, JFK's son John F. Kennedy, Jr. and many others. Albert Einstein said, "Three great forces rule the world: stupidity, fear and greed." I would add a fourth, the inestimable, unquenchable, relentless quest for power. We've all heard the saying that power corrupts, and absolute power corrupts absolutely. That is what has happened to our government and our country in the last sixty or so years. There are dark forces within our own government that will continue to control and manipulate every aspect of American life. The great Libertarian and American Neal Boortz often remarked that once the Government takes something away, they'll never give it back. Want proof? The federal income tax which was supposed to be temporary. President Abraham Lincoln signed into law the first income tax – The Revenue Act of 1862 – appointing George S. Boutwell to the office of Commissioner of Internal Revenue. The Act was passed as an emergency and temporary measure to help fund the war, and it was supposed to terminate in 1866!

I am now classified as being "elderly," but I have a passion and burning desire to see our beloved country revert back to the days when we trusted those we elected into government, when politicians – regardless of political affiliation – worked together for the good of the American people who elected them to office. These books I help write with my talented, passionate co-authors are indicative of our burning desire for the truth to finally be known, for the American public to one day be ruled by leaders who have the best interests of the people they serve at heart, God willing.

Messrs. Fannin and Ise, I salute you!

Tim Brennan   July, 2023

<u>Acknowledgements</u>

Mr. Saint John Hunt for his generous contributions to John's Biography.

Mr. Truly Ott for having the courage to step forward and share the truth.

Mr. Adam Budd for having the courage to do a live interview.

My mother Mary Ise, school teacher, for keeping me indoors one entire summer vacation so I could learn to write.

Mr. Robin Foote for teaching me all the skills needed to write and publish.

Mr. Kris Milligan for honest unbiased guidance and advice.

Ms. Lorien Fenton for her undying support and talk show opportunities.

Mr. Bruce De Torres for his endless quest for the truth and phenomenal radio shows.

Judyth Baker and the board members of the Dallas Conference who let me take the stage in sharing my research.

To Sabbie Ludovici and Frankie Sutton for teaching me a flight standard above the rest.

My co-authors Gary and Tim for making the final production of this work possible.

Ms. Victoria Sulzer for being my in-house sounding board and editor.

And finally, John Kennedy Jr. for being himself, working hard at everything he did, and trying to better the world we live in.

Damon Ise—July 2023

"I tell myself that God gave my children many gifts—spirit, beauty, intelligence, the capacity to make friends and to inspire respect. There was only one gift he held back—length of life."

Rose Kennedy

Damon Ise's Aviation biography:

Damon's aviation interests and career have spanned more than 40 years. After earning his private pilot's rating in July of 1977, Damon went on to receive the ratings of commercial pilot, instrument pilot, and flight instructor. Southern New England based, many of his training flights were flown to Martha's Vineyard and Nantucket under both visual and instrument flight conditions.

He worked for the State of Rhode Island as an airport attendant and traffic advisor at North Central State Airport. He was a founding Father of the Quonset Air Museum and served as the organization's president for several years.

In 1994 Damon led the salvage team who recovered A Us Navy F6F Hellcat off the waters of Martha's Vineyard. As a local aviation professional Damon was solicited by the Providence journal shortly after the terrible death of John Kennedy Jr., his wife Carolyn, and her sister Lauren.

Having no reason to doubt the official story Damon lent a "boiler plate" opinion of the circumstances surrounding the so-called accident. Just casual remarks with no real research. Opinion without study of the facts.

Twelve years later, while digging through a closet, Damon found the faded yellow Sunday edition of The Providence Journal. Damon re-read the quotes which had made the front page. Damon began his research after questioning the accuracy of the original "Official Story" regarding John's death. He is still uncovering the roots of deception fed to the world publicly regarding the demise of a skilled pilot and truly dynamic and charismatic individual, John Kennedy Jr.

John did not die by accident.

Gary Fannin Biography

Gary has been studying the JFK and political assassinations of the 1960's since 1980. Primarily using microfilm and dated newspapers, he originally thought Oswald was guilty of killing the President with an accomplice. He reached this conclusion based upon eyewitness testimony of shots from different locations other than the Texas School Book Depository. This all changed with his first trip to Dallas, Texas in 1987.

Before the 6th Floor Museum, Gary was actually standing in the alleged 'sniper's nest' and his viewpoints completely changed. This all started with a phone call and interview of Jim Leavelle. As the lead detective, Jim informed Gary that had they gone to trial on the evidence the DPD had collected on Oswald up until the time of his death, "he would have never been found guilty."

This first interview would lead to hundreds more with Drs., eyewitnesses, CIA, FBI, morticians, and fellow researchers including:

Dr. Charles Crenshaw, Dr. Robert McClelland, Dr. Paul Peters, Robert Groden, Autopsy personnel Paul O'Connor, Dennis David and Jim Jenkins, JFK Honor Guard members, Tom Robinson who embalmed JFK and Paul Groody who embalmed Oswald, LBJ Attorney Barr McClellan, Billie Sol Estes, Douglas Caddy, Roger Stone, J. Gary Shaw, Mark Lane, Jim Marrs, Phil Singer and even Marina Oswald Porter.

Gary has spoken at numerous conferences in Dallas since 1993. He has also spoken at conferences in New Orleans, Chicago, Los Angeles, and Washington D.C.

Gary is an avid sports fan including University of Kentucky basketball, the Atlanta Braves, and the Minnesota Vikings. He enjoys travel, golf, and spending time with his family. He currently lives in Florida.

Gary is the co-author of four books, 'The Innocence of Oswald, 2nd Edition,' 'JFK-Marked For Death,' 'RFK-Marked For Death' and 'JFK Jr.-Marked For Death and is currently working on his fifth book, 'Operation Mockingbird' which details how the CIA has influenced the Media over the past 70 years.

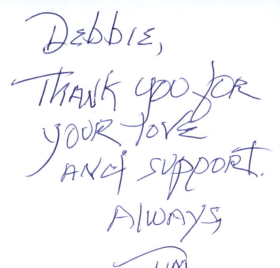

Tim Brennan Biography

Author Tim Brennan's interest in the JFK assassination (and other political murders) began shortly after November 22nd, 1963. Tim was born in Cleveland, Ohio, into an Irish, Catholic, Democratic family with politicians on both sides of the house. When he first saw Lyndon Johnson, shortly after the assassination, he said to his Mother, "I don't trust that man!" Aghast, she asked why. He replied, "He looks evil!" Quite the prescient comment for a precocious eleven-year-old!

Decades later, now in Atlanta, GA, Tim struck up a lifelong friendship with author Gary Fannin, and since 1994 their combined interest in these events has resulted in four books: The Innocence of Oswald (2nd edition), JFK – Marked for Death, RFK – Marked for Death, and JFK, Jr. - Marked for Death (with author Damon Ise). A fifth Fannin/Brennan collaboration, Operation Mockingbird will be published later this year. Tim is also the co-writer, appears in, and is the narrator of the documentary film, 'The Innocence of Oswald' DVD, with co-writer Gary Fannin. Future books on MLK, Malcolm X and others are being planned.

A baseball enthusiast at a young age, Tim is now an ardent Atlanta Braves fan. He does voiceovers, enjoys travel, music, movies and writing. He and Mr. Fannin are readily available – and thoroughly enjoy – book signings, presentations, discussions and the like. www.thejfkassassination.com

One

<u>Introduction</u>

The untimely death of John Kennedy Jr., his pregnant wife Carolyn Bessette and her sister Lauren Bessette saddened people worldwide. The aftereffects of that horrific event are felt every July 16th, the anniversary of their deaths. The story of the final chapter of Camelot has been told countless times. Periodicals, tabloids and all forms of media continue to keep the legend of John Jr. alive for an adoring world of worshipers who still find it hard to believe he was taken from them so prematurely.

Continually harassed by photographers and paparazzi, the Kennedy's wanted little more than security, privacy, and respect. John developed a keen interest in aviation at a very young age. It gave him release. It was where he went to feel solitude and reward. The privacy of his airplane afforded he and his family an oasis from the pressure of constant observation by onlookers and admirers.

John was the king at the controls of his meticulously maintained airplane. He was a well-trained and competent pilot. In the air, he was in complete control of all the factors that tugged at him daily. He could silence his internal voice and focus on one thing, the beauty and majesty of flight.

This overwhelming sense of freedom and sacred isolation would later prove to be the very vulnerability exploited by those who needed John removed from the picture.

The 'Official Story' regarding his aircraft's plunge into the Atlantic was nothing more than a deliberate whitewash of the event intended to keep the sinister forces behind the murders safely hidden behind the scenes.

To quote Dr. Judy Wood who wrote "Where Did the Towers Go?" by far, the best book written about the events of 9/11, "Examine the evidence and only the evidence and the story will tell itself."

It is our hope that this book provides the reader with deeper insight and greater clarity regarding the chain of events that led to the demise of John Jr. and his passengers on that fateful night in July of 1999.

A multitude of books have been written about John Kennedy Jr., most regarding his life, relationships, and perceived personal faults. A few books have dared to address the possibility that 'America's Golden Prince' met his fate at the hands of murderers, most containing inaccurate and incompetent accounts of the events that unfolded that fateful night.

Our book has been eight years in the making. Initially author Damon Ise felt the book would be late to market and the facts exposed by other writers. What appeared to be a liability ultimately became an asset. A former flight instructor and present-day commercial pilot who has logged hundreds of hours flying into Martha's Vineyard, Ise brings his aviation expertise into focus on one of the most memorable nights in aviation history. He provides a step-by-step analysis of the actual conditions and circumstances which led to the fabricated, "Official Story."

When the preponderance of evidence tilted the legal scales toward homicide Ise contacted noted Kennedy assassination researchers and authors Gary Fannin and Tim Brennan. With renewed and increased focus and energy, the three authors brought this final manuscript to fruition. The evidence compiled in this book is the most technical, comprehensive, and competent representation of the events that led to the death of four innocent people. The truths are scarce, intentionally hidden behind a plethora of lies, allegations, and aberrations surrounding the untimely passing of America's Golden Prince and his family. There is no greater loss than termination of life.

Read the book thoroughly, digest the evidence, then reach your own conclusions about "The Official Story." It never happened as described, and so far, they're sitting in the shadows, smug and satisfied they made it happen without being held accountable.

Two

<u>Growing Up Kennedy</u>

For John F. Kennedy Jr., life seemed to be following a script written by anonymous authors, a curious and ultimately lethal force guiding him to an inevitable conclusion. Unknowingly, he was embroiled within a previously scripted role in an epic and unchangeable play, with no understudy and no escape. No matter what he tried, no matter what he said, no matter what he wanted, his purpose in life was predetermined. This malevolent force shaped his life and ensured that he would fulfill his destiny. He was, for the most part, an unwilling participant in a screenplay that had long ago decided his fate. John F. Kennedy Jr. was trapped in an unalterable story that hung over him his entire life like a phantom in the dark. In the revered history of White House occupants, John was the first child born to a sitting President. On November 25, 1960, two births came to pass. One birth was President John F. Kennedy's first-born son, John F. Kennedy Jr. The other was the unforeseen fate that would hover above John, Jr. for his entire life and ultimately lead him to his demise.

It was a new era, a new beginning for America. With high hopes and unfailing trust, America had affectionately christened the new Kennedy administration with the sobriquet 'Camelot', and John Jr. anointed as its first Prince. Within the walls of this fairy tale castle, he would run and play, nary a care in the world, unknowing of the forces which some day would present him with the only choice he ever had, to return to this magical kingdom as its King, as President of the United States. In the 1990's, the Kennedy legacy remained viable, its mystery, tragedy, and magic still resonating and poignant for many Americans, Democrats and liberal Republicans alike. Camelot's promise remained unfulfilled, and the most important goals of the Kennedy administration were cut short on November 22, 1963. For the next several decades, John F. Kennedy's murder was the exclamation mark indelibly stamped by sinister forces determined with unchecked power and cavalier viciousness that a Kennedy would never again occupy the White House. Nevertheless, in the minds of many Americans JFK, Jr. seemed destined to become President, none of them aware of the horror that would ultimately unfold.

President Elect Kennedy, Jackie & John Jr.

This was the force that decided John Jr.'s purpose, the unseen author, the uninvited partner, the fate that allowed no alternative. Despite his reluctance to enter the political arena, he eventually bowed to the overwhelming idea that this was his destiny.

There is little doubt that had he run for Senator of New York state, he would have won. Accordingly, had he sought the Democratic nomination for President, he likely would have won, and perhaps recaptured the magic of his Father's administration those many years before. However, JFK's ascent to the Presidency was not without blemish.

Jack Kennedy became President of the United States through collusion and fraud. This is irrefutable. A deal was brokered with the devil. With the promise of unfettered access to the White House, Joseph P. Kennedy had enlisted the help of two notorious individuals, Chicago Mayor Richard Daley, and Chicago Mafia boss Sam Giancana. In November 1960, the night of the election, while the votes of 69 million Americans were being counted, the Presidency hung on the balance of votes from Illinois. According to Washington Post editor Ben Bradlee, JFK placed a late-night call to family friend and Mayor of Chicago, Richard Daley. When Daley answered the call, he addressed Jack as "Mr. President" and said, "with a little bit of luck and the help of a few close friends, you're going to carry Illinois." Daley supplied 10,000 votes from Cook County, a Ward he controlled. The votes were held back until needed, and as history would show, they were needed. The margin was razor thin, 8,585 votes going, at the last minute, to Kennedy. Daley used all the tricks to add the required votes: tombstone names, spoiling Republican ballots, and tallying votes from those who had once lived on streets bulldozed out of existence by city redevelopment. (1)

Crime boss Sam 'Momo' Giancana had a great deal of political power in Chicago. He bragged to Judith Campbell, the mistress he shared with JFK, that "if it wasn't for me, your boyfriend wouldn't even be in the White House."

The Chicago Tribune stated that "the election of November 8, 1960, was characterized by such gross and palpable fraud as to justify the conclusion that Nixon was deprived of victory." Even J. Edgar Hoover, longtime Director of the FBI, complained to friend and editor of the Newark Star Ledger, that as far as he was concerned, Kennedy "is not the President-elect."

Hoover bitterly complained that Eisenhower and Nixon had prevented him from opening an investigation into election fraud. Although Nixon knew the Presidency had been stolen from him to his credit, he would not challenge Kennedy. In his mind, America needed unification and he chose the higher road, putting the welfare of the country ahead of his own personal gain. (2)

Richard Nixon (with Pat) conceding 1960 election to JFK.

Life for JFK, Jr. didn't begin easily. He was born prematurely, requiring Jackie to undergo a cesarean procedure. Like many premature infant's baby John had respiratory complications. He spent the first six days of his fragile life in an incubator, due to inflammation in his lung's membrane. His condition was listed as 'an undiagnosed respiratory ailment.' According to the National Center for Biotechnology Information and the American Journal of Obstetrics and Gynecology, the perinatal impact of amphetamine use shows a higher risk of premature birth, coupled with lung and respiratory problems for the fetus.

It's known that JFK was being injected with amphetamines throughout much of his life by his physician, but what about Jackie? According to New York Times Best Selling author Christopher Anderson, Jackie was receiving the same treatment. In his book, 'The Good Son,' Anderson recounts that during the inaugural balls following her husband's swearing in, Jackie had run out of energy and retreated to the Queens Bedroom in the White House. Dr. Max Jacobson had been injecting JFK, Jackie, and several members of the Kennedy inner circle with amphetamines. Dr. Janet Travell, JFK's personal physician, was sent up to the bedroom where Jackie was and supplied her with tablets of Dexedrine. An hour later Jackie appeared glowing and full of energy, able to attend her husband's inaugural balls. By the time of the fourth ball, the effects of the Dexedrine had worn off and once again Jackie nearly collapsed. "It was like Cinderella and the clock striking midnight. I just crumbled," she said. "All my strength was finally gone." (3)

One wonders if her use of amphetamines could have produced the lung infection and premature birth that almost cost John's life. At that time however, the relationship between amphetamines and those specific medical complications were

Jackie and JFK at one of the many Inaugural events, January 20, 1961.

unknown. This same respiratory condition would later claim the life of John's infant brother, Patrick. In a study by the Institute of Forensic Science by Judith L. Stewart and James E. Meeker, amphetamine use during pregnancy can result in stillborn births and spontaneous abortion in the second trimester and premature birth in the third trimester. (4 & 5)

On August 23, 1956 a pregnant Jackie collapsed, and doctors performed an emergency cesarean section to try and save the baby. The girl was stillborn, and Jackie had to undergo several blood transfusions while she lay in critical condition.

On August 7, 1963, Jackie went into labor five weeks before her baby was due. The baby, named Patrick, lived for forty hours in an incubator, and died on August 9, 1963. During the 1950's and 1960's, amphetamine and methamphetamine were viewed as 'utilitarian drugs' that working class and upper middle-class individuals would use as an antidepressant, to lose weight, to increase their energy, and to meet performance and endurance goals. There is no fault to be found in Jackie's use of this drug, although it's sad to imagine that these two Kennedy children may have lived.

Dr. Max Jacobson (aka Dr. Feelgood).

For husband Jack, his use and addiction to amphetamines produced a well-known side effect: hypersexual arousal. According to the Diagnostic and Statistical Manual of Mental Disorders, also known as the DSM, a major side effect of amphetamine use is hypersexuality. Most men who use amphetamines become so over-stimulated that the need to engage in sex is overwhelming. This could certainly account for

JFK's well-known addiction to sex and his unquenchable need for sex partners. It would also explain why he risked everything in the pursuit of sexual gratification. For JFK, the drug took control of his senses and fueled his womanizing, risking his Presidency, his family, and his reputation. It became such a problem that his brother Bobby was constantly covering up these messy, sordid encounters. Even FBI Director J. Edgar Hoover, never a Kennedy fan, alerted Bobby on numerous occasions of the dangers and risks that Jack was taking. On several occasions JFK had dalliances with a glamorous Soviet agent and a Mafia mistress.

The man responsible for Jackie and JFK's amphetamine use was Max Jacobson, also known as 'Dr. Feelgood.' Born in Berlin in 1900, he fled Nazi Germany in 1936. JFK met Jacobson through an introduction by Chuck Spalding, his friend from Harvard. Jacobson treated JFK with an injection of amphetamines prior to the Nixon-Kennedy debate. He accompanied JFK on Air Force One to Vienna and Paris. JFK received an injection every morning and sometimes twice during the summit with Nikita Khrushchev. After that, Jacobson stayed on call around the clock and was given a code name 'Mrs. Dunn.' White House records show that during 1961 and 1962, he visited the President and the First Lady more than thirty times at the White House. Pilot and photographer Mark Shaw flew the good doctor many times to Hyannis Port and Palm Beach. When brother Bobby criticized the doctor, JFK exclaimed, "I don't care if it's horse piss, it's the only thing that works." (6)

Although JFK's womanizing was well known to Jackie and many members of the press, it remained a taboo subject, not to be reported on. The image of Camelot was not to be tainted. This was the power of Camelot. John was born into this world, and thirty some years later, the power still held, beckoning him to return. As we will see, this force manifested itself in many ways, several which the government and media used to explain the circumstances surrounding his death. His daredevil and reckless nature, his need to challenge himself and push the limits regardless of safety. These were all part of the Kennedy mystique. The myth of the Kennedy's, and the mention of the 'Kennedy curse,' would play a huge part in explaining John's death. But for now, he was just a child, and enjoyed childish things.

After Jackie's recuperation, she forged ahead full steam, converting sections of the White House into areas where she and the children would feel more comfortable. She disliked the grand emptiness of the White House and set up a school on the third floor which was attended by Caroline, children of friends and White House staffers. "I want my children to be brought up in more personal surroundings" she insisted, "and I don't want them raised by nurses and Secret Service agents." Next, she designed an outdoor play area just outside of the President's Oval Office window. Outfitted with a slide, a leather swing, a barrel tunnel, a rabbit hutch, and a trampoline, she surrounded it with trees to insure some privacy from the Secret Service detail. As if that weren't enough, she had a tree house with a slide built in Herbert Hoover's favorite white oak tree. There is much to credit Jackie's insistence that her children be brought up in the most normal conditions possible.

To a Presidential family 'normal' was quite different from most, but to Jackie it meant that she wanted to raise her children without media intrusion, without an overbearing Secret Service presence. Although her husband was President of the United States, she loved that Jack took time to play with both children several times each day. The children would play quietly during

JFK with Caroline and John, Halloween 1963.

staff meetings in the Oval Office, and when they got too rambunctious Jack would call their nanny to take the children out.

It was during the late summer and fall months that John Jr. became enthralled with airplanes. He especially loved JFK's White House helicopter and watched with fascination and excitement as it took off and landed on the White House lawn. Jack soon started allowing John to sit in the pilot's seat and move the controls as it sat parked in its hanger.

John was given the nickname 'helicopter head' after the President saw him twirling around, arms flailing like helicopter blades and making helicopter sounds! John's most cherished toy was a small plastic airplane that Jack had given him, promising his son that one day he would buy him a real one. Sadly, Jack

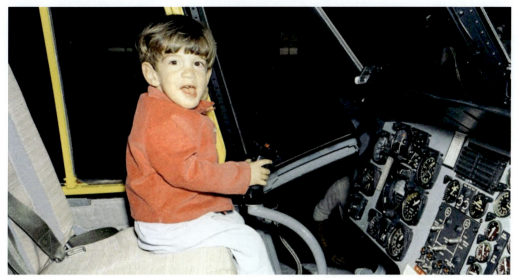
JFK Jr. sitting in Marine One.

would never live to fulfill the promise. The horrific events that took place in Dealey Plaza on November 22, 1963, would forever end all considerations normally ascribed to 'normal.'

The Warren Commission ruled that JFK's assassin, Lee Harvey Oswald, acted alone and was not connected in any way with any intelligence arm of the United States Government. After years of research by hundreds of scholars, we now know that John Kennedy Jr.'s father was killed as the result of a conspiracy. One week after JFK's death, Jackie and Bobby Kennedy confided to friend William Walton that they believed Dallas was the work of a high-level domestic plot. Later, Walton was given a letter written by Jackie and Bobby to be delivered to Georgi Bolshakov, a Soviet journalist who'd served as a back channel between the Kennedy administration and the Soviet government.

The letter stated that they knew JFK had been killed by his enemies within the U.S. Government as part of a domestic conspiracy. Walton conveyed the Kennedy family's belief that JFK had not been the victim of a Soviet or Cuban plot, which LBJ had initially been intimating to the Warren Commission before switching gears and directing them to rule that Oswald acted alone. (7) In fact, the official verdict by the United States House of Representatives Select Committee on Assassinations (HSCA) in 1978, concluded that JFK was assassinated as a result of a conspiracy.

Jackie with family friend, William Walton.

Years later, the adult John Kennedy Jr. would secretly make inquiries into his father's death. "Sometimes I can't remember what really happened, and what I saw in pictures." His words are easily understood. They are honest. For the Kennedy myth, it would have been romantic if John, as an adult, remembered saluting his dead father at the funeral procession. It would somehow raise his stature to even greater proportions. Having to carry the memory, the pain, the loss, and the fear in that tiny little boy, for all those years into manhood is fitting for a Kennedy. Because somehow, with all the sadness and death within their family, they still looked at humanity with hope and wonderment. They advocated and cared for the common man.

There is no question that the Kennedy's came from a wealthy and privileged background. It is also without question that they regarded themselves as protectors of the rights and liberties of the common folk. They were blessed with a life of privilege and sought to use their status and position to represent those less fortunate. There is a quote often used by both JFK and JFK Jr. that goes, "To those whom much is given, much is required." It was a noble calling, and it was just as much a part of the myth as the rest of the Kennedy mystique. Yet people felt that despite their money, they stood for what was moral, righteous and just in America. The myth always triumphs. The truth is much less romantic. Given the choice, the adoring public always chose to believe in Camelot. They wouldn't have it any other way.

The President and First Lady were young, glamorous, and exciting. After the likes of Eisenhower, Truman and FDR, the handsome, attractive, vibrant Kennedy's represented promise for the future.

When that dream ended in Dallas, it seemed all hope was gone. It wasn't until RFK ran for President in 1968 that the dream burst into life again. Again, sadly, inexplicably this dream was also struck down, and retreated into the shadows. It was this sense of unfulfilled promise that haunted John his entire life. He understood his place as the torch bearer of the Kennedy promise. Everyone knew it was his destiny to resurrect the Kennedy promise and lead America to its rightful place of glory. The world watched as the little boy slowly grew into young manhood.

In 1963, John John, as the press called him, did his best to support the Kennedy image. For that little boy to salute his father's casket was beyond every photographer's dream. It spoke with words beyond description and broke hearts around the world. Something so important, so poignant, had to have come from greatness, even at three years of age. "I've seen that photograph so many times, and I'd like to say I remember that moment," he would say years later. "But I don't." On the day of

JFK Jr. saluting his father's coffin, November 25, 1963.

his father's funeral, he would turn three and like many three-year-old boys, spent his day in a happy, carefree mood, opening presents and blowing out the three little candles on his birthday cake. John and his sister Caroline celebrated Birthdays together, him being born on November 25, and her on November 27, three years earlier. Despite the all-too-recent tragedy, their gifts were abundant and beautifully wrapped, and the children were delighted opening them and enjoying the day's festivities. In another week, they would move out of the White House and many precious memories would float dreamily into the past.

Caroline kissing John just after her 3rd birthday.

With all the strain of her husband's murder, a funeral she could never have imagined, and the seemingly endless official duties a widowed First Lady had to attend to, the magic potions of Dr. Feelgood were in high demand. Jackie was on the brink of complete physical and emotional exhaustion. She had barely gotten any sleep since that horrible day, staying up nights writing and rewriting a five-page letter to her dead husband. She cried until she could cry no more, and still she shook uncontrollably. Yet as each day began, she somehow pulled herself together for the children. In a sense, the children were her rock, and she would not let them see her fall apart. So, she called for the good Doctor Jacobson. She welcomed his injections of amphetamines, knowing that this was the only way she could make it through the day. Jacobson stayed nearby, and she summoned him often. "I was there when she needed me," he would say later, "and she needed me quite a lot." (8)

Sometime after Thanksgiving, Jackie invited Ted White of LIFE magazine to commemorate her recollections of that horrible day. This was unusual, because Jackie had been so guarded in the past, always protecting her and the children's privacy. This time she didn't hold back and gave her all for the interview. There was another reason she needed the LIFE article. She wanted to leave the American people with a lasting sense that there would be other great Presidents again, but there would never, ever be another Camelot. It was at this moment that Jackie created the myth of a President that was a king, of a man who somehow in his few short years in office gave the American people more hope and more confidence than any President before him. She told White that she had always been described as a fairy tale princess, and now she wanted JFK to take his place in history as a modern-day King, like King Arthur, the mythical English King. (9) Theirs would be just as mythical, just as romantic, the King, his Queen and John, the Prince and heir to the throne. In his later years, John professed to ignore this expectation, yet in the end he embraced it.

And so, as the new President and his family took their place in the White House, they did not reside in Camelot, for Camelot was no longer of this world. It had hardly existed for more than the blink of an eye. As the years pushed Camelot farther into mythology, its legend grew, and its voice cried out for a new King. Jackie had laid the groundwork for this great American myth. Seeking to resurrect the myth of Camelot, in 1968 another Kennedy brought his name forward, seeking the Presidency. He too would be murdered, martyred like his Brother before him and passing the torch to John, the Prince who would be King.

In the first few years after the death of his father, John grew closer to Bobby Kennedy than perhaps anyone else. Bobby made it a point to visit Jackie and the kids almost every day at their temporary lodging at the estate of Averell Harriman in Georgetown, a fashionable area near Washington D.C. Less than a month after the assassination, Jackie purchased a three-story colonial house just down the street from the Harriman's. She even had the children's rooms decorated to match their rooms at the White House. Besides Jackie, Caroline seemed to be hit hardest over the loss of her father. Being older than John by three years, she understood what had happened and was keenly aware of the agony her mother was experiencing.

"I cry all the time" Caroline confessed to one of her schoolteachers. For her part, Jackie continued to rely on the amphetamine injections from Dr. Jacobson. Now it would seem, she was addicted, if she hadn't been before. The euphoria and energy that one gets when high on amphetamines helped Jackie

Robert playing with John Jr.

through those difficult times yet according to Jacobson, Jackie felt that her life was empty and over.

Jackie and the kids would visit Hickory Hill, Bobby's home, in McLean, Virginia several times a week. JFK and Jackie had lived there for a year and then sold it to Bobby and his wife Ethel. It was a place where Jackie felt safe, and Bobby's eight children made it a virtual playland for young Caroline and John. There, they could relax and be themselves. It was noted that Bobby spent a great deal of time with John, playing kickball, wrestling on the grass, and going for walks.

Even with all the support from family and friends, Jackie was unhappy living in Washington D.C. There were too many reminders of the recent past. She moved again, this time to New

York, where she felt much more at home. It was an important move for John and Caroline. Located across from Central Park, they lived on the fifteenth floor, away from the prying eyes and clicking cameras that had plagued them at their first-floor apartment in Georgetown. Central Park was vast and offered a zoo, bike paths, lakes, and a carousel. They had many wonderful times there. Bobby also moved to New York when he announced his run for the Senate. Yet not all was well for the Kennedy's. Teddy Kennedy, the youngest of the brothers, was involved in a plane crash in June of 1964. The pilot and one of Teddy's aides were killed, and Teddy's back was badly broken.

Entrance to Jackie's 1040 5th Avenue Apartment.   15th Floor Suite

This would not be the only time that an accident would take a life while Teddy miraculously escaped. It was no wonder that Jackie started feeling that the Kennedy's had "unusually bad luck." After Teddy's accident, life for the Kennedy's seemed to return to normalcy. There were lots and lots of vacations interspersed with school and homework. Caroline snapped out of her depression and Jackie rebounded, newly immersed in New York society.

In 1966, after Jackie went to Spain by herself, she gave John what his father had once promised him. Although missing an engine, the World War II Piper Cub airplane was intact. John was ecstatic! He was one lucky kid. How many six-year-olds have an actual (non-working) plane for a toy? 1967 was a year of travel for Jackie and the children, this time to Ireland, to the Kennedy ancestral home. She was introducing John and Caroline to the world, a little bit at a time.

1968 was a year marked by major and profound changes for the small Kennedy family. For the last year or two, Jackie had been receiving telephone calls and letters from Aristotle Onassis. He was an incredibly wealthy Greek tycoon who had made his fortune in the shipping business. As one of the wealthiest men in the world, he boasted of owning a fleet of ships, an airline, a 325-foot yacht, a 500-acre private island, a villa in Monte Carlo, a penthouse in Paris, a hacienda in Montevideo, and a mansion outside of Athens. (10) Onassis had met Jackie on his yacht Christina O in 1959, when Winston Churchill came aboard. Onassis hosted Churchill in a sort of meet and greet. Jackie and JFK were both aboard, and as history tells, Churchill was not impressed. However, Onassis was. In 1963, after Jackie's pregnancy, and baby Patrick's death, Onassis offered her his yacht as a place of sanctuary. She accepted, and the genesis of their complicated relationship began there. (11) Onassis was known as one of the greatest womanizers of the time and had bedded some of the most glamorous women on the planet. Bobby considered him "a rogue."

It perplexed Jackie that this Greek tycoon, who could have any woman in the world, would be so persistent in his desire to meet her. Cautiously she warmed to the idea and eventually they arranged to meet. Onassis knew that if he could have the

President's widow at his side, he would finally attain the status that had eluded him. True, he was already known throughout the world as a tycoon and playboy, but that kind of notoriety lacked class, and Jackie was regarded as a woman of unique and esteemed stature. To Jackie, Onassis represented wealth, protection, and seclusion. His private bodyguards numbered up to 75 armed men and highly trained attack dogs. With Onassis, she might finally find refuge from the frenzied swarm of media and paparazzi. Still, Jackie was not prepared to seriously consider Onassis as a husband. He would first have to gain the approval of Caroline and John.

As rumors of their budding relationship became public, Bobby wondered what effect it might have on his yet unannounced bid for the presidency. Once he made his candidacy known, he asked Jackie to postpone any announcement she might make regarding her relationship with Onassis. Out of respect to the Kennedy's, she agreed. Once Bobby announced that he would seek the Democratic nomination for the White House, Onassis felt Jackie would be left without Bobby's protective attention.

When Bobby was assassinated in 1968, Jackie received the call while on board Onassis' luxury yacht. Upon hearing the news, Jackie cried out, "I hate this country, I despise America and I don't want my children living here anymore!" She continued, "If they're killing Kennedy's, my kids are number one targets!" (12) For John, it was another horrifying death, much like his father's. The difference was that he was now seven years old, and he would remember this event with more clarity than his father's death, which he didn't remember at all. The brutality of RFK's murder drove Jackie into the arms of her Greek savior, Aristotle.

There was more to Bobby's murder than the official conclusion would have us believe. It's credible that Jackie, at this point, believed that Bobby's death was not another freak killing by some random lone gunman. She was heard to have screamed, "Oh no, it can't happen again." (13) Yet it did. JFK's death had never been thoroughly investigated, and the official ruling on RFK's death would also never be satisfactorily investigated. There were persistent witnesses that testified that the accused killer Sirhan Sirhan was in front of RFK at the time of the shooting. The official autopsy showed that RFK had been hit *from behind* by four bullets, the fatal shot having been fired from less than an inch behind his right ear. This shot would be considered by most firearms experts as a "military" kill. Interestingly enough, the only other gun in the room was owned by a CIA operative, Thane Eugene Cesar, who was hired as a Security Guard two weeks before the assassination. Witnesses placed him directly behind Bobby Kennedy when the shooting began. The LAPD never investigated Cesar, and he died in the Philippines in September, 2019. One witness to the shooting was brutally interrogated by L.A. police for hours in an attempt to make her change her story. She told police that she had seen a woman dressed in a polka dot dress running from the killing scene yelling "we got him." (14) The 'Kennedy curse' was not a curse of whimsical fate. The 'curse' was that these men, along with Martin Luther King were assassinated to prevent them from assuming positions of power. Someone obviously had it out for the Kennedy men.

Robert Kennedy's murder convinced Jackie that it was imperative that she distance herself from the Kennedy family. With Bobby gone, there was really no one left for her. Her next move had to be made in the best interests of her and her children. She decided to marry Onassis and leave the country.

Onassis' private army would protect her and her young family. They could live on his private island, fly on his private jet, and sail on his private ship. On October 25, 1968, Jackie married Onassis on his Island Paradise. According to insiders, he paid Jackie $3 million to marry him. In addition, he bought her a one million-dollar, forty carat Cartier ring, a pair of sapphire, emerald and ruby earrings, and an allowance of $1.5 million for the first year. (15)

Mr. & Mrs. Aristotle Onassis with John Jr. & Caroline (L)

Jackie had done well for herself and her children. Considering that this was such an epic event, the guest list was small, with only twenty-two family members attending. After the wedding and honeymoon, Jackie and the kids returned to New York and spent the school season in Manhattan. For Easter they flew to Greece, and from time to time, Onassis joined them in New York.

Holidays were usually spent with Onassis on his island or his yacht. One must give credit to Onassis for offering such a strong guiding hand to young John. He explained to the youngster that he could never take the place of his real father, JFK. John would nod his head, understanding what he could, but John didn't remember his father at all, so in some ways, Aristotle Onassis became the first 'father' in John's memory. They grew close and by all accounts, Onassis treated John as if he was his own son. For a time, life felt safe. But even one of the richest and most powerful men in the world could not shield the Kennedy's from events that were about to unfold. 1969 held another horror for them to endure.

On July 18, 1969, Teddy, the youngest Kennedy brother, drove his Oldsmobile off the Dyke Bridge on Chappaquiddick Island, killing a passenger who was in the car with him. The passenger was an attractive assistant named Mary Jo Kopechne. Teddy, Mary Jo and several other girls had been attending a reunion party at Lawrence Cottage, a small cottage on the island. The reunion was for the 'Boiler Room Girls.' They were girls, assistants, and secretaries who worked on RFK's campaign until his death in 1968. By all accounts the party was wild, with unbridled drinking and carousing. Around 11:15 p.m. Mary Jo and Teddy left the party to return to Edgartown where they were staying. Whether she intended to or not, Mary Jo left her purse and room key at the cottage. What happened next has been the subject of much speculation.

As Teddy and Mary Jo drove towards the ferry, Teddy made a wrong turn which took him to Dyke bridge. In the darkness, the big Oldsmobile plunged off the small bridge and into the dark waters of Poucha Pond. According to Kennedy, he broke free of the vehicle and realizing that his passenger was still trapped, he

Boston Sunday Globe headlines, July 20, 1969.

dove down several times attempting to free the young girl. The
depth of the water was about 8 feet. After several attempts, he
gave up and crawled onto the banks of the pond. He rested for
about 15 minutes and walked back to Lawrence Cottage.
Enlisting the help of two men at the party, the three of them left,
and upon reaching the accident scene, tried in vain to rescue
Mary Jo Kopechne. The two men then returned to the cottage
and in accordance with Teddy's wishes, did not inform the other
girls or the police. Teddy swam across the 500-foot channel back
to Edgartown and retired to his hotel room.

By 7:30 the next morning Kennedy had still not reported the
accident to authorities. Around 8:00 a.m., the three men took
the ferry back to the scene of the accident, where Kennedy
phoned several friends asking for advice. At around 8:20 a.m.

two fishermen discovered the car in the water and called the police. At 10:00 a.m., Kennedy walked into the police station and reported the event. John Farrar, the diver who recovered Kopechne's body testified that she had been alive in the car for 2-3 hours and died of suffocation rather than drowning. Kennedy waited 10 hours before notifying the police. He failed to mention that there were several well-lit houses near the bridge, anyone of whom he could have gone to for help. (16)

There is another version of events that night, where Kennedy and Kopechne stopped the car after seeing police ahead. Not wanting to be seen drunk and with a single woman, Kennedy left the vehicle and walked back to the cottage, leaving Mary Jo to drive the rest of the way to the ferry. Being completely unfamiliar with the road, she took the wrong turn and drove off the bridge. The car flipped over and lay upside down in the dark water. (17) This could explain why Kennedy took so long to report the incident. He didn't realize that the accident took place. Yet another version suggested that Ted Kennedy was drugged and set up to take the blame for Mary Jo's death. Perhaps someone did not want another Kennedy to run for President.

Either way, the incident tarnished Kennedy's image and ended any chance of his becoming the new King of Camelot.   In the final conclusion of Judge Boyle, he stated that:

(1) Kennedy did not intend to drive to the ferry,
(2) At a speed of 20 mph, Kennedy was guilty of operating a motor vehicle negligently, and
(3) Kennedy failed to exercise due care as he approached the bridge, and this appears to have contributed to the death of Mary Jo Kopechne.

No charges were ever brought against him, although his license was suspended. Mary Jo's family was awarded $140,000 from the Senator. In time, several books would be written; 'Senatorial Privilege', 'Chappaquiddick, the Real Story,' 'Left to Die,' 'Death at Chappaquiddick.' JFK Jr. was still too young to remember but provided Jackie with one more reason why she needed to protect John and Caroline from the 'Kennedy curse.'

Chappaquiddick takes on an interesting and curious perspective when it was revealed that Nixon's White House 'plumber,' E. Howard Hunt, was sent to Chappaquiddick to investigate and dig up dirt on Ted Kennedy. According to Hunt's son Saint John, the elder Hunt often muttered "we should have finished the job and hit Ted." (18) Were the Kennedy men just naturally unlucky, or were they victims of murder and contrived 'accidents?'

Kennedy family plot, Holyhood Cemetery, Brookline, Massachusetts.

On the heels of Chappaquiddick, another Kennedy tragedy quickly followed. On November 18, 1969 at the Kennedy compound in Hyannis Port, Joseph P. Kennedy, patriarch of the Kennedy family died at the age of 89. Although he died a natural death, he had suffered a debilitating stroke in 1961, suffered from aphasia and was eventually relegated to using a wheelchair. He had outlived four of his children. Joe, Jr., had died During WWII, his plane exploding while on a secret mission, his daughter, Kathleen 'Kick' Kennedy also died in a plane crash in France, and the deaths of both JFK and RFK remain shrouded in doubt as to who the real assassins were. There is no doubt, however, that the Kennedy family was continually plagued with tragedy. Their wealth, privilege, connections both legitimate and suspect, and the ability to do most anything and have most anything they wanted could not protect them from untold misfortune. The so-called "Kennedy curse" has often been used as a convenient explanation, which is fine if you believe in witches, wizards, druids, and dragons. With no doubt whatsoever, sinister forces and thoroughly evil people were behind some of these atrocious events. And they weren't done just yet.

Three

<u>Becoming His Own Man</u>

Time marched inexorably on, and John was maturing into a young man. He came to realize that he would always be in the public eye and was determined to forge his own way in the world, despite anyone's expectations. He was a Kennedy in every sense of the word but chose to distance himself from much of that world, instead walking his own difficult path, ignoring the ever-present criticisms and whisperings of those who felt he should live that lifestyle. When asked if he wanted to become President of the United States, he would answer honestly "I don't know." Deep down in his heart, even at such a young age, he did know, and the answer was not the answer that most people wanted to hear. He continued to reach, not for the heights of politics, but to the heights of tactical human feeling. He embraced the notion that he had been sheltered throughout much of his life, and as an antidote, he felt the need to experience struggle, survival, and live life on the edge.

In August 1971, he and his cousin Anthony Radziwill spent two weeks at the Drake Island Adventure Center, off the southwest coast of England, near Plymouth Sound. It was his first opportunity to test himself, along with sixty-four other boys. He wanted to be one of them. No special treatment, no undue attention for the Kennedy boy.

He learned sailing, rock climbing and nature studies. When he completed the course, he begged Jackie to enroll him in similar camps the following season. Something else happened to

John during Christmas that year: he took a small part in a stage production of Charles Dickens' 1838 Novel, 'Oliver Twist.' The part was small, one of Fagin's boys, but for the second time, John was doing something he wanted to do. The little boy who saluted his dead father's casket was growing up. (1)

The danger associated with the Kennedy name reared its ugly head in July of 1972, when the FBI thwarted a plan to kidnap John. The plot, to be carried out in Greece, involved two gangs. One gang was made up of four West German terrorists of the 20th of October Group. The second group consisted of eight Greek leftists who carried out a series of kidnappings, robberies, and bombings. John was chosen as someone who would bring a high profit for their efforts. This may have been the first time that John became aware that he was a target. It wouldn't be the last. (2)

(L to R) Aristotle Onassis speaking with his son, Alexander.

By the beginning of 1973, the Kennedy/Onassis marriage was falling apart. Onassis was still very much in love with opera star Maria Callas, the love of his life before Jackie, and had continued a relationship with her, albeit from a distance. Apparently, the prestige of marrying one of America's most respected and loved woman had worn off. In 1973 on the eve of what should have been their divorce, Aristotle's son Alexander died at age 24 in a plane crash. Onassis fell into a deep and unending depression. He withdrew and became sullen, despondent, and paranoid. He claimed that the CIA had engineered the plane crash to murder his son and offered $1 million to anyone who could provide him with evidence of a CIA plot. (3) Similar to Larry Flynt, who on January 8, 1978, printed a full-page advertisement in the Dallas Morning News in which he offered $1,000,000 in cash rewards to anyone who could provide him and his research team concrete evidence to solve the mystery of John F. Kennedy's assassination in Dallas' Dealey Plaza on November 22, 1963.

A temporary period of sympathy and support ensued, and Jackie did her best to console the shattered billionaire. Putting their difficulties aside, they clung to each other, perhaps fearful that parting might inflict an emptiness and aloneness which would destroy all that was left of their wounded hearts. They needed each other more than ever. Jackie and John tried their best to rally the stricken Onassis. In the end, he had no joy for life. Onassis died in France two years later of respiratory failure.

In 1975 the American media was experiencing unprecedented change. Prior to then, certain topics concerning JFK and other luminaries were off limits to the press. During his Presidency JFK's numerous affairs were whispered about but never reported. Whether by agreement or just from recognizing the sanctity of one's personal life, the extra marital affairs of JFK were not disclosed. However, this delicate arrangement was broken forever by the revelations of Judith Campbell Exner, mistress to both Mafia boss Sam Giancana and President Kennedy. Exner had testified before The Church Committee, and her identity was leaked to and published by The Washington Post. Undoubtedly, Bobby and Jack would have been appalled.

(L to R) President Kennedy, Judith Campbell Exner & Sam Giancana.

Exner had numerous licentious stories, and she revealed all the lurid details in a press conference. Newspapers everywhere were screaming over her admission that she was having sex with Giancana one day, and sex with JFK the following day.

Once the media realized that Kennedy's affairs sold papers, the veil of secrecy was stripped away once and for all. It's almost a blessing that JFK and RFK were not alive to see their private lives revealed before a nation hungry for scandal. Bobby Kennedy had prosecuted the Mafia with unrelenting zeal, yet his Brother was consorting with a Mafia trollop! With certainly, the public's knowledge of JFK's many indiscretions caused Jackie, her children, and the entire Kennedy family a shame that would never be forgotten. Camelot was showing signs of wear and tear, the impenetrable veil of perfection slowly deteriorating. John Jr. surely heard the sensational press reports. Jackie, ever the wounded widow, would never comment on these accusations. It was beneath her. Year after year she was voted America's most admired woman.

When Onassis died, his plans for divorcing Jackie remained unfulfilled. He was buried next to his son, Alexander, in the small chapel where he had married Jackie just seven years before. In the next months, Jackie began to distance herself from his family and associates. However, one more business matter needed to be resolved. The will that Onassis left called for John and Caroline to receive $25,000 each. Jackie was outraged! She eventually renegotiated the will with Christina Onassis and received $20 million! (4)

Although the death of his surrogate father was unfortunate, John's relationship with Onassis had chilled, a result of the protective feelings he had for his mother. He had noticed that Aristotle and Jackie had drifted apart, due to Ari's infidelities. He was maturing, and part of his emotional growth meant that he started to understand the dynamics of relationships. For the first time he saw Jackie as vulnerable, and this brought out his protective side. Jackie had continued to shield and protect him, but now he felt responsible to protect her.

John was always somewhat of a maverick, one who would often push back, but Jackie was usually able to keep him in check. When he began 11th grade at Phillips Academy at Andover he was met with the unfamiliar and necessary shock of responsibility. Now a mere equal among his student peers, he was at once liberated and uncomfortably on his own. Growing up having been raised to this point within the confines of a tightly structured regime, his new-found freedom was unsettling. He could do anything he wanted, but no one would be there to pick him up if he fell. He had always wished for independence, but this new taste of life was bittersweet.

With his blossoming freedom, John found new ways to express himself. He began acting, embracing this new craft with fervor. In 1975, he appeared in a play called 'Petticoats and Union Suits.' The play was reviewed by the New York Times. They wrote, "One can't help but be aware of the 15-year-old John Kennedy in his role, although like others in his celebrated family, he seems to be trying painfully to avoid special attention." (5) He continued acting in other roles at Andover. In 1977 he starred in 'Comings and Goings.' In 1978 he appeared in William Shakespeare's 'A Comedy of Errors.' (6) Although he drank moderately, he used pot regularly. According to Holly Owen, head of Andover's drama department, "John smoked grass, but it didn't appear to affect him." Although he had several incidents with campus security guards, every time Andover officials called Jackie to inform her that her son had been caught smoking marijuana Jackie never overreacted. John would apologize and promise not to do it again. Jackie regarded it as John trying to fit in as one of the boys. (7)

John also developed an interest in girls, and by sixteen, he had a girlfriend. Her name was Meg Azzoni, and by all accounts

JFK Jr. with Meg Azonni.

she was very attractive. She was also a senior, and two years older than the young JFK Jr. This was considered quite an accomplishment and became a pattern for the rest of his life. He always got the hottest, best-looking girl.

Sports, acting, and girls were John's new priorities. His schoolwork, as reflected in his grades, was of little interest. He failed math, and barely passed his other classes. His teachers advised him to spend less time at the gym, and more time with his books. At the end of his eleventh-grade year, his grade point average was so low he should have been expelled, but Jackie phoned Andover and begged them not to expel him. They agreed on one condition, that John repeat eleventh grade. (8)

From all accounts, being held back a grade didn't seem to bother John, at least outwardly. However, the pressure to succeed as the flag bearer for the Kennedy family must have been overwhelming. His poor grades became fodder for the tabloids. During a weekend break in New York, a reporter asked him quite bluntly, "Are you a poor student?" With an embarrassed grin, John replied, "well, I don't know. It depends on what you call a poor student." John handled the media spotlight with grace, and rarely displayed the outrage that he surely must have felt.

During the next school year, John continued with his passions: acting, sports and girls. He had split up with Meg Azzoni and then taken up with a slender, blond, sixteen-year-old named Jenny Christian. Their relationship continued for four years. Although John had lost his virginity in high school, he wouldn't consummate his relationship with Jenny until they had been together for a year. (9) His grades continued to suffer, as Jackie attempted to find new ways to inspire John to a higher standard. Summer was approaching, and Jackie searched for something for John to do to build up his character. A Wyoming ranch owner and friend of JFK's suggested John come work as a ranch hand. This was a paying job, with no frills attached. He would be bunking with the other hands and be expected to carry his fair share of the workload. According to fellow ranch hand, Melody Harding, "he worked hard for those six weeks, and never complained once." When he returned to Andover, he found a new passion, helping disadvantaged children. He joined an outreach program and taught English to immigrant students twice a week.

Jackie pulled out all the stops for John and Caroline's eighteenth and twenty first combined birthday party, held at Le Club, a fashionable Fifth Avenue venue. The guest list was a who's who of the elite. Politicians, movie stars, financial barons, and all the Kennedy's, along with dozens of John and Caroline's friends attended. President Jimmy Carter had been invited but couldn't make it. He sent Secretary of State Cyrus Vance in his place. Senator Ted Kennedy made a heartfelt toast after dinner. "I shouldn't be doing this tonight. By rights it should be the father of these two children. Young John and Caroline bring new life to the family." By 1:00 a.m., the older crowd had left. John and his pals continued drinking heavily, smoking weed and carousing. At 4:00 a.m., the club manager had to close the place. John's friend and partner in crime, Billy Noonan, peeked out a window and noticed that their taxis had not yet arrived. He also noticed a small hoard of photographers who had waited outside all night despite the freezing cold, hoping for the chance to snap a few pictures of the eighteen-year-old star. Noonan recognized one photographer as Ron Galella. Galella had become a thorn in the side of the Kennedy's. He pestered Jackie so much that she was granted a restraining order against him. By law, Galella had to stay 100 feet away from the Kennedys, yet here he was, standing outside the door in violation of the order.

Noonan opened the door slightly, and egged on the photographers, "I'm giving you fair warning, don't start any shit." When the partier's left, they surrounded John in a protective shield. The photographers lunged at the group. Other photographers came running from across the street, where they had been staying warm inside their cars. Things turned ugly, and as John and Jenny tried to make a run for it, someone knocked him down.

Knocked flat, with his sunglasses askew, Noonan and the other boys started throwing punches at the press. It was all over in a few minutes. The next day, the pictures were on the front page of all the tabloids. LIFE magazine also ran the story, complete with photos! Jackie mentioned the incident only a few times, usually when John and Billy Noonan wore dark glasses. "Dark glasses, are you boys going out looking for a fight?" (10) Billy Noonan had been friends with John since 1974. Billy's Irish parents were neighbors to the Kennedy clan in Hyannis Port. The two boys had known each other since the age of three. Noonan's book, 'Forever Young,' is a light but interesting read.

In the summer of 1979, John journeyed to Kenya, Africa to study environmental issues. He also worked with troubled teens at the Massachusetts State House. For the rest of his life, he demonstrated a strong interest in environmental concerns and in educating the underprivileged. In October, 1979 he made his first public speech at the dedication ceremony for the John F. Kennedy Library near Boston.

(L to R) Caroline, John Jr. & Jackie at dedication of JFK Library.

The following year, John started college at Brown University. Although he had been accepted at Harvard, Yale, and Columbia, he chose Brown due to its more lenient academic demands. John wasn't the academic type, and Brown offered a middle of the road curriculum. With the press clicking away, John registered, allowing the press ten minutes of photo ops if they would just let him enroll. He joined the Phi Psi fraternity after completing their 'hell night' initiation rituals. Not one to demand special treatment, he willingly wallowed in animal entrails, guzzled beer, swallowed a goldfish, and streaked across campus completely naked. He wanted to be known as a regular guy.

When his uncle Teddy began campaigning again, John graciously offered to support him by going on the campaign trail. Teddy had seen the magnetic Kennedy charisma inherent in John during the Kennedy Library dedication ceremony the previous October and was grateful that John was willing to publicly support him. John made short speeches on behalf of his uncle and let it be known that he was available to student groups. He answered questions about Teddy and deflected questions that he considered off limits, such as the Chappaquiddick episode. (11)

Acting continued to be important to John and he honed his skills by appearing in several Brown plays, most notably, 'The Tempest,' 'Playboy of the Western World,' and 'Short Eyes.' Was John considering an acting career? Jackie certainly felt threatened by it and put her foot squarely down against the very thought. Although they rarely argued, friends claimed that Jackie and John engaged in terrible fights over his acting. A Brown classmate recounted that Jackie told John in no uncertain terms that "acting was beneath him, that he was his father's son and that he had a tradition of public service to uphold." Yet despite these fights, John continued acting. He even reached out to close family friend, actor Peter Lawford for advice and help.

Peter Lawford, was a famous Hollywood actor from the 1950's through the 1970's. A strikingly good-looking man, he had married JFK's sister Pat. A member of Frank Sinatra's 'Rat Pack' he added class and could sing, dance and carouse with the rest of the pack. However, his position in the Kennedy family was delicate. He was only a Kennedy by marriage, and he did whatever he could to please Jack and Bobby. By the same token, his position in Sinatra's Rat Pack was secure only if Frank was pleased with him. He existed between both powerful groups and found himself anointed as a date fixer, arranging trysts for JFK and Sinatra. He knew all the Hollywood starlets, most all-too willing to consort with such powerful men. When JFK Jr. asked Lawford for advice he was honored that the young Kennedy trusted and respected him. By the 1980's, Lawford's career had diminished considerably, and he had fallen into serious alcohol and cocaine abuse. Some said that he blamed himself for Marilyn Monroe's death.

Peter Lawford & Marilyn Monroe at Madison Square Garden.

He and Monroe were very close friends and Marilyn confided everything to him. Lawford knew that both JFK and RFK were having affairs with Marilyn. He had introduced her to the President. He knew that she had been feeling used by both brothers and was threatening to call a press conference to expose the affairs. He also knew that on the day of her death, RFK had secretly visited Marilyn twice, trying to convince her not to go public. In fact, Lawford arrived at Monroe's house with Bobby the afternoon of her death. A second visit ended with Bobby and Marilyn in a violent argument. Marilyn's house had been bugged, and some of those who heard the secret tape recordings suggested that she was accidentally murdered to keep her quiet. As Marilyn lay dying from an overdose, she called Lawford on the phone, and he did nothing. As a member of the Kennedy inner circle, and a member of the Rat Pack, Lawford was privy to all the sordid sexual escapades involving the Kennedy brothers. He was also responsible for cleaning up any messes they left behind. He was allowed the pleasure of Kennedy company only if it suited them. He was witness to the Kennedy's involvement with the Mafia, witnessed the Sinatra/Kennedy war, and suffered greatly from Sinatra's vengeance when JFK snubbed Sinatra's invitation to stay at his estate, preferring a less Mob connected host, Bing Crosby. Lawford kept all this sensational information locked away, deep inside, eventually turning to alcohol, pills, and cocaine to dull the shame and guilt he felt for his involvement in the dark underbelly of Camelot. (12)

All of that was ancient history and John Jr. probably knew little or nothing regarding the Kennedy's involvement in Monroe's death. Now, as Lawford neared his own end, he found a measure of redemption by helping John, absolution he desperately needed. When Jackie became aware of Lawford's support, she wrote him a stern letter advising him not to encourage John, because she wanted him to be a scholar. He continued supporting John's interest in acting despite her letter.

Actress Katherine Hepburn once commented that, "All actors hide behind masks. It's the perfect way to cope with celebrity because people are only seeing you play a character." (13) When John announced that he intended to enroll in Yale's Drama School after graduating, Jackie threatened to disinherit him. "I'll disinherit you unless you go to law school," she said. (14) In April of 1983, John made his final appearance on stage in the Leeds Theater production of 'Short Eyes.' Jackie had won. John would attend law school, but first he would travel to India for a year. He attended the University of Delhi, studying food production and health care, and worked with the poor. According to friends, John's time in India was the calmest period of his life. After a few months alone in India, John invited his latest girlfriend, Sally Munro to join him there. He and Sally had met at Brown, and she bore a startling resemblance to Caroline Kennedy, as if she was Caroline's physical double. Some men might not be attracted to a girl who looked exactly like their sister, but it didn't seem to bother John. Caroline and Jackie had always been the two closest women in his life, and he and Caroline were best friends growing up. She was his protector and playmate. They celebrated Birthdays together. Sadly, time, age, and circumstance injected distance into their relationship.

When John and Sally returned from India, John moved in with his friend Robert Littell, finding work as Deputy Director of the 42nd Street Development Corporation which Jackie had co-founded. His life seemed to be coming together, but pressure to accede to Jackie's will was never far away. In the meantime, Bobby and Ethel's son David died of a drug overdose. David and

JFK Jr. with girlfriend Sally Munro. (Close resemblance to Caroline)

John was not close. Jackie had always tried to keep John away from Bobby's sons. Those Kennedy's were regarded as troublemakers and compared to them John was a quiet angel. Still, another death in the Kennedy family followed a long line of Kennedy family tragedies. Later in the year, John's ally, Peter Lawford died at age sixty-one. John took it hard, Lawford being the only one who supported John's desire to act. Despite their disagreement regarding acting, Jackie genuinely cared for Lawford and was devastated by his death. Now that he was gone, Jackie increased her pressure on John to enroll in law school. Caroline sided with her Mother, and John finally relented. He was quoted as saying, "All of these people have expectations of me because of my father, but I believe he would have wanted me to do whatever the hell I wanted."

Yet another death in the Kennedy family occurred when Jackie's half-sister Janet passed away from lung cancer at the age of thirty-three. They were very close, and Jackie mourned her death deeply. Amidst all this sorrow and death, John and Sally Munro's relationship fell apart, leaving John in search of a new girlfriend. John never had a problem finding girls to share his bed, in fact they often threw themselves at him. On one occasion, housemate Robert Littell answered the door to find six-foot-tall Sports Illustrated model Ashley Richardson asking for John, wearing only a mink coat and Prada boots! John also had a very publicized affair with Superstar singer/celebrity Madonna. (15)

At the time, Madonna was cultivating her Marilyn Monroe image and to John was the perfect combination of Madonna and Marilyn. She pursued John aggressively, leaving dozens of messages on his answering service. Finally, he agreed to meet her, and their bizarre affair became front page tabloid news. Although opposites in many ways, the two were equals in terms of fame. Madonna craved publicity; John hated it. Madonna was a sexual predator, using it to control and shock. John was laid back and not nearly as kinky. John enjoyed watching porno movies with his girls, while Madonna was a porno movie, live and in color! Madonna loved the nightlife. Although John also enjoyed going out, he preferred kayaking, mountain climbing, scuba diving, endurance trials and solitude. They eventually became just friends, and Jackie breathed a huge sigh of relief when their fling was over. John continued with his acting career, calling it a hobby, and in 1985, he signed on to play a lead role in 'Winners' by Irish playwright Brian Friel.

One time love interest of JFK Jr., 'Boy Toy' Madonna dressed like Monroe.

The lead female role was played by a young beauty named Christina Haag, who had known John since he was fifteen. This was to be his professional debut on stage, and he couldn't have been happier. Jackie and Caroline agreed to attend provided critics were kept out. She worried that people would come to see the play just because it showcased her son. In the end they both boycotted the show hoping John would get the message. There were only six performances, but they provided a measure of success for John, and many thought he could forge a career in acting. Within a few months John and Christina began a passionate affair. (16)

1986 proved to be a year of significant change for John. Caroline married Ed Schlossberg in July, and that fall John enrolled in classes at New York University School of Law. At Jackie's insistence, John moved from his shared apartment into a swanky residential hotel called The Surrey. John seemed focused in his new life, and surprisingly worked in Washington, D.C. as a clerk for Ronald Reagan.

1986 was also the year that 'Manwatchers' declared John F. Kennedy Jr. "one of the most eligible bachelors of the year." Ten thousand 'Manwatchers' voted, and John accepted this curious honor with his usual cavalier attitude. Los Angeles Manwatchers President Suzy Mallery said, "he has that Kennedy magic, he has that style and charisma." Just two years later, People magazine named him "America's Most Eligible Bachelor." John was now attracting attention normally reserved for superstars. (17) As Law School loomed ever closer, John seemed ready to apply himself and do his best.

Jackie could now breathe a little easier. In the fall of 1987 John embarked on his first year of law school. Perpetually in need of some sort of diversion, he secretly enrolled in flying lessons at Martha's Vineyard Airport. No one knew, including Jackie.

Local pilot Arthur Marx was impressed with John, especially his dedication and perseverance. "I was impressed with him immediately because he rode his bike to the airport from his mother's house at the other end of the Island, and it was freezing." Marx also noted that the young Kennedy would "rather be flying than working." (18) Marx accompanied John on many flights, with John at the controls. Marx insisted that "he was always focused on the airplane. I never saw him as a pilot act in an impulsive way. In fact, John was probably better than he thought he was." (19) When John eventually brought Arthur

Marx to meet Jackie, hoping that she would tolerate the idea if she met his flight instructor, she acted as if she had no problem with John taking flying lessons. This made John extremely happy. Yet soon thereafter, Jackie began having nightmares of John crashing in a plane. She made such an issue of it that John promised he would stop his flying lessons. He kept his promise, and once again Jackie's wishes overrode John's newfound passion for flying. He had always shown incredible restraint and respect for his mother. She didn't like John's acting, so he stopped. She didn't want him flying, so he stopped. Obviously, he preferred to put his plans on hold rather than fight with Jackie.

For many people, John F. Kennedy Jr. stepped into the role that he was destined to play at the 1988 Democratic National Convention. He was there to introduce his uncle Ted, but by all accounts, it could have been him who was running for office. Stepping up to the podium, John seemed completely relaxed, confidant, and every bit as charismatic as his father had been. He was born to become a United States president. He looked the part, sounded the part, and as some have said, he could have been reading from the phone book for all that it mattered. It was a sign from the ages that Camelot might yet rise again. The young prince was nearly ready to assume the throne. "Over a quarter century ago, my father stood before you to accept the nomination of the presidency of the United States. So many of you came into public service because of him and in a very real sense it is because of you that he is with us today." The reaction to his short speech was astounding! John stole the show. Jackie was beyond excitement. Her iron will to steer John in the right direction had prevailed. She was confident he was finally instilled in the Kennedy family business, politics.

JFK Jr. introduces Uncle Teddy at 1988 DNC.

Jackie clearly felt that the only son of John F. Kennedy should be more than a movie actor, that he was destined for greater things. More than anyone, she knew Politics was part and parcel within John's DNA, and that he would be successful in that realm. Her plans for her son become harder to rationalize given the litany of Kennedy family tragedies she endured, including the deaths of her husband and brother-in-law. Perhaps she believed that Camelot could be reborn.

Jackie, JFK Jr., and Caroline Kennedy.

Four

<u>Headlines in the Tabloids</u>

When John's appearance at the Democratic convention immediately fueled a rash of media questions about his political future, another news item took center stage, and John was once again the object of media sensationalism. On September 12, 1988, People magazine christened John F. Kennedy Jr. as the 'sexiest man alive!' Jackie was crushed with this latest example of tawdry journalism at the expense of the Kennedy name. John didn't seem to mind. When asked by Barbara Walters how he felt about the People Magazine honor, he said, "listen, people can say a lot worse things about you than you are attractive, and you look good in a bathing suit."

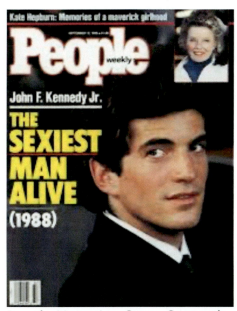

People Magazine Cover September 1988.

That may have been a perfect answer, but the flip side of it was that John would now face more scrutiny from the tabloids and media than ever before. Giving him this dubious crown made him fair game. Like it or not, anyone in the spotlight is fair game. When John failed to pass his law exam, he was hounded by tabloid headlines proclaiming, "the hunk flunks." Years later, a well-placed source who had once been a confidante of John's attributed his failure to the use of cocaine. An unnamed lawyer who had taken a bar-review course with John the previous summer recalled how wired he had seemed, possibly being high on cocaine. (1) Over the next decade John was tabloid gold with front page headlines and photos including 'JFK Jr. & Model in Sex Scandal: Kennedy Furious but Elle Macpherson Laughs' (from National Enquirer) and 'JFK Jr.'s Secret Life' (The National Examiner). In 1990, he failed his second attempt at passing the bar exam. Of course, the tabloids (New York Post) screamed "the hunk flunks...again!"

NY Daily News Cover.

He faced the reporters waiting for him and said, "Obviously, I'm very disappointed. But you know, God willing, I'll go back there in July, and I'll pass it then. Or I'll pass it the next time, or I'll pass it when I'm ninety-five. I'm clearly not a major legal genius." On his third attempt, he passed! John was relieved. He deserves credit for dealing with all that pressure.

Before he had passed the bar exam, he joined the Manhattan District Attorney's office as a junior assistant prosecutor. Although this wasn't anything like stepping into local politics, it was looked upon by many as an early first step into a position that could lead to a political future. After all, how many politicians have law degrees? True to form, John started at the bottom, working in the complaint room where prosecutors met with defendants several times each week. According to fellow rookies, he never complained, even though this was considered one of the worst jobs in the D.A.'s office. Apart from the hundreds of fan letters from female admirers, John was just one of the guys. John stayed with the assistant prosecutor's job for four years. He really enjoyed helping people less fortunate. He had always been that way. During those four years John enjoyed several on-again, off-again relationships, some with well-known models and actresses. He had brief flings with Sarah Jessica Parker of Sex and the City fame, model Julie Baker and occasionally with Christina Haag, although that relationship had all but fizzled out. His strongest relationship around that time was with actress Daryl Hannah. She was involved in a relationship with musician Jackson Browne, and although she had promised John that she would leave Browne for good, she eventually went back to him, leaving John somewhat brokenhearted. (2)

1991 was a year marked by yet another Kennedy scandal. William Kennedy Smith or 'Willie' as John called him was charged with raping Patricia Bowman, a twenty-nine-year-old. The alleged rape was said to have occurred on the lawn of the Kennedy estate in Palm Beach, Florida. Willie was a fourth-year medical student at Georgetown University, a nephew of John F. Kennedy, Robert F. Kennedy, Ted Kennedy and John and Caroline's cousin.

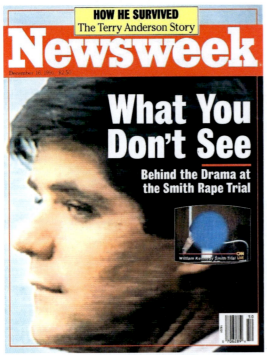

Newsweek coverage of Smith trial.

Patricia Bowman had no connection to America's royalty. At best she was the stepdaughter of a former Chairman of the Board of General Tire and Rubber Co. in Akron, Ohio. Various members of the Kennedy family attended the trial at different times. John showed up twice and commented to reporters that he was certain Willie was innocent. RFK's widow Ethel attended with two of her sons, RFK Jr. and Michael. Patricia Kennedy Lawford and three of her children were there. Teddy Kennedy was there as a witness. Earlier on the night in question Teddy had called Willie up, insisting they go out drinking. That was the night Willie met Patricia Bowman. Teddy, who had been drinking heavily and behaving rather indecently, left the couple and Patricia offered to give Willie a ride back to the Kennedy Compound. It was after a stroll on the beach that she claimed he attacked her. He claimed the sex was consensual. (3)

Sargent and Eunice Kennedy Shriver, Willie's brother and two sisters rounded out the Kennedy family show of support. Jackie and Caroline did not attend. In fact, Jackie had pleaded with John not to attend. Apparently, John had confided to a friend that, "they (the Kennedy family) should have done something about Willie years ago when he first started doing this," (meaning get help for him when he first started raping women.) John suspected that Willie the rapist was guilty.

So why did the otherwise honest and trustworthy JFK Jr. agree to show support for someone he knew was guilty? The friend that John confided in was James Ridgway De Szigethy. James was so upset with John's refusal to tell the truth that he provided a sworn deposition to Ohio Congressman James Traficant. The deposition was officially entered into the Congressional record. In addition, De Szigethy passed a polygraph examination regarding his conversations with John. Even more startling is that John had told De Szigethy that he was being pressured by someone to show support for Willie, or certain private information about John would be leaked to the press. John had even used the word 'blackmail' when describing the pressure he was under. This was one of the lowest points in John's life. (4)

One wonders what this 'private and personal information' could have been and who was blackmailing JFK Jr.? As a prosecutor in the District Attorney's office, John was going against everything he believed in. What could possibly be so damaging? We may never know. When powerful people become embroiled within the legal system, justice becomes a stranger. Another anomaly of the trial involved three other women who had been raped or sexually victimized by Willie Smith and were prepared to testify, proving a pattern of predatory behavior. The judge ruled their testimony was inadmissible. Smith was ultimately acquitted.

Notwithstanding a Kennedy curse, the truth is that rich, powerful, connected people get away with crimes that other people don't. There are no curses, Kennedy or otherwise, only victims. Years later William Kennedy Smith would be accused of two federal sexual misconduct charges. Both were "settled amicably" out of court.

On May 21, 1992, John made a rare appearance on ABC-TV's Prime Time Live with Jay Schadler. When asked about JFK's legacy John answered with honesty. "I think (Caroline and I) have a strong sense of my father's legacy and how important it is, and we both respect it enormously. But at the same time, there is a sense of, a realization that things are different and that he would have wanted us to go on with our own lives and not re-enact his. You have to remember that both my sister and I, particularly myself, view my father's administration through the color of others and the perception of others and through photographs and through what we have read. And so, it's difficult for us to discern much about him independently of what other people's impressions are." When John was once asked whether he'd ever enter politics, he replied, "If your father was a doctor, and your uncles are doctors, and all your cousins are doctors, and all the family ever talks about is medicine, there's a good chance maybe you're going to be a doctor too. But maybe you want to be a baker." (5)

In 1993, Jackie was thrown from her horse when it stumbled after jumping a stone fence. Jackie was rushed to the hospital, unconscious for thirty minutes. During her recovery, doctors found a swelling in her abdomen. She was given antibiotics and the swelling subsided. She appeared fine until December when she became ill while on holiday. Maurice Tempelsman, her companion since 1982, rushed the stricken woman to the hospital where they found lymph nodes in her neck, indicative of an aggressive form of non-Hodgkin's lymphoma. She would need chemotherapy immediately. Her prognosis was not positive, and she promptly informed John and Caroline of her medical condition.

1994 saw John find and lose two of the most important women in his life. He met his soulmate, Carolyn Bessette and lost his mother to cancer. Carolyn Bessette was blond, tall, and absolutely stunning. She carried herself with grace and poise, as if she came from royalty. She worked for Calvin Klein as a high fashion adviser and shopper to the rich and famous. John met her while jogging in Central Park, and the attraction was immediate and mutual. John, ever the gentleman, allowed his deteriorating relationship with Daryl Hannah to play itself out before making his move for Carolyn. Although John had spoken of marriage to Daryl, that idea now seemed to be cooling. Daryl may have brought that upon herself by always having someone else to run back to. John invested himself fully in his significant other. He always had a 'roving eye' but generally remained faithful in his romances.

Maurice Tempelsman with Jackie Kennedy in Central Park, April 1994.

Daryl went back temporarily into the arms of musician Jackson Browne. Jackie and Caroline were happy for John. They never approved of Hannah and made it clear that if Daryl attended any Kennedy gatherings, they would not come.

As Jackie's condition worsened, she remained cheerful and dignified. She walked in Central Park with John and Maurice almost every day, despite the cold or rain. As news of her condition became public, she remained poised and uncomplaining. Always the one to carry her burdens with stoic grace, she became even more of an icon to women all over the world. Somehow, she kept that glamorous Jackie 'O' image until the end. Just before she passed away, she wrote a letter to

Caroline and John.

To John, who had just told her of his plans to launch a 'politics meets entertainment' magazine, she said, "I understand the pressures you'll forever have to endure as a Kennedy, even though we brought you into this world as an innocent. You especially have a place in history." Jackie was making one final attempt to convince John that he was destined to be Camelot's king. (6)

Jackie died on May 19, 1994 with John, Caroline, and Maurice at her bedside. John's maturity showed when he announced her passing to the media. He was poised, in control and his voice never faltered. "Last night, around ten-fifteen, my mother passed on. She was surrounded by her friends and family and her books and the people and things that she loved. And she did it in her own way, and we all feel lucky for that, and now she's in God's hands."

When John acted as spokesperson, he indirectly sent a message that he was now the patriarch of the family. Could this be a step towards a renewed Camelot? As the world mourned the passing of this great Lady, it waited breathlessly to see what John would do next. In the days that followed, John met with Presidents and heads of state from many countries. Funerals were one thing that the Kennedy's did masterfully. Daryl Hannah came back briefly to offer support. By July, after it was clear that John was not ready for marriage, she went back to Jackson Browne and this time she stayed. Later that month John was quoted as saying, "A person never really becomes a grown up

Jacqueline Kennedy Onassis funeral, Arlington Cemetery, May 23, 1994.

until he loses both his parents." As if Jackie's death had stripped away the last vestiges of a by-gone era, John F. Kennedy Jr. subsequently headed in a completely unique direction.

The media relentlessly inquired about any political plans John might be considering, and at times he gave mixed signals. He told Barbara Walters, "I don't rule out anything. Public service should be something that you bring yourself wholly to and...I have sort of a life to live before I think about that." Not quite satisfied with that answer, Barbara then asked what he would do if he were elected President of the United States. He responded, "I think I would have to call my uncle Teddy and gloat for a moment, and then...I think I would offer a big tax cut before the next election and hopefully in between try to do some good." (7)

In an issue of Good Housekeeping John explained "I have to admit it, it is something I consider a lot. Once you run for office, though, you're in it. Sort of like going into the military...you better be damn sure that it is what you want to do, and the rest of your life is set up to accommodate that." (8)

John had nurtured the idea of starting a politically oriented magazine for several years. He thought of it as a combination of politics and entertainment meets Vogue. Something glossy and chic, a new type of magazine for a new generation who had grown up disillusioned with their elected officials. The seventies had spawned Vietnam and Watergate. The country was suffering from a malaise of distrust and apathy. John had always regarded politicians as public servants. Presumably, they ran for office to better the lives of their fellow Americans. They were 'servants' and as such led difficult and often misunderstood lives.

Since many Americans seemed to hold movie stars and entertainers in high esteem, John felt if he could publish a magazine that combined leading entertainers with politics, without liberal or conservative bias, it might inject renewed interest into the political spectrum. It's true that at that time actors, musicians and celebrities were becoming involved in noteworthy causes, and many were announcing support for their candidate of choice. It had been decades since this kind of political activism had occurred.

Previously, the opinions of those outside of the political sphere, although esteemed in their own right were not held in high regard. In fact, there was a time when movie stars were accused of being part of the international communist conspiracy. They were followed by the FBI, their phones were tapped, their movements scrutinized, and many dragged in front of cameras and subjected to intense and demeaning interrogation by publicity seeking senators and congressmen. A deep divide developed between politics and entertainment. Fear reigned in

Hollywood, and most celebrities were reluctant to speak their mind.

That all began to change in the early sixties. JFK helped to engender that change. When Frank Sinatra and his fellow 'Rat Pack' pals offered to help the young senator from Massachusetts, JFK readily accepted, acutely aware of the growing fascination young America had with movie stars. It was a win/win situation. It made Kennedy look youthful and glamorous, in touch with the 'new' generation, and gave the celebrities recognition and awareness regarding important issues. This is exactly what JFK Jr. wanted in his magazine. He may not have realized just how important his father had been in creating this fusion of entertainers and politicians, nor how relevant his Father's legacy still was within the political arena. He also had no idea of the impact any political leanings of his would have, nor the fear any intentions he had in that regard would strike within the hearts of those who had been responsible for the deaths of his Father and Uncle.

The only competition John's new magazine would have come from The National Review and The New Republic, both which ignored the relationship between politics and pop culture. John had a great concept, and with the right backing, and the look and feel of magazines like Elle or Vogue, it just might be successful.

Finally, John was doing something to which he was deeply committed. Now he needed a partner. He met Michael Berman in 1983 while working in New York's Office of Business Development. Michael was founder of a public relations firm called PRNY. They became good friends, and in 1993 they conceived of John's new magazine, 'George.' They began discussing their ideas within elite New York society, and soon thereafter the rumor mill was atwitter with whispers regarding John's ideas for the publication. While perusing the gossip column of New York magazine, David Pecker, CEO of a consortium called Hachette Filipacchi Magazines read about the buzz. He called Michael and arranged a meeting. After meeting JFK Jr. and believing in the premise for 'George' magazine, he invested $20 million. (9) After attending a two-day seminar on magazine publication, John was ready to hire a small, loyal staff.

JFK Jr. introduces, 'George,' September 8, 1995.

On September 8, 1995, John F. Kennedy Jr. launched his dream at a news conference in Manhattan. For the first issue he interviewed former governor George Wallace. For the all-important cover he and art director Matt Berman placed super model Cindy Crawford dressed in George Washington regalia and some very tight spandex. The idea for the pose was taken from an Alberto Vargas pin up drawing from the 1940's. The cover perfectly dramatized the 'politics as pop culture' theme of the magazine. The first 500,000 copies quickly sold out.

Undoubtedly, 'George' was well received due to the Kennedy mystique. Still, John refused to exploit that. For the second issue, co-editor Eric Ethridge wanted John to interview film director Oliver Stone. Stone's new movie "Nixon" was being released around the same time as the second issue of 'George.' Eric felt that if the man who brought the idea of conspiracy to the mainstream public was to grace the cover of the second issue, and be interviewed by John, it would be another sell out, perhaps bigger than the first. It would have been the first time that John discussed his father's murder in depth.

John emphatically declined. He was not interested in assassination conspiracies and considered Stone as somewhat of an eccentric. Still, he saw the potential selling value and agreed to meet with Stone for lunch. Stone apparently made John feel uncomfortable by asking too many questions John couldn't answer. Did he really believe the lone gunman theory? What did he think of the Warren Report? How many bullets did he think his father had been shot with? Finishing lunch as quickly as possible John politely excused himself, ending their discussion. (10)

It is easy to understand how John felt. Stone was known for asking tough, direct, to-the-point questions. When Stone was directing the Nixon film, he invited E. Howard Hunt to act as technical adviser for the scenes relevant to Hunt's involvement. Hunt was one of the Watergate burglars and had a long, infamous history involved in the CIA's darkest operations. There was also speculation that he was involved in JFK's assassination. Hunt's son David accompanied him to meet Stone, actor Anthony Hopkins and the cast. In the midst of one lively lunch Stone blurted out, "Well Mr. Hunt, how much money is it going to take to get you to reveal that the CIA killed Kennedy?" The table fell silent, and you could hear that everyone was holding their breath. The silence at the table was palpable. Hunt looked calmly at Stone, eye to eye, and with no hesitation whatsoever replied, "if you're serious, I would have to ask for three million, now pass me the pepper, would you?" (11)

The idea of John Kennedy Jr. launching an investigation into his father's murder and publishing it in 'George' would have had historical significance, impact and results, but John would have none of it. He felt that such a venture would be regarded as a cheap and dishonorable way to make money. (There are theories that he was planning or had already undertaken his own investigation into his father's assassination and was intent on revealing his findings in 'George.') Some issues of 'George' sold better than others, and for the next four years John worked tirelessly to keep it his magazine relevant in an ever-changing world.

Keeping 'George' in the public eye meant that John would have to agree to do some occasional television interviews. To everyone's amazement, he agreed to appear on the eighth season premiere of Candice Bergen's television sitcom, 'Murphy Brown.' The episode was actually taped in August of 1995 and was aired a month later in September. The appearance was quite clearly an effort on John's part to publicize 'George' magazine. John played himself and Bergen played her Murphy Brown character. The episode involved Bergen (as Murphy Brown) mistaking John, who had his back turned to her, as her new secretary. When he turns around, he explains that he's brought her a gift in honor of her upcoming wedding. Handing it to her, she opens it while John explains it's a special cover of his magazine 'George,' featuring a picture of Murphy. When Murphy responds with little enthusiasm, John storms off. (12)

John must have enjoyed his one-and-a-half-minute debut on national television, all for a good cause. Following Murphy Brown, John was interviewed on the Oprah Winfrey show.

Obviously trying to raise awareness for his magazine, he continued to answer the same worn questions: As a public figure do you have a right to privacy? How did the Kennedy family feel about his 'Marilyn' cover? How did he grow up to be so normal? Will he ever run for office? His answer to that question was always elusive and non-committal, "I've certainly thought about it...I really grew up in a political environment, going to fundraisers, seeing that stuff and it was important to me to really do something different. John Adams said that you should become a politician at the end of your life when you bring a wealth of life experience to bear on that office. For me, I think I was eager to try something different, to see another part of life...and I had an idea to be an entrepreneur." (13)

On September 21, 1996, John F. Kennedy Jr. married Carolyn Bessette in a private ceremony on Cumberland Island, Georgia, held at a tiny wooden chapel built by freed slaves after the Civil War. About forty people attended, close family and friends held in high regard. Caroline Kennedy served as the Matron of Honor and her son Jack, age three and a half, was the ring bearer. The private wedding was held with dignity and reverence, and when news of the event was made public, left New York society completely surprised. John was now happily married, and his

JFK Jr. marries Carolyn Bessette, Cumberland Island, Georgia.

magazine was doing well. Over the years, 'George' became known for its covers. In addition to Cindy Crawford, Drew Barrymore, Barbara Streisand, Demi Moore, Kate Moss, and Elizabeth Hurley, many others graced the covers of 'George.' John and his staff worked hard at keeping the covers just racy enough to catch the eye. 'George's' success wasn't just about the covers. The main attraction from the advertiser's perspective was John's interviews and editorial page. When the publication changed from bimonthly to monthly, John began having difficulty finding people to provide compelling interviews. He reflected on his own dislike for being interviewed. He hated the obvious, repetitive questions. Whether it was Barbara Walters, Peter Jennings, or Oprah, it was always the same. Now it was him asking the questions and he found it more difficult than he would have imagined. Routine questions were boring and intellectually stifling. He wanted the interviews to be relevant, insightful, and provide his readers with stimulating subject matter. Over time he became more confidant. He began to relax and trust his instincts when conducting the interviews, but his honesty began to get in the way. If he wasn't enthused about a proposed interview, he would put it off, and began publishing them sporadically. Every issue without his interviews meant lost revenue and fewer advertisers.

In October of 1997, John flew to Havana to meet with Cuban Premiere Fidel Castro. In April, 1961 Castro had defeated the Kennedy administration's attempted coup at the Bay of Pigs. During their meeting, Castro spoke of his admiration for JFK, and suggested that if Lee Harvey Oswald had been granted an entry visa to Cuba, he would not have been in Dallas a few weeks later, supposedly to assassinate the President. The New York Times termed John's visit 'mysterious.' Nancy Haberman, spokesperson for 'George' magazine said, "He's there as a journalist." (14)

Castro (L) and JFK Jr. (R) having dinner before interview.

John, as CEO and editor in chief, always had final oversight for the contents of the magazine. Most of the time his projects were well received, however one particular article was a disaster. It was written by Geula Amir, the mother of a young man who had assassinated Yitzhak Rabin, the Israeli Prime Minister. Geula Amir felt her son had been falsely accused of this horrible crime. More than that, she claimed that her son had been set up by the Israeli secret police. She also claimed that the assassination was supposed to be a 'pretend' or false assassination. Her son, Yigal Amir had been recruited to shoot at the Prime Minister with a gun ostensibly loaded with blanks. The Israeli secret police would 'foil' the attempt, thereby making themselves appear to be heroes while claiming it was the right-wing party behind the attempt. Something, she claimed, went terribly wrong. The gun had real bullets and Amir actually shot and killed the Prime Minister. Her claims sounded far-fetched and bizarre.

No one at 'George' thought John would publish such a conspiracy-related article. There was little evidence to support the mother's claims, yet John published the article in the March 1997 issue of 'George.' No one understood John's motivations. Richard Blow, 'George's' editor, thought that it may have been John's way of floating the possibility of doing an article on his own father's assassination.

When the story ran, the murdered Prime Minister's wife lambasted John for publishing such a hurtful and baseless article. The New York Daily News reported on the story with the headline 'Rabin's Wife Blasts JFK Jr.' Leah Rabin said, "she was enraged when the son of the late President Kennedy gave a platform in his magazine, 'George,' to the mother of my husband's murderer! How could he, of all people do such a thing?" Leah Rabin furiously excoriated John in front of the National Press Club saying, "I would expect John Kennedy, who lost his father to an assassin's bullet when he was a mere child and grew up in the shadow of that horrible tragedy, to adopt a higher moral standard in his paper." (15)

As fall turned to winter, problems for John's magazine mounted. Although 'George' was doing better than any other political monthly, it was hovering around $400,000 in monthly sales. In order to be profitable, it had to sell around $500,000. (16) Still, it was doing better than the other political magazines that were being published at that time.

Co-editor Eric Ethridge and co-founder Michael Berman pressured John to add his name on the cover to promote the interviews but he remained adamant, unwilling to use his name for the sake of promotion. Michael wanted John's picture on the Editor's page as well as pictures showing John interviewing his subjects.

It wasn't such a bad idea, and Eric and Michael were merely trying to boost sales. But John rejected their ideas. An inevitable rift between Michael and John soon developed, punctuated by slammed doors and shouting matches. John was also losing his temper with the media circus continually hounding his wife, Carolyn. She had grown tired of the constant harassment and complained bitterly. She couldn't even walk outside the apartment without being surrounded by press. Unhappiness reigned in the Kennedy home, and at the Kennedy workplace. John had no refuge, no sanctuary, and it took its toll. (17)

There was the much publicized and photographed altercation between husband-and-wife, where a photographer captured John and Carolyn in what appeared to be a physical brawl. One minute they were walking their dog in Washington Square Park and the next they were shouting, pushing, and crying. It was all over the tabloids and the national mainstream news. It looked bad for John, it looked bad for Carolyn, and it was bad for 'George' magazine. There was also a domestic incident where John was rushed from their home to the hospital after suffering a deep cut to his hand. (18)

In Hyannis Port, John threw a bucket of water on a photographer who called one of John's neighbors an "asshole." "You don't call women assholes!" John shouted. "Didn't your mother teach you that?" In another incident, John grabbed a photographer by the coat and threw him against the hood of his Jeep Cherokee. (19)

These actions were not typical of John's behavior. He could take the frenzy of the press but when it concerned Carolyn, he defended her with a rage never seen previously. John was in crucial need of some form of escape, and he found refuge in his one unfulfilled passion, flying. In 1997, he began taking flying lesson again. Since 1996 he had made do with flying an ultra-light 'powered parachute' which he thoroughly enjoyed. Even Carolyn didn't mind. It was more like powered gliding, and he didn't need a license. For a time, it satisfied what he really desired, his pilot's license, his own airplane, and the privacy he sought.

Another Kennedy tragedy struck on New Year's Eve, 1997. John's cousin Michael Kennedy was killed in a freak skiing accident. According to some of John's friends, he was stunned by this unexpected random death and confided that Michael's death made him that much more aware of his own mortality. Carolyn was beside herself and persuaded John to drop any thought of flying lessons. She seemed to truly believe believed in the Kennedy curse. John's desire to continue flying consumed him and within a few weeks he convinced Carolyn to accompany him to Vero Beach, Florida where he resumed his lessons.

Despite rumors of a breakup, John and Carolyn attended the Kennedy family 4th of July festivities at Hyannis Port, and in August they flew to Italy to attend the wedding of Christiane Amanpour. Outwardly they seemed to be doing fine. In private, there were problems in their marriage. John was volatile regarding 'George' magazine's up and down revenue. The Monica Lewinsky story created a strange new symmetry between politics and pop culture, something that 'George' had been reporting on for several years. Finally, people were catching on. Politics as pop culture was happening. John's political aspirations, if any, were still the topic of constant speculation.

The biggest political buzz that spring and summer was whether Hillary Clinton would run for the New York senate seat in

2000. John was completely opposed to her running. He wanted to shout it out to the world, yet he worried that if he publicly condemned Hillary, he may be denied media access from an angry Hillary camp. After much consideration he decided it was better to keep media access open in case Hillary made a bid. There was another buzz making rounds in the press: would John consider running for the Senate? According to 'George's' editor and John's confidant Richard Blow, he had been considering the idea. In fact, John had been approached by several influential New York Democrats with offers of financial support and campaign strategies. If he decided to run, he and everyone else knew that he was unbeatable. The entire country would support him, and the press would have been eating from the palm of his hand. The Prince of Camelot was poised to assume his throne!

When Hillary announced her intention to run, John quietly re-focused on his magazine's floundering sales. Many regarded his reluctance to run as a missed opportunity that would have led John to the White House. Some of John's close friends then suggested he should run for Mayor of New York City. To them, he seemed a natural. John's response was that he might run for office at some point, provided he felt he'd earned the right. (20)

That summer, John purchased a Piper Saratoga airplane and could often be seen flying the Vineyard coastline. He even convinced Carolyn that she might enjoy flying as well. In fact, Carolyn and actor Harrison Ford's wife Melissa Mathison had agreed to take flying lessons together. Their decision wasn't based on their love of flying, rather out of fear of not knowing what to do in case John or Harrison Ford became incapacitated while piloting their aircraft. John had thoughtfully given Carolyn a book called 'The Pinch Hitter;' a guide showing non-fliers how to pilot and land a plane in an emergency. (21) As if to lessen the sting of all the recent Kennedy-related deaths, a Kennedy wedding was being planned, and John and Carolyn were planning to attend. Rory Kennedy was getting married on July 17, 1999, and John prepared for the short flight to Martha's Vineyard.

Five

<u>TWA Flight 800 and the NTSB</u>

Author's Note: Most of this manuscript was compiled before the discovery of the Classified FBI Report recovered by Mr. Sherman Skolnick. The reader will encounter numerous references to that report in the following pages of text. These direct references to the FBI Report were inserted to substantiate the evidence gathered by the authors and their references.

<u>TWA Flight 800, July 17, 1996</u>

<u>Compromise and Cronyism within the NTSB and the FBI</u>

Undoubtedly, the reader will ask, "why are we discussing the elements of the TWA Flight 800 disaster when this book is about the demise of John F. Kennedy Jr.?" The answer is pure and simple. The investigation of TWA Flight 800 was compromised at the highest levels of U.S. Government. Never in the history of aviation disasters has an investigation been so corrupted, deliberately fraudulent and adulterated.

The actions of high-ranking members of the NTSB, the FBI, the CIA, and the White House serve as alarming examples of high-level corruption. Many of the same officials who intentionally hid the truth of what really happened to TWA Flight 800 remained in place nearly three years later, the night John F. Kennedy, Jr. was murdered.

The magnitude of witness intimidation, alteration of evidence and media manipulation cannot be overlooked. The murder/coverup of John Jr. pales in comparison to the intentionally nefarious activities surrounding the demise of TWA Flight 800.

The plethora of outrageous lies, and the preposterous findings of the agencies involved in the "investigation" of TWA Flight 800 served as the perfect dress rehearsal for the subterfuge involved in the investigation into the tragedy that took the lives of JFK, Jr., his pregnant wife Carolyn, and her sister Lauren. Their fateful flight proved to be an 'accident' of much less magnitude. The NTSB is the ultimate authority regarding response, investigation, documentation and official conclusions of all transportation-related accidents and incidents. Any other agencies, such as the FAA, the Coast Guard, Civil Air Patrol, municipal police and other search and rescue organizations all report back to the NTSB.

When a catastrophe such as an airplane crash occurs, the NTSB is immediately notified by the responding agency. A team of NTSB investigators is rapidly deployed to the scene. The investigation is initiated upon their arrival. The magnitude of the disaster determines the number of investigators dispatched to a crash site. Aviation and railroad accidents can sometimes command dozens of field investigators who are responsible for compiling Field Reports. These reports are then condensed into the Final Report, referred to as the Full Narrative. Until the early 1990's those same field investigators worked together to prepare the Full Narrative, which served as the NTSB's official report and their conclusions.

"THEN THINGS CHANGED!"

Several months ago, co-author Ise spoke with Henry 'Hank' Hughes, former lead investigator for the NTSB. Hank is credited with more than twenty-six years' service with the NTSB. Hank has spent his life serving with counterintelligence, a career detective. He led the team of investigators tasked with the investigation into the TWA Flight 800 disaster. The tragedy that doomed the fully loaded Boeing 747 occurred ten miles south of Long Island on the night of July 17, 1996. Nearly one hundred onlookers who witnessed this disaster, including aviators, observed up to three proximity missiles rising from the sea. These missiles are designed for targets such as planes, missiles, ships at sea, and ground forces. One of the projectiles arced toward the aircraft and exploded near the left wing. The high energy explosion shattered the spar and other structural components of the aircraft. The fully fueled jumbo jet bound for France exploded in midair, killing all 230 people on board. Upon his arrival at the scene, Inspector James Spear observed at least 1,000 law enforcement officials. It gave him the impression that the investigation was operating under martial law. To the NTSB team the situation seemed very unusual for an accident investigation.

The FBI supervised the transportation of the recovered wreckage, which was loaded on National Guard trucks and driven to the reconstruction hangar located ten miles away at Calverton, NY. The inspectors observed an unusual amount of friction between FBI agents and agents from the Bureau of Alcohol, Tobacco, and Firearms, who had significantly more experience regarding investigations that involved explosives. Hughes said, "The ATF agents were relegated to sitting at picnic tables where they were not allowed to do anything." (1)

Inspector Spear found a structural sample of the aircraft which had three holes blown through it. He said, "it was like a .22 shot through a tin can with an obvious entrance and exit side of the penetration." As he raised his camera to photograph the evidence, FBI agents ordered him to stop. As the investigation continued, Inspector Spears found other structural parts with similar holes. Structural sections of the aircraft tested positive for nitrates, and sophisticated FBI analysis showed the presence of high explosive residue. FBI agents who were stationed in the field lab at Calverton operated the highly sensitive Egis Mac machines that yielded those atypical findings.

When NTSB investigators questioned the FBI agents regarding the positive results the agents stated that the Egis Mac machines delivered frequent false positive results. However, Dr. Fred Whitehurst, Supervisory Special Agent for the FBI Laboratory said the agent's claim regarding false positives was untrue. Furthermore, Dr. David Fine, inventor of the Egis Mac stated, "the characteristics of the Egis Machine were quite to the contrary. The machine is very sensitive and extremely accurate in the measurement of nitrates. The machine is seldom, if ever, incorrect in the detection of nitrates."

FBI agents then ran the tests four more times but would not allow any of the inspectors to observe them performing the tests. The agents claimed the four tests were all negative, then calling the initial test a false positive. The structural samples were removed from the premises and subsequently sent to the FBI lab in Washington D.C., never to be seen again. Dr. Whitehurst did

Kallstrom (holding evidence) in front of reconstructed TWA Flight 800.

not understand why the FBI removed the samples, since transportation could expose the samples to potential contamination. James Kallstrom, an FBI Regional Director was questioned as to how the samples could have disappeared. He laughed and replied, "To my knowledge everything came back, nothing disappeared."

FORENSIC TAMPERING

Chief Medical Examiner, Dr. Charles Wetli remarked, "Many of the bodies had parts of metal embedded in the bodies, pieces of metal we could not identify. We initially separated out these particles of metal. They were put into plastic containers categorized by a number we gave them. We could then address whether they came from the surface of the body, or they came from the internal tissues of the body. The samples were then turned over to the FBI." (2)

Retired Colonel, Dr. Dennis F. Shanahan, Senior Consultant Medical Forensics said, "Normally I would expect to receive the parts as Dr. Wetli had discharged them from his office. But then at some point someone from the FBI presented some plastic containers with metal parts in them. They weren't separated as Dr. Wetli described. They were pretty much together. We certainly lost identification as to who the parts were associated with. If you can associate a wound with a certain particle, it tells you something about direction. It also tells you something about the velocity of those parts. But once they were combined there really wasn't much analysis we could do." (3)

Inspector Hughes said, "Virtually nothing that the FBI learned about the investigation was provided to us." Inspector Spears added, "We didn't have much cooperation from the FBI on any part of the investigation. The FBI controlled all access to the wreckage, and no one from the NTSB could see it until all the evidence technicians from the FBI had looked at it and decided that NTSB Inspectors could see it." This type of concealment was previously unheard of in NTSB history.

Inspector James Spear also noticed missing time frames in salvage video recorded by remotely operated vehicles. He demanded to see the unedited version. An agent from the FBI responded in an adversarial tone and informed him that he could not view the entire video.

Remains of TWA Flight 800 fell into three debris fields. Color coded tags indicated which debris field the parts were recovered from, noted with latitude and longitude coordinates and the date they were recovered. About one month into the investigation, Inspector Hughes noticed that the materials in the hangar had been disturbed. Investigator John Desmond also noticed that the tags had been changed. Only two people had keys to the hangar. Hank Hughes had one and the security chief had the other. The FBI then set up video surveillance inside the hangar. They discovered that three FBI agents from another office had entered the hangar in the early hours of the morning.

The inspectors were told that these were new agents who were never identified. On one occasion an agent from California was brought in. Agent Ricky Hahn was found in the hangar in the middle of the night hammering on a piece of wreckage trying to flatten it out. His actions violate every rule of normal investigation into events of this type. No one is allowed to alter or destroy evidence. These actions by the FBI were brought to the attention of the NTSB Investigator in Charge, Al Dickinson, but nothing was ever done. To the frustration of the investigators, every time there was a problem, it was ignored.

FBI Witness Manipulation and Intimidation

The FBI interviewed more than seven hundred witnesses, all providing similar descriptions of what had happened. They all had seen streaks of light heading toward the aircraft, followed shortly by an enormous fireball. Outraged by the FBI's malfeasance Dr. Vernon Gross stated, "What the FBI did which was so onerous to me is that they did all the interviewing of eyewitnesses." Dr. Gross is the most interviewed analyst in the world regarding TWA Flight 800. He continued, "What the FBI did by being sole interrogators is they kept the NTSB out." Inspector Hughes added, "The vast majority of witnesses were never interviewed by the NTSB. I find this unconscionable."

Olympic Airlines pilot Vasylis Baconis was flying that evening at 2,000 feet over the shore of Long Island. He observed a 'light coming out of the sea.' He followed the light throughout its path. It rose past his altitude, turned to the right and exploded near TWA Flight 800. He described the impact as "an umbrella of flames."

The official story released by the NTSB claimed the explosion was caused by faulty electrical wiring that ignited vapors in the aircraft's center section fuel tank. Their story is absurd.

Evidence of a missile strike, not vapor inspired electric spark explosion.

First, the aircraft had just departed JFK International Airport fully fueled. This left very little space in the fuel tank for vapors to develop.

Second, the only wiring anywhere near the sealed tank connected to the fuel level sensor operates on very low voltage. It would have taken 1200 volts to produce an electrical arc capable of penetrating the tank.

Third, aviation jet Grade A fuel is little more than K1 kerosene. It would need to be atomized in order to ignite in such an environment. If a match is tossed into a bucket of kerosene it will extinguish. With no doubt whatsoever whatever caused the aircraft to explode had to be something other than simple electronics.

House Subcommittee Hearing on TWA Flight 800

When the FBI and the NTSB were questioned under oath, some very interesting answers were brought forth. Kallstom blatantly lied to Representative Roy Blunt from Missouri "approximately 200 people described 'events' in the sky, none of which reported seeing a missile." The FBI abstract is replete with witnesses who said they had observed a missile. This issue became such a point of concern for Government officials that the CIA was brought in to produce their own documentary, an unimaginable fantasy which emphasized there was never a missile. Their 20-minute lame/laughable/lamentable and completely unbelievable docu-falsity is still available for public viewing at no charge on Amazon Prime. It is obvious that the production is total horse pucky. Actual witnesses who viewed the CIA animation testified that, "The animation did not even closely resemble anything they had seen." The honest, truthful, and believable hour-and-a-half documentary of TWA Flight 800 produced by outraged investigators may be rented for $3.00. It is well worth the money for those seeking the truth. Kallstrom lied and defended the FBI and NTSB by stating, "Not a missile, never was, never will be."

INTIMIDATION

One of the Flight 800 witnesses, whose name was not identified in the documentary appeared to be a refined, credible woman. She spoke of her interview with the FBI. She said, "All of a sudden, this rocket went up into the air. Then there was a big explosion. Days later the FBI came to visit, and they sat down, and they were talking to me, and they were asking me questions, and I told them my story. They had this little pad. Then when the interview was over, they looked at me and they

CIA documentary of TWA Flight 800.

said, "You have your papers in to become an American citizen, don't you?" She replied, "Yes I'm waiting to be called." The agents continued: "Well it would be very wise of you, if you want to become an American citizen, to keep very quiet about this and to not talk about it."

ADMINISTRATIVE CORRUPTION NTSB

At the time of the TWA Flight 800 tragedy, David Mayer was a relatively new NTSB employee. He had no training or experience in any aspect of transportation accident investigation. When James Hall, NTSB Executive Director testified during a public hearing on TWA Flight 800, he mentioned Mayer, saying that "Almost a year after the investigation began, I noticed that he had come to my hangar and started to change evidence tags, never bothered to ask me, just started changing them. The things that he did were technically illegal. There are ten or twelve pieces of evidence where he altered the location from which they were recovered. (4) It became blatantly clear that this was an agenda driven investigation. The agenda was, 'this was an accident, make it so." Hall went on to say, "These hearings are an exercise in public accountability." (5) Inspectors were not allowed to ask any questions or speak at the public hearing. Moreover, eyewitness testimony was disallowed. When questioned by reporters, Hall stated, "there was no reason in his mind to think this was a bomb or a missile and he felt that the NTSB had done all that it could to look at the issue."

The report compiled by Hank Hughes contained 497 pages and photographic supplements. Without his knowledge or approval, the report was cut and amended to 28 pages. When he complained about the butchery, nothing was done. The inspectors were required to provide a factual report but ordered not to write an analysis. In every other investigation Hank had been involved in, the group chairman wrote a factual report, and based upon that report wrote an analysis. Hank's analysis stated that the explosive forces came from outside of the airplane, not from the center fuel tank. James Hall stated, "Let me tell ya, this is an honest investigation and that it is being conducted in an honest and open fashion." When questioned before the House Transportation Committee, Hall, was asked if there was any conclusive evidence to prove that it was a mechanical failure that caused the explosion of the center fuel tank. Hall replied, "No."

When Kallstrom was questioned whether any explosive chemicals were found in the plane, he answered, "In the affirmative." Officials then lied regarding an explosives training session that was conducted aboard the aircraft less than one hour before its departure for France. The TWA Flight 800 tragedy was a watershed moment in the history of the United States and gave its perpetrators confidence that they could execute such a horrific event, cover it up and not be held responsible.

Hank Hughes stated that as an American he was, "Ashamed of the coverup. The malfeasance and nefarious activities on the part of the NTSB bother me to this day." He continued, "Despite repeated efforts to inform them of the facts, the media and reporters refused to look at the facts regarding the crash." Some of the most telling evidence was the splatter pattern found over the top section of the center wing tank. This indicates that the splatter was deposited prior to the explosion of the center wing tank. Samples of this splatter pattern which ran across the fracture boundaries of the center fuel tank were sent to NASA.

At the space center, Charlie Bassett ran nitrate tests on the samples. The report that came back to NTSB indicated that the samples contained a significant level of 7.5 micrograms of nitrates. Despite the NASA findings, despite knowing that nitrates are commonly associated with explosives, NTSB officials stopped requesting further examination of the samples. Extensive further testing should have been ordered. Subsequent explosive tests staged independently by the investigators produced fractures in the wing structure identical to the fractures found in TWA Flight 800. Captain Ray Lear sued the CIA and received the agency's own simulation software, which did not support their claim that the airplane reached a climb attitude before breaking apart and falling into the sea.

MORE FORENSIC EVIDENCE OF A HIGH ENERGY EXPLOSION:

Hank Hughes stated, "Typically, you will see damage patterns that correlate with the injuries. The center tank blowing up or an explosive device within the airplane would have caused a burn pattern which would have emanated from one area and would have progressed in a direction away from the area where the explosion originated. In the instance of TWA Flight 800, there is no such correlation. From front to back and right to left, the injury patterns were completely atypical. One person might have been severely burned and the person sitting next to them didn't have a mark on their body, and the person sitting next to them was completely destroyed." (6)

Forensic investigators found pieces of bone which were shot through or imbedded in sections of the fuselage. These fragments were telling examples of the tremendous force involved in the explosion. The damage to the seats and the injuries to the passengers was random. According to Hank Hughes, this indicated a high ordinance detonation, as opposed to a low-speed explosion such as a center tank blowing up. Hughes stated, "Considering that we could not determine a point from which the explosion emanated, I think it was external to the aircraft." (7)

In April 2000, the NTSB decided to go down to Edwin Air Force Base and shoot stinger flares and fireworks. They placed witnesses on the ground in different locations at various distances from the launch point. Basically, the theory was intended to prove that the witnesses didn't actually know what they were seeing. If proven, the results could then be used to eliminate the veracity of those who witnessed the TWA Flight 800 debacle. Therefore, it could be brought up to refute the eyewitnesses at the hearing. To the NTSB's surprise the three missile launches were easily and correctly identified by all the eyewitnesses.

PHYSICAL EVIDENCE OF A HIGH ENERGY EXPLOSION (RADAR)

Radar data recorded during the first few seconds after the airplane lost electrical power showed debris moving away from the airplane at a speed of nearly Mach 4. This is greater than four times the speed of sound or 3,050 miles per hour. This was clear evidence of a high energy explosion and certainly not the eruption of a center fuel tank. This evidence is the smoking gun which proves the entire case for a high energy explosion. Witness upon witness saw three missiles explode near TWA Flight 800, one launched from land and two by sea. Eyewitnesses reported seeing a boat with bright mast lights from which the third missile was launched.

THE LAST INSULT

At the final NTSB hearing on TWA Flight 800, eyewitnesses who were not allowed to testify listened to NTSB's Dr. Dave

Mayer give an hour-long speech on why their reports were deemed unreliable. Mayer is the same man who was found altering evidence in the reconstruction hangar at Calverton. He deliberately lied about witness testimony during the hearing. According to Hank Hughes, "Mayer was Mr. Fix It." There is no doubt he was well paid for his performance. 16 years after the crash of Flight 800, a Petition for Reconsideration was filed with the NTSB. The petition contained the signatures of investigators, eyewitnesses, surviving family members and concerned citizens.

Hank Hughes on CNN discussing lies about TWA 800 Crash.

The Petition for Reconsideration was flatly denied by NTSB officials. According to Inspector Hughes, this tragedy bore witness to one of the most compromised investigations in NTSB history. Hank said, "We used to compile our own Final Narratives. All the actual Field Investigators would sit at a big table for days and compose the Full Narrative. It was a condensed version of all the field reports. That was it. Our word is law."

THEN THINGS CHANGED

Hughes said, "At the tail end of the Bush years, we had a lot of people in administration who were retiring. They never had any part in preparing our reports. Our knowledgeable administrators were replaced by political appointees who had little or no experience in the field. We were appalled. They knew nothing about their own jobs and much less about ours." He continued, "Suddenly we were faced with a very disturbing change in professional protocol. Our Field Notes were now directed to these agenda-driven officials so that they could prepare the Final Reports. These people were professional spin doctors who altered and adulterated our findings. It was an outrage. TWA Flight 800 was a prime example of this illicit and illegal activity. The subversion of evidence was unlike anything any of us had ever seen in our careers. This was a felony beyond imagination. And they got away with it." (8)

The tragedy of TWA Flight 800 is without doubt the result of three, surface to air proximity missiles. But it was not the first time in U.S. history that a military 'accident' was made to look like one.

Six

<u>Iran Air Flight 665</u>

If you walked into any high school classroom in the United States and asked the students to describe their country's relationship with Iran, you'd probably hear words like, 'enemy,' 'threat,' 'distrust' and 'nuclear.' But ask them why the number 655 is relevant, and you'd be met with silence.

Repeating that exercise in an Iranian classroom, asking about the United States, and you'd probably hear the same words. Mention the number 655 though, and it's a safe bet that at least a few of the students would immediately know what you were talking about.

U.S.S. Vincennes in the Persian Gulf.

On July 3, 1988, near the end of the Iran-Iraq war, a U.S. Navy ship, the U.S.S. Vincennes was exchanging fire with small Iranian ships in the Persian Gulf. The U.S. Navy keeps ships deployed there to protect oil trade routes. As the American and Iranian ships skirmished, Iran Air Flight 655 departed from nearby Bandar Abbas International Airport, bound for Dubai. The airport was used for both civilian and military aircraft. The Vincennes mistook the lumbering Airbus A300 civilian airliner for a much smaller and faster F-14 fighter jet, and fired two surface-to-air missiles, killing all 290 passengers and crew members on board. It was alleged the aircraft failed to identify itself.

The incident brought Tehran closer to ending the war, but its effects have lingered for much longer. "The shoot-down of Iran Air Flight 655 was an accident, but that is not how it was seen in Tehran," former CIA analyst and current Brooking's scholar Kenneth Pollack wrote in his 2004 history of U.S.-Iran enmity, 'The Persian Puzzle.' Pollack continues, "The Iranian government assumed that the attack had been purposeful. Tehran convinced itself that Washington was trying to signal that the United States had decided to openly enter the war on Iraq's side." (1)

That belief, along with Iraq's increased use of chemical weapons against Iran, led Tehran to accept a United Nations cease-fire two months later. But it also helped cement a perspective in Iran, still common among government hard-liners, that the United States is committed to the destruction of the Islamic Republic and will stop at almost nothing to accomplish this. It is one of several reasons distrust for the United States is still prevalent within Iran.

If Iran believes that the United States would knowingly shoot down a plane carrying Iranian civilians, then Tehran has every reason to distrust America. It would also lead them to fear an inevitable U.S. invasion. Americans might not remember Flight 655, but Iranians will never forget. (2)

The toughest question to ask regarding the incident is this: How does an entire crew of highly trained American military personnel mistake a huge, fully loaded Airbus A300 (top speed 518 MPH) for a much smaller military fighter jet capable of attaining a speed of Mach 4? (3069 mph) When considering the fiasco associated with TWA flight 800 discussed earlier, a likely comparison provides an ominous answer: People high in Government authority engaged in subterfuge, deceit, and cover-up.

Airbus A300 civilian jet.

Grumman F-14 Tomcat.

Seven

John F. Kennedy Jr.—Pilot

TWO YEARS OF INTENSIVE FOCUSED TRAINING

- At least 200 hours flying hang gliders and ultralights thru 1982 (estimated)
- 46 hours Dual and 1 hour solo from 1982 thru 1988. Jackie terrified: John promised her he would fly no more.
- Jackie dies May 19, 1994 : John resumes training December of 1997, Departs for FSI. 43 hours dual, 10 solo.
- Buys C182 N529JK, logs 65 dual and 114 solo hours during 8, months average 5.5 hours per week.
- Passes Instrument written exam on March 12, 1999 with a 78% score. Returns to FSI April 05, 1999.
- Receives 13.3 hours Dual IFR, 17 hours Simulator time. Departs FSI April 24th and buys Saratoga N9235N.
- Three different CFIs log 96 hrs. dual training; 17 hrs. of night training and 8 hrs. instrument training.
- Receives Complex endorsement May, 1999.

Two years intensive training focuses on December 1997-July 1999.

The following information was taken directly from the official NTSB Accident Report Full Narrative.

NTSB Identification Number: NYC99MA178

On October 4, 1982, John F. Kennedy Jr. started receiving flight instruction. Through the next six years, he flew with six different Certified Flight Instructors (CFI's). During this period, he logged 47 hours, consisting of 46 hours of dual instruction and one hour without a CFI on board. John made no entries in his logbook from September 1988 to December 1997.

In December 1997, after the death of his mother, John enrolled in a training program at Flight Safety International (FSI), Vero Beach, Florida, to obtain his private pilot certification. Between December 1997 and April 1998, he flew approximately 53 hours, 43 of those accompanied by a CFI. The CFI who prepared John for his private pilot certification flight stated that the pilot had "very good" flying skills for his level of experience.

On April 22, 1998, John passed his private pilot flight test. The designated pilot examiner who administered the check ride stated that as part of the flight test, John conducted two unusual attitude recoveries. In both instances, John recovered the airplane while wearing a hood and referencing the airplane's flight instruments. He could not reference anything beyond the airplane's instrument panel. After receiving his private pilot certificate, John flew solo in his Cessna 182 and received instruction from CFI's local to New Jersey. He also received instruction at Million Air, a flight school in New Jersey, and flew their airplanes. During calendar year 1998, John flew approximately 179 hours, including 65 hours without a CFI on board. On March 12, 1999, John completed the FAA's written airplane instrument examination and received a score of 78%.

On April 5, 1999, John returned to FSI and began an airplane instrument rating course. During the instrument training, John satisfactorily completed the first 12 of 25 lesson plans. John's primary CFI stated that John's progression was normal and that he grasped all of the basic skills needed to complete the course.

John attended this training primarily on weekends and accumulated 13.3 hours of flight time with a CFI on board. In addition, he logged 16.9 hours of simulator time. John left FSI for the last time on April 24, 1999.

He continued to receive flight instruction from CFIs in New Jersey in his newly purchased Piper Saratoga, the aircraft he flew until his untimely death. One CFI flew with John on three separate occasions. One of the flights was on June 25, 1999, from Caldwell Field to Martha's Vineyard. The CFI stated that their departure, flight, and descent were executed under visual flight conditions, but an instrument approach into Martha's Vineyard was required because of a 300-foot overcast ceiling. The CFI requested an instrument flight rules (IFR) clearance and demonstrated a coupled instrument landing system (ILS) approach to runway 24. The CFI stated that John performed the landing to his satisfaction. He also noted that John's aeronautical abilities and his ability to handle multiple tasks while flying were average based on his level of experience.

A second CFI flew with John between May 1998 and July 1999. This CFI accumulated 39 hours of flight time with him, including 21 hours of night flight and 0.9 hour flown in Instrument Meteorological Conditions (IMC). John used this CFI as a safety pilot and for instruction on cross-country flights. In May 1999 the CFI conducted a 'complex airplane' evaluation on John, giving him full authorization to pilot the Saratoga. On July 1, 1999, the CFI accompanied John on a flight to Martha's Vineyard. The flight was conducted at night, and instrument conditions prevailed at the airport. The CFI stated that, during the flight, John used and exhibited competence with the autopilot, adding that during the flight John wore a non-plaster cast on his leg, which required the CFI to taxi the airplane and help John with the landing. He also noted that John had the ability to fly the airplane without a visible horizon. He also stated that as of July 1, 1999 John was not ready for an instrument evaluation and needed additional training, also noting John was methodical about his flight planning and that he was very cautious about his aviation decision-making. He felt that John had the capability to conduct a night flight to Martha's Vineyard as long as a visible horizon existed.

A third CFI flew with John between May 1998 and July 1999. This CFI accumulated 57 hours of flight time with John, including 17 hours of night flight and 8 hours flown in actual instrument conditions. John also used this instructor for instruction on cross-country flights and as a safety pilot. This CFI had conducted a 'complex airplane' evaluation on the pilot and signed him off in the Saratoga in May 1999. The CFI had made six or seven flights to Martha's Vineyard John in the Saratoga. The CFI stated that most of the flights were conducted at night and that, during the flights, the pilot did not have any trouble flying the airplane.

John's actual flight skills were more finely tuned than one would be led to believe. The preceding excerpts taken from the NTSB Full Narrative, although fairly accurate, would cause one to conclude that John's flight training was undertaken over an extended period of time. The long and wordy nature of the summary subjectively overwhelms the reader.

We can look at John's total flight time and provide analysis in a more condensed format. John's total flight time appears as follows:

Dual time (with instructor) 250 hours minimum
Solo time (Pilot in command) at least 125 hours
Instrument time (simulator and actual) 38.3 hours
Night flight (actual) 40 hours minimum

Complex Aircraft (retractable landing gear, and constant speed prop) 96 hours

John's total time on record, 450 hours minimal, considering some of the time above was flown as dual time.

Note that John completed 38.3 hours of training for his instrument rating. This figure is only 1.7 hours short of FAA requirements to be an instrument rated pilot. John was within 1.7 hours of his certification as an instrument rated pilot. This completely contradicts the "official story" which portrayed John as an inexperienced pilot without an instrument rating. When the actual weather conditions at departure airport, enroute weather and weather at Martha's Vineyard the night of the doomed flight are examined in detail, visibility was excellent and cloud decks were well above John's flight level, in complete contradiction with the official and thoroughly false narrative.

It should be noted that John's most current logbook was supposedly lost in the crash. He had also logged significant time flying hang gliders and ultralights, which was never mentioned in the Final Narrative. Multiple media sources had already been giving false information discrediting John's flight skills.

It is interesting to analyze John's known flight time from an instructor's standpoint. John supposedly flew 46 hours of dual instruction and one hour of solo flight time between 1982 and 1988. It was during 1988 that he ceased flight lessons at his mother's behest. Jackie became terrified that she would lose her son in a plane crash. John acceded to his mother's wishes and ceased flying. From a flight instructor's perspective, the issue which immediately becomes apparent is the ratio of dual to solo flight time noted in the report. It is highly unlikely that the solo time figure is accurate, given the fact that Aviation schools typically frown on excessive dual flying time. The pilot is constantly motivated to increase his solo time and use it productively, practicing procedures and maneuvers. The typical solo to dual hourly ratio for private pilot certification is 1:1. That is, one hour dual to one hour solo time. A forty-hour private pilot regimen would typically include 20 hours of dual training and twenty hours of solo practice.

John's records would seem to indicate a concentrated period of flight training with an instructor just prior to the solo flight. Typically, preparing for any solo flight would mandate at least ten hours of consolidated dual flight training. From 1988 through 1994, in keeping with his Mother's wishes, John did not record any flight time.

JFK Jr. pre-flight inspection of Cessna 182, Tail Number N529JK.

During April of 1998, John bought a beautiful Cessna 182. He registered the aircraft choosing Tail Number N529JK in memory of his father's birthday. The 182 was the perfect 'family airplane' for someone of John's flight experience and financial means. It was the ideal airplane to transition to more complex aircraft. The 182 is noted for its versatility, stability, reliability, and ease of flight. To this day the 182 is one of the most dependable and trustworthy airplanes flying the skies. This particular model would cruise at 125 knots or 140 miles per hour.

The NTSB Final Narrative states that using this plane from April through December of 1998 John flew 65 hours of dual instruction and 114 hours of solo time. Those figures equate to 179 hours of flight time in 8 months or 5.5 hours per week. There were also days of inclement weather which were below minimums required for visual flight. The hours flown by John would indicate a good cohesive and progressive transition into higher performance aircraft.

The 182 serves as an excellent platform for pilots receiving instrument flight training. A pilot with John's level of experience would normally require 10-12 hours of instructor time before receiving his endorsement for the 182. Insurance requirements are typically in the same range. The numbers in the Final Narrative are suspiciously askew. Though the factors are unspecified in the NTSB report, it is almost certain that John began some of his instrument training in his Piper Saratoga.

Most reputable flight schools who produce high quality pilots' frown on over-training. The FAR's (Federal Aviation Regulation) are very specific as to the minimum training requirements for each rating. If flight training centers exceed these minimums significantly, they subject themselves to FAA scrutiny. Typically, when dual training exceeds the minimum requirements by 10-15 hours the Chief Flight Instructor intervenes to correct the student's expected progress. Good schools monitor these times very closely.

Most assuredly airplanes have improved technologically over time. However, the art of competently piloting those planes has changed very little. An airplane is a three-axis motor vehicle which operates within the confines of pitch, roll, and yaw. For decades, pilots have been trained using the same techniques as their predecessors. The examination standards have remained basically the same. If the student fails any of the mandatory maneuvers, he fails the overall exam. He is issued a 'pink' failure slip by the flight examiner and must demonstrate competence in performing the failed task at a later date. The student's primary instructor is informed of the deficiency and is responsible for providing the training necessary to bring the student up to performance standard.

The hourly requirements are much lower than one would think. For example, the private pilot rating requires a minimum of 40 hours total dual and solo time before being recommended for a flight examination. If the flight school is using an FAA approved integrated course of study, which most schools do, then the total time requirement is reduced to 35 hours. These hours may seem minimal however, the numbers are an accurate reflection of the traditional study time necessary to train and certify safe pilots.

John's final flight log was supposedly never found. The NTSB clearly states its figures are only estimates based on flight school records and past logbooks. In that vein, it is likely the reports lack complete, accurate data. More than likely John logged a great deal more solo flight time than we are being led to believe. For example, here's a quote from a CNN article in which a Federal Pilot Examiner who tested John's flying skills describes his abilities. John McColgan of Vero Beach, Florida, told the Orlando Sentinel, "He was an excellent pilot." He continued, "I put him through the paces, and he passed everything with flying colors." He said Kennedy had a lot of flight experience for someone who had his pilot's license for a mere 15 months. "He flew a lot," McColgan said. "In fact, by now he probably has enough hours to be a Commercial pilot." At the time of his death, John had logged at least 200 hours in excess of the commercial certification requirement.

The Final Narrative issued by the NTSB reads: "The pilot obtained his private pilot certificate for 'airplane single-engine land' in April 1998. He did not possess an instrument rating. He received a 'high performance airplane' sign-off in the accident airplane in May 1999. His most recent Federal Aviation Administration (FAA) second-class medical certificate was issued on December 27, 1997, with no limitations."

A copy of the pilot's (John) logbook from October 4, 1982 through November 11, 1998, was provided to the Safety Board. The pilot's most recent logbook was not located. The Board used the copied logbook, records from training facilities, copies of flight instructors' logbooks, and statements from instructors and pilots to estimate the pilot's total flight experience. The pilot's estimated total flight experience, excluding simulator training, was about 310 hours, of which 55 hours were at night. The pilot's estimated experience flying without a certified flight instructor (CFI) on board was about 72 hours. The pilot's estimated flight time in the accident airplane was about 36 hours, of which 9.4 hours were at night. Approximately 3 hours of that flight time was without a CFI on board, and about 0.8 hours of that time was flown at night, which included a night landing. In the 15 months before the accident, the pilot had flown about 35 flight legs either to or from the Essex County/Teterboro, New Jersey, area and the Martha's Vineyard, Hyannis, Massachusetts, area. The pilot flew over 17 of these legs without a CFI on board, including at least 5 at night. The pilot's last known flight in the accident airplane without a CFI on board was on May 28, 1999." (2)

On March 12, 1999, John passed his instrument written exam, the most difficult test a pilot will take in his aviation career. His score in the 78th percentile is regarded as a good overall score. According to the official record, John returned to Flight Safety International where he had received previous training. During his stay he logged 13.3 hours of actual instrument flying and 17 hours of simulator time. John logged 30.3 hours of instrument time in 21 days. He departed Flight Safety on April 24, 1999.

On April 28th, 1999, John purchased a used 1996 Piper Saratoga II HP, Tail Number N9235N for an estimated $300,000. It is unclear when he sold N529JK, though the sale would certainly be recorded in the FAA Archives. The Saratoga is a 300-horsepower, single-engine six-seater that pilots compare to a sport utility vehicle. It was originally owned by a private North Carolina company, then by Munir Hussain of Hasbrouck, New Jersey, who sold it to John through a broker. Government and company records indicate no history of mechanical problems. The aircraft could attain a cruise speed of approximately 166 knots or 192 mph. With this transaction, John was stepping up. Had he lived there undoubtedly would have been additional steps up to more complex, sophisticated aircraft, and John's abilities as a pilot would have continued to improve.

JFK Jr. piloting Piper Saratoga II HP, Tail Number N9253N (undated photo)

Pilot Credentials

KNOWN FLIGHT TIME TOTALS

DUAL   250 HOURS
SOLO   125 HOURS MINIMAL
INSTRUMENT   38.3 HOURS MINIMAL
NIGHT   40 HOURS MINIMAL
COMPLEX   96 HOURS MINIMAL

450 HOURS TOTAL ESTIMATED TIME NOT INCLUDING ULTRALIGHTS

ONLY 250 HOURS REQUIRED FOR COMMERCIAL CERTIFICATION

Eight

July 16, 1999

A Late Departure—The Phone Calls

A whirlwind of speculation surrounds John's activities prior to leaving Caldwell airport. According to Adam Budd, John Jr. contacted Martha's Vineyard Airport Operations at 1:30 p.m. on July 16, 1999, informing them that he planned to arrive at 7:30 p.m. that evening. He planned to drop his sister-in-law Lauren there and continue on to Hyannis Port for his cousin Rory's long-awaited wedding. John reportedly picked up Lauren around 5:00 p.m. and headed to Caldwell Airport, hoping for an early departure. Moderate traffic was reported.

What happened next is subject to speculation. John was observed placing several phone calls to Carolyn, who was very late. He appeared agitated. Some theorize that John was desperately trying to reach his flight instructor who was supposed to accompany him on the flight. This is false.

Others suggest that a 'Manchurian Candidate,' MK-ULTRA instructor left in the airplane with John and his family, and proceeded to sabotage the airplane while it was enroute to the Vineyard. This is false as well. John was totally qualified, comfortable, and in no need of an instructor to accompany him. Arguments to support the Manchurian Instructor theory surround revolved around the missing right front passenger seat which was reportedly never recovered in the wreckage. Further speculation relates to the Fuel selector valve which was found locked in the

OFF position. Proponents of the Manchurian Instructor theory attribute the valve position to a deliberate act of sabotage by the attending instructor. There is no evidence that indicates anything of this sort ever occurred. The fuel valve position will be discussed in a later chapter.

So, what were John's frequent phone calls in the terminal lobby about? All pilots are required by law to check weather conditions before departing on any flight. The registration number of the aircraft is logged into the National Weather Service Data Base. Should a pilot experience an incident or accident on any given flight, his tail numbers must be on record for a weather check. It is the first question asked by investigators in the event a pilot is involved in a mishap. John is on record as having checked the weather that evening. Seeing that John was delayed, he may have made one or more calls, checking the weather. His remaining phone calls, which surfaced in 2003 were accounted for by hair colorist Colin Lively. (1) Speaking publicly for the first time, she told author Edward Klein, "It was late at the end of the day on Friday, and she (Carolyn) was right next to me, sitting in the same line of people getting pedicures. She had a little piece of sheer fabric about three inches square, almost white with a hint of lavender, and she wanted her toenail polish to match the swatch." After the pedicurist applied the polish, Carolyn went to the window and put her foot up next to the fabric, examining the color. She asked the pedicurist to redo the color three times.

Lively said that whenever Bessette's phone rang she would answer. "What? She'd say impatiently into the phone. I told you I'm getting a pedicure, the more times you call me the longer it's going to take." Lively said, "She was not overtly bitchy, but she was so self-involved. If this was a key to her personality, then I would say she was obsessive about a lot of things." Finally, Lively said, her phone rang again. It was her driver, who had been waiting for her. Carolyn said, "If you can't park, circle the block, I'll be down in a few minutes." Lively said, "Only when the nails were done to her satisfaction did Carolyn finally leave the salon." Carolyn's driver dropped her off at the Caldwell airport around 8:00 p.m. The extended Kennedy family then boarded John's Piper Saratoga and flew into a fate no one could have foreseen.

ROUTE OF FLIGHT

In the aftermath of the crash, media sources and official agencies circulated the following maps depicting John's flight path. Note that each chart positions the flight path directly over Long Island and Montauk Point. His last reported contact with the FAA was depicted as being ten miles east of Block Island, in complete contradiction with the official reports that there was no communication with the airplane after its departure from Caldwell airport.

Kennedy's intended route

A plane piloted by John F. Kennedy Jr., carrying his wife and her sister, disappeared Friday night en route to Martha's Vineyard. Luggage and debris from the aircraft was found and search parties continue to look for more evidence of a crash.

20 miles
20 km

MASSACHUSETTS

Boston

Intended route →

N.Y.

CONNECTICUT

R.I.

West Tisbury
Intended arrival
10 p.m.

Hyannisport

Newport

Martha's Vineyard

Fairfield
Departure about
8:30 p.m.

Philbin Beach
Luggage, debris
from plane
found on beach.

Montauk

9:39 p.m.
Last contact
with FAA.

N.J.   Long Island

AP

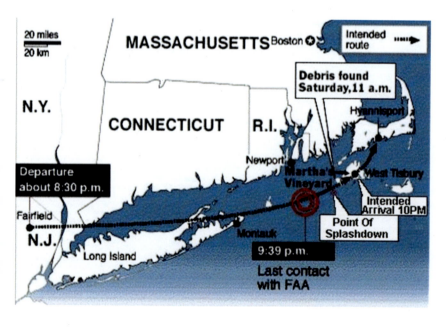

20 miles
20 km

MASSACHUSETTS Boston

Intended route

Debris found
Saturday, 11 a.m.

N.Y.

CONNECTICUT   R.I.

Hyannisport

Newport

Martha's Vineyard

West Tisbury

Departure
about 8:30 p.m.

Intended
Arrival 10PM

Fairfield

Point Of
Splashdown

N.J.

Montauk

Long Island

9:39 p.m.

Last contact
with FAA

114

The two illustrations shown on the previous page were circulated by Associated Press. They clearly depict John's airplane passing straight through the restricted airspace above Kennedy and La Guardia Airports. Supposedly he then flew directly over the open water of Long Island Sound, grazing the Hamptons. The airplane then passed over Montauk, flying twenty miles over open ocean, passing just south of Block Island and continuing on to fly another forty miles over open ocean to Martha's Vineyard.

No pilot worth his salt would choose such a route flying at night or during the day. The safety net of a highway or a beach is lost over open ocean. Should the airplane's power plant fail for any reason the pilot would be outside of the parameters required to reach an alternate landing point. The actual flight path is shown in aqua below, instead of plan indicated on next page.

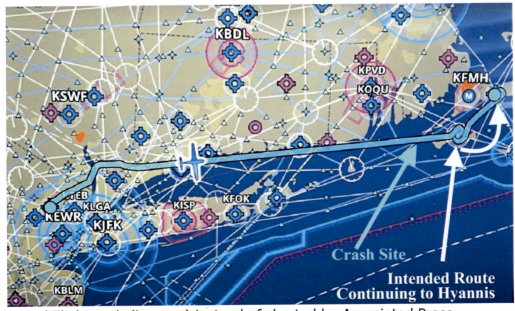

Actual Flight path (in aqua) instead of charted by Associated Press.

Kennedy's intended route

A plane piloted by John F. Kennedy Jr. carrying his wife and her sister disappeared Friday night en route to Martha's Vineyard.

Intended route

Boston

20 miles

N

MASSACHUSETTS

CONNECTICUT

R.I.

Hyannisport

Debris found

Departure
Friday, 8:30 p.m.

Martha's Vineyard

Last contact
Friday, 9:40 p.m.

Fairfield
N.J.

Long Island

Montauk

ATLANTIC
OCEAN

AP / MSNBC

MSNBC graphic depicting JFK Jr.'s flight path.

Another graphic circulated by MSNBC illustrating the same flight path shown in the previous charts. (page 114)

The graphic on page 117 was also shown to the general public, source unknown. This is the grand slam of misrepresentation regarding John's flight path. The airplane leaves Jersey, which is in the wrong place, to travel the south coast of Long Island. Midway through Long Island the pilot chooses to fly thirty miles out to sea only to arc back northeast to make the Vineyard. The very thought of John's choosing such an obtuse route is preposterous. What appears to be deliberate and intentional disinformation had to have been provided to the press by 'Official Sources.' Throughout the entire process of researching this book have we failed to locate any graphic or map depicting John's actual flight path.

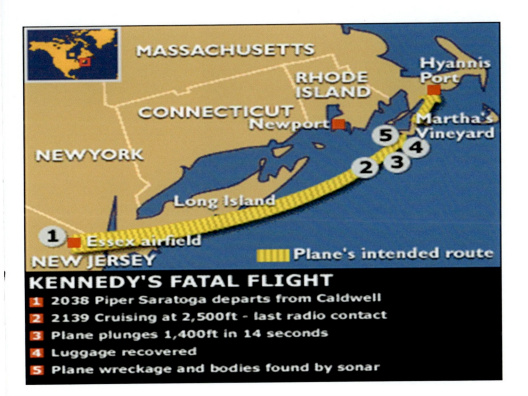

KENNEDY'S FATAL FLIGHT

1. 2038 Piper Saratoga departs from Caldwell
2. 2139 Cruising at 2,500ft - last radio contact
3. Plane plunges 1,400ft in 14 seconds
4. Luggage recovered
5. Plane wreckage and bodies found by sonar

ACTUAL ROUTE OF PATH

The map shown on page 118 is called a 'sectional.' This is the actual map pilots use to plot and navigate before and during flight. Illustrated below is an accurate plotting of the ACTUAL FLIGHT PATH of John Kennedy's airplane. Note the true course line running west to east. Disregard vertical line in center of photo, it is simply an unavoidable crease in the map. John's flight path was plotted using the coordinates and references provided in NTSB accident report; NYC99MA178. New York and Long Island are clearly visible in the left half of the map. Rhode Island Sound, Block Island, Noman's Land and Martha's Vineyard are depicted in the right half.

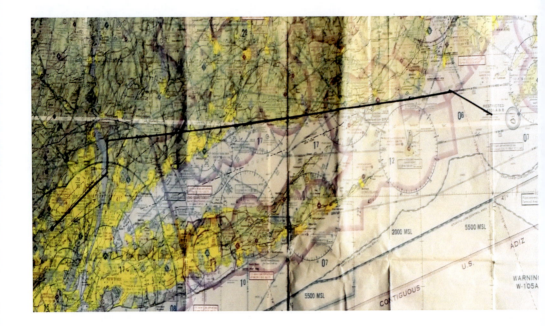

John Kennedy clearly departs Caldwell New Jersey and maintains a Northeasterly heading until intersecting the Hudson River. He flies eight miles due North in order to clear overlying airspace, then executes a right turn to a near Easterly heading while climbing to 5,500 feet. An extension of this segment of the true course line intersects the Vineyard directly, as quoted in the Accident Report.

Kennedy begins his descent from 5,500 feet, 34 miles west of the Vineyard. His airspeed is 160 knots and his descent rate as quoted from the report; 'Varied from 400-800 feet per minute.' Cruise descents in lighter aircraft are usually initiated at a rate of 500 feet per minute. It is a standard figure which has been used in flight training for years. It is also the standard descent rate taught to pilots using the Instrument Flight Rating (IFR) environment.

At a point somewhere south of Rhode Island Sound, John initiates a turn to a southeasterly heading, supposedly to fly over his Mother's property on the south shore of Martha's Vineyard. Seven miles southwest of Gay Head, John and his passengers plummet out of control into the sea below. The airplane disintegrates as it hits the water at more than 4,700 feet per minute. The impact forces are similar to driving a car into solid concrete at 60 miles per hour. Moments later, according to ABC News, FAA radar showed the plane went into a dive and dropped 1,200 feet in just 12 seconds. (2)

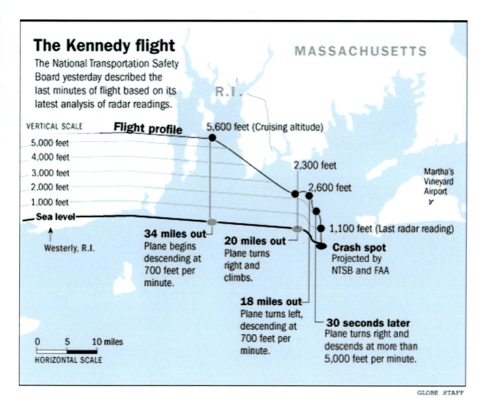

The Kennedy flight

The National Transportation Safety Board yesterday described the last minutes of flight based on its latest analysis of radar readings.

MASSACHUSETTS

R.I.

VERTICAL SCALE   **Flight profile**   5,600 feet (Cruising altitude)

5,000 feet
4,000 feet
3,000 feet   2,300 feet   Martha's
2,000 feet   2,600 feet   Vineyard
1,000 feet   Airport
Sea level

Westerly, R.I.   1,100 feet (Last radar reading)

34 miles out   **20 miles out**   **Crash spot**
Plane begins   Plane turns   Projected by
descending at   right and   NTSB and FAA
700 feet per   climbs.
minute.

                        18 miles out
                        Plane turns left,   **30 seconds later**
0   5   10 miles   descending at   Plane turns right and
                        700 feet per   descends at more than
HORIZONTAL SCALE   minute.   5,000 feet per minute.

GLOBE STAFF

In a diagram released by The Associated Press, John's airplane is shown to have made final contact with the FAA directly over Montauk Point Long Island. We already know through initial reports that his last call was made to the Control Tower at a position approximately 13 miles SW of Martha's Vineyard. His flight route is also grossly misrepresented in this depiction.

These graphics were circulated by The Associated Press, MSNBC, and BBC, billed as Kennedy's Intended Route of Flight. The red line or 'intended route' has been deliberately shifted 20 miles South of the ACTUAL KNOWN FLIGHT PATH, justifying the diversionary search in the Horton Point area.

Kennedy's intended route
A plane piloted by John F. Kennedy Jr. carrying his wife and her sister disappeared Friday night en route to Martha's Vineyard.

Intended route

Boston

20 miles

N

MASSACHUSETTS

CONNECTICUT

R.I.

Hyannisport

N.Y.

Departure
Friday, 8:30 p.m.

Debris found

Martha's Vineyard

Last contact
Friday, 9:40 p.m.

Fairfield
N.J.

Long Island

Montauk

ATLANTIC OCEAN

AP / MSNBC

Falsely printed 'intended route' of JFK Jr.'s flight plan 7/16/1999.

Location of Horton Point, original search point (diversionary).

"The plane took off from Essex County Airport in Caldwell, New Jersey at 8:38 p.m., Friday and lost contact with the FAA on its final approach to Martha's Vineyard, Massachusetts," said Coast Guard spokesman, Steve Carleton. First District Coast Guard Spokesman, Lt. Gary Jones said, "the Coast Guard was notified about the missing plane at around 3:00 a.m., EDT, and the search started immediately." According to WCVB-TV News in Boston, at 9:39 p.m., Friday, Kennedy radioed the airport, reporting he was 13 miles from the airport, 10 miles from the coast, and making his final approach. WCVB-TV said Kennedy advised controllers at the airport that he planned to drop off his wife's sister and then take off again between 11:00 p.m. and 11:30 p.m., for Hyannis Airport.

An emergency beacon thought to belong to the plane was activated and heard by the Coast Guard in Long Island, N.Y., at 3:40 a.m. As the search continued, authorities seemed to discount the relevance of the beacon signal. Kurt Hartman, spokesman for the U.S. Coast Guard's district headquarters in New Haven, Connecticut, said this morning, "We received a call from our district office in Boston directing us to conduct a shoreline search off Horton Point, in Long Island Sound, for an emergency locating transmitting beacon." (3)

During the early morning stages of the search, The Coast Guard, acting in its own rightful capacity, released an approximate location of the downed aircraft to ABC News WCVB TV Channel 5 Boston. Note: The estimated location of the crash is within 15 miles of the actual crash site provided by the U.S. Navy. The video map seen below was broadcast before the Pentagon took control of the search effort. It was never seen again as the possible point of impact during the search.

Diagram from WCVB-TV Boston of U.S. Navy's crash site.

Every airplane is fitted with an ELT: Emergency Locator Transmitter. It is nearly bulletproof and designed to activate upon any impact of significant G force. Activation is automatic, requiring no input from the pilot. The ELT is an exceptionally reliable device which is tested during routine mandatory aircraft inspections. Without an ELT beacon, search and rescue efforts would not have an immediate pinpoint location to find a downed aircraft. The ELT distress signal is heard audibly as a loud warble, much like an emergency vehicle responding to an accident. That warble is transmitted through several aircraft frequencies, and broadcast through satellite receivers as well.

The reference map on page 121 illustrates the bogus search area near Horton Point, Long Island. Horton Point is nowhere near John Kennedy's known flight path nor is it even close to the airplane's last known location provided by the **N Tap** results. Search efforts were deliberately concentrated at an appreciable distance from the known crash site. Linda Killian from People Magazine attempted to question Lt. Col. Steve Roark, the Director of the U.S. Air Force's National Search and Rescue School (at the time former director of the Air Force Rescue Coordination Center), about the time discrepancy regarding official notification of the missing plane. Raw, uninterrupted static cut her off before she could finish her question. This question never got answered, was never asked again and was never mentioned again in any media outlet.

When Col Roark was asked why his search was scattered all over a wide area of the Atlantic, when the **'N-Tap' Report** pinpointing the location of the crash was available eight hours earlier, he replied in rehearsed indifference, "we have nothing that absolutely pinpoints to one area as opposed to another, so we can't rule out the entire flight." When asked again about the radar position of the crash site, Roark lied and said, "it was just a possible position."

All conversations with air traffic control indicated a calm, relaxed pilot in full command of the flight, with no difficulties on final approach. Seconds after the last communication, the explosion was observed by several eyewitnesses and contact with the plane was lost. The headrest, steering yoke, pieces of the cowling, plexiglass and carpeting were literally torn apart from the plane and ended up floating up on Gay Head Beach. Debris from the crash was washing up on the West end of Martha's Vineyard, indicating a widespread area of destruction. This indicates a mid-air explosion, not a stall and crash.

Nine

<u>(Falsified) Weather Reports</u>

Every pilot who operates an aircraft is required by law to check weather conditions along their scheduled flight path in advance of departure. If unable to do so, they are compelled by law to obtain a briefing as soon as practical once airborne. A standard weather briefing contains the following elements:

. **Adverse Conditions.** Significant meteorological information (SIGMET) (for example, thunderstorms, icing, turbulence, low ceilings, or visibility) that might influence the pilot to alter their proposed route of flight or even cancel the flight entirely.

· **Synopsis.** A brief statement about the cause of the weather (for example, fronts or pressure systems) that is pertinent to the proposed route of flight.

· **Current Conditions.** When the proposed departure is within 2 hours, current conditions include a summary of the current weather, including Pilot (weather) Reports (PIREPs) and radar weather information applicable to the planned flight.

· **Enroute Forecast.** The briefer will summarize the forecast conditions (unless requested to read the forecasts verbatim) along the proposed route in a logical order (that is, climb out, enroute, and descent).

· **Destination Forecast.** The briefer will provide the destination forecast at the estimated time of arrival, including any significant changes expected within 1 hour of the planned time of arrival.

- **Winds Aloft.** The briefer will summarize Forecast Winds Aloft (FD) for the proposed route. Temperature information will be provided on request.

- **Notices to Airmen (NOTAMs).** The briefer will provide current NOTAMs pertinent to the proposed route of flight in a standard briefing. "Information on Global Positioning Systems outages, Long Range Navigation Military Training Routes (MTRs) and Military Operations Areas (MOAs) and published NOTAMs must be specifically requested." (1)

According to Weather Service International (WSI) personnel, a search of their briefing logs indicated that JFK Jr., or someone using his user code, made two weather requests from WSI-'s PILOT brief Website on July 16, 1999. The first request, made at 18:32:59 was for a radar image. The second request, made at 18:34:18, was for a route briefing from TEB to HYA with MVY as an alternate. (2)

The information provided to John included enroute weather observations from BID, BLM, EWB, EWR, FMH, FOK, FRG, ISP, JFK, PVD, and TAN. These observations indicated that visibilities varied from 10 miles along the route to 4 miles and haze at CDW. The lowest cloud ceiling was reported at 20,000 feet overcast at PVD. These observations were made about 18:00. (3)

No records exist of the pilot, or a pilot using the airplane's registration number, receiving a weather briefing, or filing a flight plan with any FAA, FSS (Flight Service Station) for the accident flight. Further, no record exists of the pilot, or a pilot using the airplane's registration number, contacting any FSS or ATC tower or facility during the duration of the flight, except for those at CDW. (4)

Federal investigators confirmed that Kennedy received an Internet weather forecast at 6:30 p.m. EDT for the flight from New Jersey to Massachusetts. The report indicated good visual flight conditions with a visibility of six to eight miles. Kennedy did not take off until 8:38 p.m. (5)

A certain ambiguity exists within the Official NTSB Report: The first two quotes state John contacted WSI not only once, but once for a radar report and a second time for enroute conditions. Oddly, in a subsequent paragraph the report states that John did not check weather, nor did he contact any Flight Service Facility or any Air Traffic Control facility or Control Tower! We know this to be false. Someone at NTSB who compiled the final report should have proofread the document before releasing it.

Field Observations

Field observations, measured hourly, by the AWOS and ASOS measuring systems located at enroute aviation facilities, provide us with the most accurate accounting of the meteorological conditions affecting a given flight. These are high tech machines which record and archive actual weather at given locations. Most of these stations are located at airports, though some are constructed in significant geographical locations such as Mt. Washington and Blue Hills near Boston.

The quality of the archived evidence furnished by these machines is superior to any other weather observations. These precision readings provide far greater accuracy than estimated values taken by a human observer. The automated archival process also leaves little chance for human tampering with evidence. Once the readings become archived, they are disseminated throughout multiple weather search engines which duplicate the data. To repeat: **The tamper proof nature of these readings provides the best evidence as to actual weather conditions.**

Automated Surface Observing System (ASOS)

In the United States the **Automated Surface Observing System** (ASOS) units are operated and controlled cooperatively by the NWS, FAA and DOD. After many years of research and development, the deployment of ASOS units began in 1991 and was completed in 2004.

These systems generally report at hourly intervals, but also report special observations if weather conditions change rapidly and cross all aviation operation thresholds. They generally report all the parameters of the AWOS-III, while also having the additional capabilities of reporting temperature and dew point in degrees Fahrenheit, present weather, icing, lightning, sea level pressure and precipitation accumulation.

AWOS units are also operated by state or local governments and some private agencies. The American National Weather Service (NWS) and Department of Defense (DOD) play little to no role in the operation, maintenance or deployment of AWOS units. These systems are among the oldest automated weather stations in the United States, and many of them predate ASOS." (6)

Automated Weather Observing System (AWOS)

A commercial AWOS   Laser Visibility Sensor   Ceilometer

Field observations recorded hourly by these precision weather measuring instruments lend the strongest testimony to the weather conditions encountered by JFK Jr. along his flightpath from Caldwell, New Jersey to Martha's Vineyard. These observations also present us with an excellent perspective as to when conditions may have begun to deteriorate that night.

PIREPS are pilot reports of unexpected weather or flight conditions such as turbulence. There were none issued along John's route.

Martha's Vineyard used an automated surface observing system (ASOS) that could be edited and augmented by ATC tower personnel if necessary. Despite insinuations by the tabloid press, the NTSB found no anomalies regarding the ASOS at the Vineyard. During an interview, the tower manager stated that no actions were taken regarding the ASOS during his shift, which ended just after the accident occurred. He also stated, "The visibility, present weather, and sky condition at the approximate time of the accident was probably a little better than what was being reported. I say this because I remember aircraft on visual approaches saying they had the airport in sight between 10 and 12 miles out. I do recall being able to see those aircraft and I do remember seeing the stars out that night. To the best of my knowledge, the ASOS was working as advertised that day with no reported problems or systems log errors." (7) A Tower Manager does not make these statements casually. His intention was to lend a degree of credibility to the official report. The Tower Manager's word is by definition: Impeccable, Legitimate, Authority.

Actual Weather Conditions

A careful analysis of the actual weather conditions encountered along John's route of flight provides some of the strongest evidence that at no time did he encounter instrument flight conditions. He never lost sight of the horizon. He never flew into opaque haze. He never inadvertently entered a cloud deck. And most importantly he was never disoriented, nor did he enter a proverbial 'Graveyard Spiral' which escalated into an accelerated stall, killing Carolyn, Lauren, and himself.

The hourly field observations measured by the automated data collection systems described above clearly indicate that the lowest visibility readings were observed at John's point of departure, Caldwell, N.J. The most favorable visibility was measured at his destination point, Martha's Vineyard.

Briefly stated: Visibility at Caldwell was reported as being 'four miles in haze.' That visibility reading increased significantly and proportionately as John progressed along his route of flight. Visibility readings at the destination airport, Martha's Vineyard, taken minutes before and after John's demise indicate that he had at the very minimum, eight miles of visibility.

Hourly Field Observations

Time	Temp	Dew Point	Humidity	Spread	Visibility	Wind Direction	Wind speed	Code
8:53	88	66	41%	22	5mi	SW	5.8	CDW
8:45	76	69.8	78%	5.4	4mi	WSW	11.5	KBDR
8:54	84	70	69%	11	7.5	WSW	5.8	KGON
9:00	77	69.1	79%	5.9	7.0	SW	7	KEWB
9.30	74	65	73%	9	9	WSW	10	MVY
9:53	69	68	96%	1	4	WSW	13	KACK

The table above lists the actual hourly automated recordings of the weather conditions encountered by JFK Jr. along his actual flight path.

The column on the far left illustrates the actual times the Saratoga would be passing over the corresponding airports listed by code on the far right. John did not pass over KACK which is the code for Nantucket. The reading provides a comparison of the weather conditions 15 miles further out to sea. The readings on Nantucket were recorded one half hour later than the impact of John's airplane with the Atlantic Ocean.

Temperature, dewpoint, relative humidity, temp/dewpoint spread, and visibility are the key elements to examine during the progression of John's flight path. The authors dispute the readings provided by Caldwell (CDW). The temperature dewpoint spread, and relative humidity do not substantiate a 5-mile visibility reading. The numbers in question would necessarily support a visibility reading of at least ten miles. The closer temperature and dewpoint approach each other, the greater potential for thick haze. This inconsistency could be due to transcription errors, measuring instrument error or visual observations taken in the event of instrument error. There were no notations in the records referencing any malfunctions.

Apart from a few air routing procedures commonly used around the New York metro area, John's flight path ran nearly perfectly west to east. He encountered the thickest haze between Caldwell and Bridgeport (KBDR). Groton, Connecticut (KGON) reported visibility of 7.5 miles. New Bedford (KEWB) recorded 7 miles visibility at 9:00 p.m. Martha's Vineyard (MVY) records 9 miles visibility with a relative humidity of only 73%. These conditions reinforce the Control Tower Manager's statements made to the NTSB. Pilots had Martha's Vineyard in sight 10 to 15 miles out and the tower manager could see the stars in the sky.

On page 133 is a depiction of New York area Radar recorded at the time of John's demise. Haze and fog are clearly visible from Long Island, North, north to central Connecticut. The Easterly boundary of this weather clearly terminates at Groton on the state's south shore. The island of Martha's Vineyard is clearly visible in the top right segment. The green code letters MVY are superimposed over the diagram of the Island. Martha's Vineyard is completely in the clear as indicated by the absence of density sensitive color-coded radar return. The dark area surrounding the island extends westward to Block Island. Aircraft flying in this zone could expect visibility of ten miles or greater. The radar interpretation clearly illustrates that John's flight path originated in conditions considerably more obscured than the conditions indicated at the destination airport of Martha's Vineyard. John did not get disoriented in haze and fog as was so widely speculated.

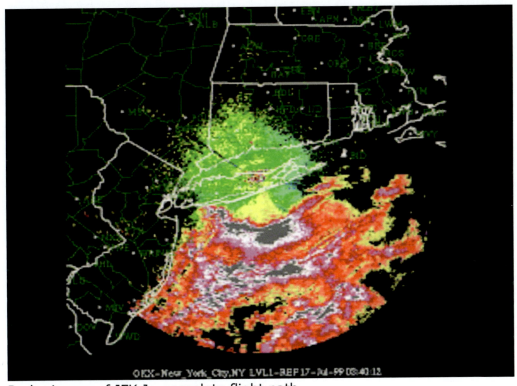

Radar image of JFK Jr. complete flight path.

Air Traffic Control—mandated and optional flight services.

John's departure from Caldwell placed him within the high-density traffic area of Kennedy and La Guardia Airports. Aircraft operating within such areas must be equipped with a device called a Mode C Transponder. The transponder is a device which encodes aircraft information to an interrogation radar facility on the ground. Typically, any aircraft entering high density traffic areas or restricted airspace must contact ATC before entering the airspace. The pilot states his intentions to a controller who issues an identification code which the pilot enters into the transponder display. As the interrogation radar beam is processed by the transponder, the aircraft appears on the controller's screen with a unique display which provides the controller with specific information about the aircraft. Altitude, Heading, Ground Speed and Aircraft Identification are all provided to the controller who also sees an enhanced image of the airplane's return echo. Use of the transponder is mandatory in such areas of congested airspace.

Despite the FAA's denial of any ATC contact we know John was in contact with ATC and had to be using his transponder as mandated by law. If he hadn't, rest assured the NTSB would have been all over the issue in its final report. Once clear of the aforementioned airspace, John would have been directed to 'Squawk 1200' on his transponder for the remainder of the flight. This is a standard VFR (visual flight rules) code used by all aircraft flying in fair weather.

Flight Watch Option

Once John was released by the terminal controller in New York it is most likely that he chose to use a flight following service provided by ATC called, 'Flight Watch.' Essentially, a controller will follow an airplane along its intended flight path, advising the pilot of conflicting traffic. Most day and night pilots are well rehearsed in the use of this service. It does not cost anything and is an added blanked of security for pilots and passengers flying at night, over water, or in congested airspace. Since John was presented with two of these factors on the night of his trip it would only be fair to assume he used Flight Watch. It would have been a natural progression, as the terminal controller released him from the restricted airspace, for him to call Flight Watch for the remainder of his flight. If something goes awry, someone on the ground is watching and can dispatch help.

Ten

Adam Budd Testimony & Final Descent

An employee of Martha's Vineyard Airport alerted federal aviation officials that John F. Kennedy Jr.'s plane was unaccounted for nearly four hours before a phone call from a Kennedy family friend early Saturday morning triggered a massive air and sea search. The first phone call, placed by airfield attendant Adam Budd cited Kennedy by name yet prompted no action by the Federal Aviation Administration. It was made at 10:05 p.m., Friday, only 25 minutes after Kennedy's plane was lost on radar and had presumably crashed into the ocean.

Adam Budd (self-portrait) In Hyannis Port, MA.

Speaking with family members waiting for the plane, Budd told an unidentified FAA employee at the Bridgeport Automated Flight Service Station, "Actually, Kennedy Jr.'s on board. He's, uh, they wanna know, uh...where he is?" A transcript of Budd's call, obtained by 'The Globe,' adds fuel to questions whether the FAA responded as promptly as it should have, and as quickly as its own regulations specify, to concerns about Kennedy's missing plane. FAA officials maintained they responded appropriately to the call.

Kennedy was flying to Martha's Vineyard to drop off Lauren Bessette, after which he planned to fly to Hyannis to attend the wedding of his cousin Rory Kennedy. A well-dressed couple with a child who had come to the airport to meet Lauren Bessette grew concerned when the plane did not arrive at 10:00 p.m. as expected. They sought help from Budd, 21, a Bridgewater State College student from Sharon, Massachusetts. Budd was also a licensed pilot who had worked for the past month as a ramp attendant at the airstrip.

Budd said he called the airport tower first but was told Kennedy's plane was not expected. Kennedy had filed no flight plan and had made no radio contact. Budd then called the FAA outpost in Bridgeport, Connecticut, a repository for flight plans that also provides pilots with weather information and notices about flight restrictions. During his conversation with the unidentified FAA employee, Budd asked if the FAA could track an airplane. Budd was with airport operations at Martha's Vineyard, mentioned Kennedy's name and provided two possible aircraft numbers for Kennedy's plane.

The FAA employee asked Budd repeatedly who he was and where he was calling from. After Budd gave his name, the FAA employee asked if he was, "in fact, with airport operations?" He ultimately told Budd, "We don't give this information out to people over the phone." Feeling dejected, at that point Budd gave up saying, "I'll just have'em wait," and then, "All right, it's no big deal." In the interview, Budd said the transcript tells only part of the story.

"You have to hear his tone of voice, because the guy was kind of rude to me, making me feel uncomfortable," Budd said. He continued, "I've called before, and they were happy to help me out. The guy might have been having a bad day or something. I don't know."

In the end, no action was taken until a 2:05 a.m. Saturday phone call from Carol Ratowell, a Kennedy family friend. Her call to the Coast Guard set in motion a multi-agency search that began with calls to regional airports and officially became a search and rescue mission at 3:28 a.m. (1)

The Critical Timeline

Excerpts from "South Coast Today" July 21,1999

1.30 PM John calls MVY Operations informing them of anticipated arrival at 7:30PM. (tie down space)
6:30 PM Carolyn still having her nails done at NY Boutique.
8:15 PM Late departure from Essex New Jersey
10:00 PM Adam discovers a couple with child waiting for John. ETA between 8:30 and 9:30
10:01 PM Adam calls control tower which is in process of shutting down for the night. Tower has no info.
10:05 PM Adam calls Bridgeport Flight service to see what they might know and receives no cooperation. Adam felt put off by the person he spoke with but did not pursue the matter. Adam specifically states that "Kennedy Jr. is on board" to no avail
2:05 AM Search and rescue executed by Coast Guard after family members become frantic.
6:30AM Authority for search and rescue is stripped from the hands of the Coast Guard, handed to the Pentagon, and in an unprecedented move, the US Air Force becomes the official Search Agency in charge.

Timeline of events, 7/16/1999 (1:30 p.m.) to 7/17/1999 (6:30 a.m.).

The Federal Aviation Administration Backpedals

" Several aviation experts and the FAA said the agency acted appropriately"

"An FAA spokesman said the agency does not provide any information on private citizens and private aircraft over the telephone and that the call from Budd gave no indication of any serious problem."

" We wish very much that we had more information. But we had nothing to indicate that the plane was overdue or that it was in trouble." Eliot Brenner FAA spokesman".

Eliot Brenner, a senior FAA spokesman said, "We've researched the matter and found the FAA was not told that the aircraft was overdue, or that there was any indication there was a problem or a cause for concern that would raise warning flags." Brenner said the problem with the tone was Budd's. He said, "There was no tone of concern in the voice or anything out of the ordinary," Brenner continued, "There needed to be some expression that this airplane is overdue."

THE AOPA AND MIT CHIME IN

A plane that landed intact could typically float about 15 minutes r so. A plane that breaks apart would sink much faster, said John Hansman, an aeronautics professor at the Massachusetts Institute of Technology

"The first question is, was it a survivable crash? If it was survivable, it would have potentially made a difference. But it doesn't appear that the FAA really did anything inappropriate," said Hansman.

"In 99 percent of the cases when someone is reported overdue, they're safe on the ground somewhere and just not where people expected them to be," Hansman said.

In the world of private aviation, it's extremely common for plane to be an hour or two late, said Drew Steketee, senior vice president of the Aircraft Owners and Pilots Association

Conversations with Adam

Visibility was good, a very thin fog directly on the ground. He could see stars overhead . Entire periphery of the airport was visible to the eye.
Could not recall any aircraft movement after 10PM.
Closed up shop, went partying with friends.
Came in for the morning shift and the Island was already buzzing with Press.
Spoke innocently, honestly with members of the press prior to hush order.
Was fired that week for violating hush order
Received a thank you call from Ted Kennedy for trying to execute a search effort.
Left the Island, returned to Bridgewater where his Father died August10th.
Never gave the crash a second thought and still buys the official story.

ADAM'S HONESTY IS NOT APPRECIATED

"Actually, Kennedy.jr's on board. He's uh, they wanna know, uh, where he is," said Budd, who generally performed clerical tasks, like taking landing fees, and assisting travelers with ground transportation and other needs

When the operator told him he wouldn't give him the information over the phone, Budd backed off "OK, well, if it's too much trouble, it's ... Ill just have 'em wait. ... It's not a big deal."

"In the end, it probably wouldn't have helped anything by the description of the wreckage," Budd said of his telephone call to th FAA. "It doesn't seem like it would have mattered."

"It sounds like they're going to fire me, " Budd said , "but I'll find out."

The operations manager at the Vineyard airport refused to discuss him.

N TAP RADAR ANALYSIS OF FINAL DESCENT

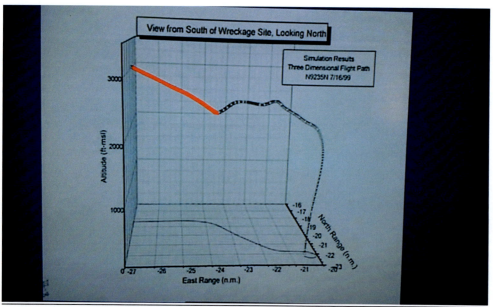

Note: this flight path has no resemblance to the flight path of the Proverbial, 'Graveyard Spiral.'

The graphic shown on page 140 illustrates the details provided by the N Tap Radar Analysis compiled by the FAA mere hours after the crash. The flight characteristics are perfectly normal until what appears to be a catastrophic control surface failure of the aircraft. The airplane plummeted 2,500 feet in less than 45 seconds. This condition does not indicate any type of spiral disorientation. The plane clearly nosedives into the water at a minus 5-degree negative angle relative to vertical. This flight condition could only have been initiated one of four ways.

(1) Pilot forcefully moves control yoke forward holding considerable, increasing pressure on yoke to maintain the nearly vertical attitude. As an airplane dives and increases in airspeed, greater coefficients of lift are produced by the wings. This additional lift causes the airplane to naturally return to level flight, hence the need for severe and deliberate control pressure by the pilot to maintain the dive. It is doubtful that John Kennedy took this action. Even if he had been incapacitated by a heart attack, or suffered death from potential poisoning, his slumping upper body pressure pushing forward on the controls would not be enough pressure to hold the airplane at such a steep dive angle.

(2) The airplane stalled and spun. A stall is not an engine failure. A stall occurs when a given wing's critical angle of attack is exceeded. This results in a sudden loss of lift on the stalling airfoil. Normally one wing will stall before the other. This will cause the airplane to roll considerably in the direction of the stalled wing and the nose of the aircraft to drop from the loss of power. If this stall was

deliberately initiated by the pilot and full rudder in the direction of the stalling wing was held constant, the airplane would enter what is referred to as a spin, a high speed accelerated stall with clockwise or counterclockwise rotation. The airplane falls straight down out of the sky with a 'corkscrew motion' very commonly seen in older aviation movies. The range breadth of John Kennedy's flight experience mandated that he spend countless hours practicing stalls and recovery from a wide range of flight attitudes. These are mandatory maneuvers which must be executed properly while riding with an FAA certified flight examiner, prior to the pilot rating being issued. Essentially, it's part of the final exam. Bear in mind, John would have to have initiated and deliberately held a spin to justify the descent rate. This is highly unlikely and almost preposterous.

(3) Portions of the tail surfaces, or the complete tail was severed from the aircraft causing the airplane to nosedive uncontrollably, straight in, vertically impacting the sea at a high rate of speed. Note: If the control cables were tampered with, let's speculate, or rigged to fail by using some sort of device, the rudder and elevator would still be hinged to the vertical and horizontal stabilizers.

(4) Assuming the airplane was trimmed for straight and level flight it would continue that flight path. John could still have landed the airplane safely by opening a door to turn the plane via adverse yaw and reduced power to descend. Highly qualified flight instructors teach student pilots

these recovery methods in case of emergency. It wouldn't have been the perfect landing but it's completely plausible that the aircraft could have landed undamaged, with its occupants intact.

Scenario number 3 is the one most likely to have occurred aboard John's airplane the night he, his wife, and sister-in-law were killed. A classified FBI document was released that detailed two key areas of the crash investigation. They were:

1) Tail of aircraft was dismembered from the plane making it front heavy. (2)

2) Tail structure was dismembered just prior to dissent. (3)

Eleven

<u>NTSB Report</u>

Reprinted on the following pages is the National Transportation Safety Board Report on John F. Kennedy Jr.'s fatal crash near Martha's Vineyard. The original report is only 28 pages long. The only change to the original report is that the font has been increased to make the document easier to read.

The authors have contributed viewpoints to several areas of the report. They are highlighted in Red Ink Font with indented paragraphs.

Location:	VINEYARD HAVEN, MA
Date & Time:	07/16/1999, 2141 EDT
Aircraft:	Piper PA-32R-301
Defining Event:	
Flight Conducted Under:	Part 91: General Aviation—Personal
Accident Number:	NYC99MA178
Registration:	N9253N
Aircraft Damage:	Destroyed
Injuries:	3 Fatal

Analysis:

National Transportation Safety Board Aviation Accident Final Report

The non-instrument-rated pilot obtained weather forecasts for a cross-country flight, which indicated visual flight rules (VFR) conditions with clear skies and visibilities that varied between 4 to 10 miles along his intended route.

The tone of the opening statement is inappropriate or prejudicial at best. It clearly states that the pilot flew VFR conditions all the way to his destination. The fact that he was not

146

yet instrument rated had no bearing on the flight conditions experienced that evening. John was acting legally and responsibly.

The pilot then departed on a dark night. According to a performance study of radar data, the airplane proceeded over land at 5,500 feet. About 34 miles west of Martha's Vineyard Airport, while crossing a 30-mile stretch of water to its destination, the airplane began a descent that varied between 400 to 800 feet per minute (fpm).

This 34 miles over open ocean which allegedly commenced over Point Judith, Rhode Island has never been verified. It is highly unlikely that John chose to leave the additional safety of the shoreline. It is far more likely that he flew to the Horseneck Beach area before crossing open water to the Vineyard. This would have given him the additional safety of the Elizabethan Islands in the event of engine failure. Pilots are trained from day one not to proceed beyond power off gliding distance capabilities of the airplane.

About 7 miles from the approaching shore, the airplane began a right turn. The airplane stopped its descent at 2,200 feet, then climbed back to 2,600 feet and entered a left turn. While in the left turn, the airplane began another descent that reached about 900 fpm. While still in the descent, the airplane entered a right turn. During this turn, the airplane's rate of descent and airspeed increased.

This description of maneuvering 7 miles from John's destination has bothered me from day one. I can't say for certain that it didn't occur. It appears fabricated. It is not typical maneuvering for a pilot descending from altitude preparing for a landing, and running late by 1.5 hrs. It suggests the beginning of pilot disorientation due to lack of visual reference outside the aircraft. Be mindful that the tower manager who only departed the field a half hour later is on record stating that, "He was talking to airplanes 10 miles from the field and could see their lights."

With his level of experience John would have more than certainly called for help. This action is stressed from day one during any comprehensive flight training. The lack of a mayday call is extremely suspicious. See further considerations in the full narrative version to follow.

The airplane's rate of descent eventually exceeded 4,700 fpm, and the airplane struck the water in a nose-down attitude. Airports along the coast reported visibilities between 5 and 8 miles.

See tower manager's statement regarding visibility in above text. Also, Adam Budd was the field attendant that night at the field. He is a private pilot and has worked in aviation his entire life. In an interview he stated to Damon that "The ceiling and visibility that night was excellent. There was no fog or haze."

Other pilots flying similar routes on the night of the accident reported no visual horizon while flying over the water because of haze.

What Pilots? Who?

The pilot's estimated total flight experience was about 310 hours, of which 55 hours were at night. The pilot's estimated flight time in the accident airplane was about 36 hours, of which about 9.4 hours were at night. About 3 hours of that time was without a certified flight instructor (CFI) on board, and about 0.8 hour of that was flown at night and included a night landing. In the 15 months before the accident, the pilot had flown either to or from the destination area about 35 times. The pilot flew at least 17 of these flight legs without a CFI on board, of which 5 were at night. Within 100 days before the accident, the pilot had completed about 50 percent of a formal instrument training course.

This is incorrect, with 38.3 hours of instrument training completed he was 95 percent through the course. He only needed 1.7 hours to complete the course and go for his certification.

A Federal Aviation Administration Advisory Circular (AC) 61-27C, "Instrument Flying: Coping with Illusions in Flight," states that illusions or false impressions occur when information provided by sensory organs is misinterpreted or inadequate and that many illusions in flight could be caused by complex motions and certain visual scenes encountered under adverse weather conditions and at night. The AC also states that some illusions might lead to spatial disorientation or the inability to determine accurately the attitude or motion of the aircraft in relation to the earth's surface. The AC further states that spatial disorientation, as a result of continued VFR flight into adverse weather conditions, is regularly near the top of the cause/factor list in annual statistics on fatal aircraft accidents.

This is true but it also is opinion inserted verifying the "Official Story,"

Page 1 of 28

According to AC 60-4A, "Pilot's Spatial Disorientation," tests conducted with qualified instrument pilots indicated that it could take as long as 35 seconds to establish full control by instruments after a loss of visual reference of the earth's surface. AC 60-4A further states that surface references and the natural horizon may become obscured even though visibility may be above VFR minimums and that an inability to perceive the natural horizon or surface references is common during flights over water, at night, in sparsely populated areas, and in low-visibility conditions.

Is someone trying to convince us of something here? Though the information in the above two paragraphs is accurate. There is nothing to suggest John's airplane flew into marginal visibility.

Examination of the airframe, systems, avionics, and engine did not reveal any evidence of a preimpact mechanical malfunction.

The airplane was meticulously maintained.

Probable Cause and Findings

The National Transportation Safety Board determines the probable cause(s) of this accident to be: The pilot's failure to maintain control of the airplane during a descent over water at night, which was a result of spatial disorientation. Factors in the accident were haze, and the dark night.

Findings

Occurrence #1: LOSS OF CONTROL - IN FLIGHT Phase of Operation: DESCENT

Findings
1. (F) LIGHT CONDITION - DARK NIGHT
2. (F) WEATHER CONDITION - HAZE
3. (C) AIRCRAFT CONTROL - NOT MAINTAINED - PILOT IN COMMAND 4. (C) SPATIAL DISORIENTATION - PILOT IN COMMAND

Occurrence #2: IN FLIGHT COLLISION WITH TERRAIN/WATER Phase of Operation: DESCENT - UNCONTROLLED

Page 2 of 28 NYC99MA178

There is no evidence of haze anywhere.

Factual Information

HISTORY OF FLIGHT

On July 16, 1999, about 2141 eastern daylight time, a Piper PA-32R-301, Saratoga II, N9253N, was destroyed when it crashed into the Atlantic Ocean approximately 7 1/2 miles southwest of Gay Head, Martha's Vineyard, Massachusetts. The certificated private pilot and two passengers received fatal injuries. Night visual meteorological conditions (VMC) prevailed, and no flight plan had been filed for the personal flight conducted under the provisions of 14 Code of Federal Regulations (CFR) Part 91. The flight originated from Essex County Airport (CDW), Caldwell, New Jersey, and was destined for Barnstable Municipal-Boardman/Polando Field (HYA), Hyannis, Massachusetts, with a scheduled stop at Martha's Vineyard Airport (MVY), Vineyard Haven, Massachusetts.

During interviews, witnesses stated that the purpose of the flight was to fly to Martha's Vineyard to drop off one passenger and then continue to HYA. An employee of a fixed-base operator (FBO) at CDW stated that he had called the pilot about 1300 on the day of the accident to verify that the pilot intended to fly the airplane, N9253N, over the weekend. The pilot informed the employee that he did plan to fly the airplane and that he would arrive at the airport between 1730 and 1800. The employee

151

informed the pilot that he would have the airplane parked outside of the hangar.

Witnesses who were at CDW on the night of the accident stated that they saw the pilot and a female near the accident airplane. The witnesses also reported that they saw the pilot using crutches and loading luggage into the airplane. One witness stated that he watched the pilot perform an engine run-up and then take off about 2040. The witness further stated that "takeoff and right downwind departure seem[ed] normal."

According to air traffic control (ATC) transcripts from CDW's tower, about 20:34, the pilot of N9253N contacted the ground controller and stated, "...saratoga niner two five three November ready to taxi with mike...right turnout northeast bound." The ground controller instructed the pilot to taxi to runway 22, which the pilot acknowledged. At 20:38:32, the pilot of N9253N contacted the tower controller and advised that he was ready to take off from runway 22. At 20:38:39, the tower controller cleared N9253N for takeoff; at 20:38:43, the pilot acknowledged the clearance. A few seconds later, the tower controller asked the pilot if he was heading towards Teterboro, New Jersey. The pilot replied, "No sir, I'm uh actually I'm heading a little uh north of it, uh eastbound." The tower controller then instructed the pilot to "make it a right downwind departure then." At 20:38:56, the pilot acknowledged the instruction stating, "right downwind departure two two." No records of any further communications between the pilot and ATC exist.

Not so, Steve Lagudi was an airport radio attendant at Long Island's Republic Airport the night of the crash. He heard John call the tower on Martha's Vineyard. Initial reports from the Coastguard to Channel 5 in Boston stated that John had indeed contacted the tower at Martha's Vineyard.

According to radar data, at 20:40:59, a target transmitting a visual flight rules (VFR) code was observed about 1 mile southwest of CDW at an altitude of 1,300 feet. The target proceeded to the northeast, on a course of about 55 degrees, remaining below 2,000 feet. The target was at 1,400 feet when it reached the Hudson River. When the target was about 8 miles northwest of the Westchester County Airport (HPN), White Plains, New York, it turned north over the river and began to climb. After proceeding north about 6 miles, the target turned eastward to a course of about 100 degrees. The target continued to climb and reached 5,500 feet about 6 miles northeast of HPN. When the target's course was plotted on a New York VFR navigational map, the extended course line crossed the island of Martha's Vineyard.

Page 3 of 28 NYC99MA178

The target continued eastward at 5,500 feet, passing just north of Bridgeport, Connecticut, and crossed the shoreline between Bridgeport and New Haven, Connecticut. The target ground track continued on the 100-degree course, just south and parallel to the Connecticut and Rhode Island coastlines. After passing Point Judith, Rhode Island, the target continued over the Rhode Island Sound.

These are the coordinates that were used to draw John's actual flight path along the coastline to Cape Cod.

A performance study of the radar data revealed that the target began a descent from 5,500 feet about 34 miles west of MVY. The speed during the descent was calculated to be about 160 knots indicated airspeed (KIAS), and the rate of descent was calculated to have varied between 400 and 800 feet per minute (fpm). About 21:38, the target began a right turn in a southerly

153

direction. About 30 seconds later, the target stopped its descent at 2,200 feet and began a climb that lasted another 30 seconds. During this period of time, the target stopped the turn, and the airspeed decreased to about 153 KIAS. About 21:39, the target leveled off at 2,500 feet and flew in a southeasterly direction. About 50 seconds later, the target entered a left turn and climbed to 2,600 feet. As the target continued in the left turn, it began a descent that reached a rate of about 900 fpm. When the target reached an easterly direction, it stopped turning; its rate of descent remained about 900 fpm. At 21:40:15, while still in the descent, the target entered a right turn. As the target's turn rate increased, its descent rate and airspeed also increased. The target's descent rate eventually exceeded 4,700 fpm. The target's last radar position was recorded at 21:40:34 at an altitude of 1,100 feet.

The preceding paragraph in this report has been one of the most perplexing issues pertinent to John's flight. As a former CFI (Certified Flight Instructor) and present day commercially rated pilot, I could not comprehend why these altitude and airspeed variations would occur during an uneventful flight while the pilot was transitioning to the landing environment.

The airplane was flying straight and on course during a cruise descent toward the airport. We experience this transition every time we fly commercially, and we are close to the destination airport. It is normally a smooth straight ride with a slight increase in airspeed due to the nose low attitude. The airplane is flying downhill in the airmass. Any digression from this stabilized flight condition is usually a minor heading correction. It is quite uncommon to experience the altitude fluctuations evident in John's approach. Linking left and right turns in tight succession along with altitude fluctuations is truly unheard of unless the airplane is flying in extremely turbulent conditions.

John would not have subjected his lady passengers to such maneuvers. The digression from normal flight just doesn't fit in.

So, what could have happened in John's cockpit to cause such a deviation from a stabilized descent? Why does John's Airplane leave the sky and career into the dark Atlantic Ocean at volatile speeds within a period of about two minutes? We analyze this scenario in greater detail in the "Smoking Guns" chapter of this book.

(For a more detailed description of the target's [accident airplane's] performance, see Section, "Tests and Research," Subsection, "Aircraft Performance Study.")

On July 20, 1999, about 2240, the airplane's wreckage was located in 120 feet of water, about 1/4 mile north of the target's last recorded radar position.

The accident occurred during the hours of darkness. In the area of and on the night of the accident, sunset occurred about 2014. Civil twilight ended about 20:47, and nautical twilight ended about 21:28. About 21:40, the moon was about 11.5 degrees above the horizon at a bearing of 270.5 degrees and provided about 19 percent illumination. The location of the accident wreckage was about 41 degrees, 17 minutes, 37.2 seconds north latitude; 70 degrees, 58 minutes, 39.2 seconds west longitude.

PILOT INFORMATION

The pilot obtained his private pilot certificate for "airplane single-engine land" in April 1998. He did not possess an instrument rating.

But John only needed 1.7 hours of additional training to go for his instrument check ride.

He received a "high performance airplane" sign-off in his Cessna 182 in June 1998 and a "complex airplane" sign-off in the accident airplane in May 1999. His most recent Federal Aviation Administration (FAA) second-class medical certificate was issued on December 27, 1997, with no limitations.

A copy of the pilot's logbook that covered from October 4, 1982, to November 11, 1998, was provided to the Safety Board. The pilot's most recent logbook was not located.

Various researchers indicate that the logbook was in the small blue duffle bag which was recovered and confiscated by police on Philbin Beach.

The Board used the copied logbook, records from training facilities, copies of flight instructors' logbooks, and statements from instructors and pilots to estimate the pilot's total flight experience. The pilot's estimated total flight experience, excluding simulator training, was about 310 hours, of which 55 hours were at night. The pilot's estimated experience flying without a certified flight instructor (CFI) on board was about 72 hours. The pilot's estimated flight time in the accident airplane was about 36 hours, of which 9.4 hours were at night. Approximately 3 hours of that flight time was without a CFI on board, and about 0.8 hour of that time was flown at night,

which included a night landing. In the 15 months before the accident, the pilot had flown about 35 flight legs either to or from the Essex County/Teterboro, New Jersey, area and the Martha's Vineyard/Hyannis, Massachusetts, area. The pilot flew over 17 of these legs without a CFI on board, including at least 5 at night. The pilot's last known flight in the accident airplane without a CFI on board was on May 28, 1999.

Pilot Training

On October 4, 1982, the pilot started receiving flight instruction. Over the next 6 years, he flew with six different CFIs. During this period, the pilot logged 47 hours, consisting of 46 hours of dual instruction and 1 hour without a CFI on board. The pilot made no entries in his logbook from September 1988 to December 1997.

In December 1997, the pilot enrolled in a training program at Flight Safety International (FSI), Vero Beach, Florida, to obtain his private pilot certificate. Between December 1997 and April 1998, the pilot flew about 53 hours, of which 43 were flown with a CFI on board. The CFI who prepared the pilot for his private pilot checkride stated that the pilot had "very good" flying skills for his level of experience.

On April 22, 1998, the pilot passed his private pilot flight test. The designated pilot examiner who administered the checkride stated that as part of the flight test, the pilot conducted two unusual attitude recoveries. The pilot examiner stated that in both cases, the pilot recovered the airplane while wearing a hood and referencing the airplane's flight instruments. After receiving his private pilot certificate, the pilot flew solo in his Cessna 182 and received instruction in it by CFIs local to New Jersey. He also received instruction at Million Air, a flight school in New Jersey, and flew their airplanes. During calendar year 1998, the pilot flew approximately 179 hours, including about 65 hours without a CFI on board. On March 12, 1999, the pilot completed the FAA's written airplane instrument examination and received a score of 78 percent.

John had even passed his instrument rating written exam which I can testify is the toughest exam anyone could have to face. 78 percent is an excellent score considering the complexity of the test.

On April 5, 1999, the pilot returned to FSI to begin an airplane instrument rating course. During the instrument training, the pilot satisfactorily completed the first 12 of 25 lesson plans. The pilot's primary CFI during the instrument training stated that the pilot's progression was normal and that he grasped all of the basic skills needed to complete the course; however, the CFI did recall the pilot having difficulty completing lesson 11, which was designed to develop a student's knowledge of very high frequency omnidirectional radio range (VOR) and nondirectional beacon operations while working with ATC. It took the pilot four attempts to complete lesson 11 satisfactorily. After two of the attempts, the pilot took a 1-week break. After this break, the pilot repeated lesson 11 two more times. The CFI stated that the pilot's basic instrument flying skills and simulator work were excellent. However, the CFI stated that the pilot had trouble managing multiple tasks while flying, which he felt was normal for the pilot's level of experience.

The pilot attended this training primarily on weekends. During this training, the pilot accumulated 13.3 hours of flight time with a CFI on board. In addition, the pilot logged 16.9 hours of simulator time. The pilot departed from FSI for the last time on April 24, 1999.

The pilot continued to receive flight instruction from CFIs in New Jersey in his newly purchased Piper Saratoga, the accident airplane. One CFI flew with the pilot on three occasions. One of the flights was on June 25, 1999, from CDW to MVY. The CFI stated that the departure, enroute, and descent portions of the flight were executed in VMC, but an

instrument approach was required into MVY because of a 300-foot overcast ceiling. The CFI requested an instrument flight rules (IFR) clearance and demonstrated a coupled instrument landing system (ILS) approach to runway 24. The CFI stated that the pilot performed the landing, but he had to assist with the rudders because of the pilot's injured ankle. (For additional information about the pilot's ankle injury, see Section, "Medical and Pathological Information.") The CFI stated that the pilot's aeronautical abilities and his ability to handle multiple tasks while flying were average for his level of experience.

A second CFI flew with the pilot between May 1998 and July 1999. This CFI accumulated 39 hours of flight time with the pilot, including 21 hours of night flight and 0.9 hour flown in instrument meteorological conditions (IMC). The pilot used this CFI for instruction on cross-country flights and as a safety pilot. On July 1, 1999, the CFI flew with the pilot in the accident airplane to MVY. The flight was conducted at night, and IMC prevailed at the airport. The CFI stated that, during the flight, the pilot used and seemed competent with the autopilot. The instructor added that during the flight the pilot was wearing a non-plaster cast on his leg, which required the CFI to taxi the airplane and assist the pilot with the landing.

The CFI stated that the pilot had the ability to fly the airplane without a visible horizon but may have had difficulty performing additional tasks under such conditions. He also stated that the pilot was not ready for an instrument evaluation as of July 1, 1999, and needed additional training. The CFI was not aware of the pilot conducting any flight in the accident airplane without an instructor on board. He also stated that he would not have felt comfortable with the accident pilot conducting night flight operations on a route similar to the one flown on, and in weather conditions similar to those that existed on, the night of the accident. The CFI further stated that he had talked to the pilot on the day of the accident and offered to fly with him on the accident flight. He stated that the accident pilot replied that "he wanted to do it alone."

A third CFI flew with the pilot between May 1998 and July 1999. This CFI accumulated 57 hours of flight time with the pilot, including 17 hours of night flight and 8 hours flown in IMC. The pilot also used this instructor for instruction on cross-country flights and as a safety pilot. This CFI had conducted a "complex airplane" evaluation on the pilot and signed him off in the accident airplane in May 1999. According to the CFI, on one or two occasions, the airplane's autopilot turned to a heading other than the one selected, which required the autopilot to be disengaged and then reengaged. He stated that it seemed as if the autopilot had independently changed from one navigation mode to another. He also stated that he did not feel that the problem was significant because it only happened once or twice.

The CFI had made six or seven flights to MVY with the pilot in the accident airplane. The CFI stated that most of the flights were conducted at night and that, during the flights, the pilot did not have any trouble flying the airplane. The instructor stated that the pilot was methodical about his flight planning and that he was very cautious about his aviation decision-making. The CFI stated that the pilot had the capability to conduct a night flight to MVY as long as a visible horizon existed.

The hours listed above have been minimized. Overemphasis is placed on training repetition which is often common with any learning experience. No one gets it "all right" in the first few sessions. Also, who are these CFI's who attest to John's competence? There are no names and no pilot numbers.

AIRCRAFT INFORMATION

The accident airplane, N9253N, was a Piper PA-32R-301, Saratoga II, single-engine, low-wing airplane with retractable landing gear. The airplane was originally certificated by Piper Aircraft Corporation on June 9, 1995. The airplane was sold to Skytech, Inc., Baltimore, Maryland, on June 16, 1995, and then resold to Poinciana LLC, Wilmington, North Carolina, on January 5, 1996.

Page 6 of 28 NYC99MA178

A review of records from an engine overhaul facility revealed that during a 100-hour and annual inspection of the airplane in May 1998, corrosion was observed on the interior surfaces of the engine cylinder walls. Additionally, pitting was observed on the surfaces of several valve tappets. At that time, the engine had a total time since new of 387.1 hours. The documents also revealed that the engine was shipped to the overhaul facility in June 1998, where the engine was disassembled, inspected, and reassembled (parts were replaced as necessary) in June and July 1998. The engine was also run in a test cell before it was shipped and was reinstalled in the airplane in July 1998.

Engine maintenance is up to date.

On August 25, 1998, the airplane was purchased by Raytheon Aircraft Company, Wichita, Kansas, and then resold the same day to Air Bound Aviation, Inc., Fairfield, New Jersey. The airplane

161

was sold on August 27, 1998, to a pilot in New Jersey. On April 28, 1999, the airplane was sold to Columbia Aircraft Sales, Inc., Groton, Connecticut. On the same day, the airplane was sold back to Air Bound Aviation and then to the accident pilot, operating as Random Ventures, Inc., New York, New York. According to maintenance personnel at CDW, the pilot kept the airplane's maintenance records inside of the airplane. The maintenance records were not recovered during the wreckage recovery operation.

Duplicate maintenance records should have been available at any facility that worked on the aircraft. Considering the infamy of the pilot and plane one would not imagine these would be too difficult to find.

According to FAA records, work orders, and a statement from an employee of a maintenance facility, a prepurchase inspection of N9253N was conducted on April 16, 1999. According to the maintenance facility employee, "the aircraft was found to be in very good condition, with only a few minor discrepancies." According to the records and the maintenance facility employee, an annual inspection was completed on June 18, 1999, at a total airframe time of 622.8 hours, and the airplane was returned to service on June 25, 1999. The records and maintenance facility employee also revealed that the airplane's return to service was delayed because of an error on the airplane's registration form about its exact make and model. A new registration form with the correct information had to be sent to the pilot for his signature.

A July 13, 1999, work order revealed that a "swing" of the compass and the horizontal situation indicator (HSI) were completed. No total airframe time was recorded on that work order. The tachometer recovered in the wreckage indicated 663.5 hours.

Normal service.

A review of other pilots' logbooks revealed that they had flown the airplane without the accident pilot on board. However, it could not be accurately determined how many other pilots might have flown the airplane without the pilot on board or how many flight hours they might have added on to the airplane.

Of course, they did. The aircraft had half a dozen previous owners. Who are these pilots if their logbooks were checked by officials?

METEOROLOGICAL INFORMATION
The following airport designators (and those previously defined) are used in this section:

ACK BDR BID BLM EWB EWR

- Nantucket Memorial Airport, Nantucket, Massachusetts.
- Igor I. Sikorsky Memorial Airport, Bridgeport, Connecticut.
- Block Island State Airport, Block Island, Rhode Island.
- Allaire Airport, Belmar-Farmingdale, New Jersey.
- New Bedford Municipal Airport, New Bedford, Massachusetts.
– Newark International Airport, Newark, New Jersey.

Page 7 of 28

NYC99MA178

FMH

FOK

FRG

ISP

JFK

PVD

TAN

TEB

- Otis ANGB, Falmouth, Massachusetts.
- Francis S. Gabreski Airport, Westhampton Beach, New York.
- Republic Airport, Farmingdale, New York.
- Long Island MacArthur Airport, Islip, New York.
- John F. Kennedy International Airport, New York, New York.
- Theodore Francis Green State Airport, Providence, Rhode Island.
- Taunton Municipal, Taunton, Massachusetts.
- Teterboro Airport, Teterboro, New Jersey.

ACK is located about 27 nautical miles (nm) east-southeast of MVY. HYA is located about 22 nm northeast of MVY.

Pilot Preflight Weather Requests

According to Weather Service International (WSI) personnel, a search of their briefing logs indicated that the pilot, or someone using his user code, made two weather requests from WSI's PILOT brief Web site on July 16, 1999. The first request, made at 18:32:59, was for a radar image. The second request, made at 18:34:18, was for a route briefing from TEB to HYA with MVY as an alternate.

The information provided to the requester included enroute weather observations from BID, BLM, EWB, EWR, FMH, FOK, FRG, ISP, JFK, PVD, and TAN. These observations indicated that visibilities varied from 10 miles along the route to 4 miles in haze at CDW. The lowest cloud ceiling was reported at 20,000 feet overcast at PVD. These observations were made about 1800. Observations for ACK, CDW, HYA, and MVY were also included. Excerpts from these observations include the following:

ACK 1753...Clear skies; visibility 5 miles in mist; winds 240 degrees at 16 knots.
CDW 1753...Clear skies; visibility 4 miles in haze; winds 230 degrees at 7 knots.
HYA 1756...Few clouds at 7,000 feet; visibility 6 miles in haze; winds 230 degrees at 13 knots. MVY 1753...Clear skies; visibility 6 miles in haze; winds 210 degrees at 11 knots.
Also included were the following terminal forecasts for ACK and HYA:

ACK (July 16 at 1400 to July 17 at 1400)...July 16...1400 to 2000...Clear skies; visibility greater than 6 miles; winds 240 degrees at 15 knots. Becoming 2000 to 2100, winds 260 degrees at 13 knots.

HYA (July 16 at 1400 to July 17 at 1400)...July 16...1400 to 2200...Clear skies; visibility greater than 6 miles; winds 230 degrees at 10 knots.

According to WSI, the pilot, or someone using his user code, did not access the National Weather Service (NWS) Area Forecast.

Aviation Forecasts and Surface Weather Observations Area Forecasts (FA)

Excerpts from the Boston FA, issued July 16 about 20:45 and valid until July 17 about 02:00,

included the following: Coastal Waters (includes area of MVY); Scattered clouds at 2,000 feet. Occasional visibility 3 to 5 miles in haze. Haze tops 7,000 feet.

Excerpts from the Boston FA, issued July 16 about 20:45 and valid until July 17 about 09:00, included the following: Coastal Waters (includes area of MVY); North of 40 degrees north latitude... Scattered cirrus. Occasional visibility 4 to 5 miles in haze. Haze tops 8,000 feet.

Aviation Terminal Forecasts (TAF)

NWS does not prepare TAFs for MVY. Excerpts from TAFs pertinent to the accident include the following:

The TAF for ACK, issued July 16 about 13:30 and valid from July 16 about 14:00 to July 17 about 14:00, was as follows: July 16 at 14:00 to July 17 at 11:00...Clear skies; visibility greater than 6 miles; winds 240 degrees at 15 knots. Becoming July 16 at 20:00 to July 16 at 21:00, winds 260 degrees at 13 knots.

The TAF for ACK, issued July 16 about 19:30 and valid from July 16 about 20:00 to July 17 about 20:00, was as follows: July 16 at 20:00 to July 17 at 02:00...Winds 240 degrees at 15 knots; visibility 4 miles, mist; scattered clouds at 25,000 feet. Temporary changes from July 16 at 2100 to July 17 at 0100...clouds 500 feet scattered; visibility 2 miles, mist.

The TAF for HYA, issued July 16 about 13:30 and valid from July 16 about 14:00 to July 17 about 14:00, was as follows: July 16 at 14:00 to July 17 at 11:00...Clear skies; visibility greater than 6 miles; winds 230 degrees at 10 knots. Winds becoming July 16 at 2200 to July 17 at 00:00...250 degrees at 8 knots.

The TAF for HYA, issued July 16 about 19:30 and valid from July 16 about 20:00 to July 17 about 20:00, was as follows: July 16 at 20:00 to July 17 at 02:00...Winds 230 degrees at 10 knots; visibility 6 miles, haze; scattered clouds at 9,000 feet. Temporary changes from July 16 at 20:00 to July 17 at 0000...Visibility 4 miles, haze.

In-flight Weather Advisories

No airmen's meteorological information, significant meteorological information (SIGMET), or convective SIGMETs were issued by the NWS Aviation Weather Center in Kansas City, Missouri, for the time and area of the accident. No in-flight weather advisories were in effect along the route between CDW and MVY from 20:00 to 22:00.

Surface Weather Observations

MVY had an Automated Surface Observing System (ASOS), which was edited and augmented by ATC tower personnel if necessary. The tower manager at MVY was on duty on the night of the accident for an 8-hour shift, which ended when the tower closed, about 2200. During an interview, the tower manager stated that no actions were taken to augment or edit the ASOS during his shift. He also stated the following:

"The visibility, present weather, and sky condition at the approximate time of the accident was probably a little better than what was being reported. I say this because I remember aircraft on visual approaches saying they had the airport in sight between 10 and 12 miles out. I do recall being able to see those aircraft and I do remember seeing the stars out that night...To the best of my knowledge, the ASOS was working as advertised that day with no reported problems or systems log errors."

ASOS observations for the night of the accident include the following: ACK

20:53...Clear at or below 12,000 feet; visibility 4 miles, mist; winds 240 degrees at 11 knots; temperature 21 degrees [Celsius] C; dewpoint 20 degrees C; altimeter setting 30.10 inches of [mercury] Hg.

21:53...Clear at or below 12,000 feet; visibility 4 miles, mist; winds 240 degrees at 12 knots; temperature 21 degrees C; dewpoint 20 degrees C; altimeter setting 30.11 inches of Hg.

BDR

20:54...Clear at or below 12,000 feet; visibility 8 miles, haze; winds 230 degrees at 4 knots; temperature 27 degrees C; dewpoint 21 degrees C; altimeter setting 30.08 inches of Hg.

CDW

19:53...Clear at or below 12,000 feet; visibility 4 miles, haze; winds 230 degrees at 4 knots; temperature 33 degrees C; dewpoint 18 degrees C; altimeter setting 30.07 inches of Hg.

20:53...Clear at or below 12,000 feet; visibility 5 miles, haze; winds 220 degrees at 5 knots; temperature 31 degrees C; dewpoint 19 degrees C; altimeter setting 30.08 inches of Hg.

HPN

20:45...7,500 feet broken, 15,000 feet overcast, visibility 5 miles haze; winds 140 degrees at 4 knots; temperature 28 degrees C; dewpoint 22 degrees C; altimeter setting 30.08 inches of Hg.

HYA

20:56...Few clouds at 7,000 feet; visibility 6 miles, mist; winds 230 degrees at 7 knots; temperature 23 degrees C; dewpoint 21 degrees C; altimeter setting 30.07 inches of Hg.

21:56...Few clouds at 7,500 feet; visibility 6 miles, mist; winds 230 degrees at 8 knots; temperature 23 degrees C; dewpoint 22 degrees C; altimeter setting 30.08 inches of Hg.

MVY

20:53...Clear at or below 12,000 feet; visibility 8 miles; winds 250 degrees at 7 knots; temperature 23 degrees C; dewpoint 19 degrees C; altimeter 30.09 inches of Hg.

21:53...Clear at or below 12,000 feet; visibility 10 miles; winds 240 degrees at 10 knots, gusts to 15 knots; temperature 24 degrees C; dewpoint 18 degrees C; altimeter 30.10 inches of Hg.

U.S. Coast Guard Station (USCG) Weather Observations

From the previous weather observations, it is clear that John left the worst weather in Caldwell, New Jersey and flew into better conditions as he progressed eastward. Highlighted above are the USCG surface observations for Martha's Vineyard proximal to the time of the crash. Note 10 miles visibility in the 9:00 p.m. read and 8 miles at the 10:00 p.m. read. Given the impact was close to 9:30 p.m. one would interpolate the visibility to be at least 9 miles. Note: The ceilings are reported at 12,000 ft.

Safety Board staff reviewed weather observations from USCG stations. Excerpts pertinent to the accident include the following:

Point Judith, Rhode Island
17:00...Cloudy, 3 miles visibility in haze, winds south-southwest at 10 knots. 2000...Cloudy, 3 miles visibility in haze, winds south-southwest at 10 knots. 2300...Cloudy, 2 miles visibility, winds southwest at 10 knots.

NYC99MA178

Brant Point, Massachusetts
17:00...Clear, 8 miles visibility. 2000...Overcast, 6 miles visibility. 23:00...Scattered clouds, 6 miles visibility.

The Brant Point report stated that two observations were reported by ships. About 20:00, a ship 1 nm north of buoy 17, which was about 8 miles north of Martha's Vineyard, reported that the seas were 2 to 3 feet, and that the visibility was 5 nm. About 23:00, another ship reported that the winds were west-southwest at 10 to 15 knots, the seas were 2 to 3 feet, and the visibility was 6 nm in light haze.

   Note: Observations made on Nantucket are another 20 miles out to sea.

Pilot Weather Observations

Three pilots who had flown over the Long Island Sound on the night of the accident were interviewed after the accident.

   John did not fly over Long Island Sound. His entire route to Horseneck Beach Massachusetts was flown north through New York and then along the Connecticut coastline.

One pilot kept his twin turboprop airplane at TEB, and on the evening of the accident, he flew from TEB to ACK. The pilot stated that he drove to TEB from New York City and that the traffic was the second heaviest he had seen in 15 years. The pilot stated that he had called the TEB FBO and estimated that his arrival time would be about 18:50; however, he did not arrive until between about 19:30 and 20:00 because of traffic. The pilot also stated that this delay changed the flight from one that would have been conducted entirely during the day to one that would have to be conducted partially at night. The pilot further stated, "Our car took route 80 to Teterboro Airport. Caldwell Airport, where [the accident pilot] flew from is another 14-minute drive west on route 80 past TEB."

Before departing the city, the pilot had obtained current weather observations and forecasts for Nantucket and other points in Massachusetts, Connecticut, New York, and New Jersey. He stated that the visibility was well above VFR minimums. He also stated that he placed a telephone call to a flight service station (FSS) before leaving the city, while driving to TEB. Regarding the telephone call, he stated the following:

"I asked if there were any adverse conditions for the route TEB to ACK. I was told emphatically: 'No adverse conditions. Have a great weekend.' I queried the briefer about any expected fog and was told none was expected and the conditions would remain VFR with good visibility. Again, I was reassured that tonight was not a problem."

The pilot stated that he departed TEB "...in daylight and good flight conditions and reasonable visibility. The horizon was not obscured by haze. I could easily pick our landmarks at least five [miles] away." The pilot also stated that he did not request or receive flight information after his departure from TEB. Once clear of the New York Class B airspace, he stated that he climbed his airplane to 17,500 feet and proceeded towards Nantucket. He reported that above 14,000 feet, the visibility was unrestricted; however, he also reported that during his descent to Nantucket, when his global positioning system (GPS) receiver indicated that he was over Martha's Vineyard, he looked down and "...there was nothing to see. There was no horizon and no light....I turned left toward Martha's Vineyard to see if it was visible but could see no lights of any kind nor any evidence of the island...I thought the island might [have] suffered a power failure."

He stated that he had his strobe lights on during the descent and that at no time did they illuminate clouds or fog. He also stated, "I had no visual reference of any kind yet was free of any clouds or fog." The pilot stated that when he contacted the ACK tower for landing, he was instructed to fly south of Nantucket about 5 miles to join the downwind for runway 24; however, he maintained a distance of 3 to 4 miles because he could not see the island at 5 miles. The pilot stated that, as he neared the airport, he had to make a 310-degree turn for spacing. He stated that, during the turn, "I found that I could not hold altitude by outside reference and had to use my [vertical speed indicator] VSI and HSI to hold altitude and properly coordinate the turn."

Another pilot had flown from Bar Harbor, Maine, to Long Island, New York, and crossed the Long Island Sound on the same evening, about 19:30. This pilot stated that during his preflight weather briefing from an FSS, the specialist indicated VMC for his flight. The pilot filed an IFR flight plan and conducted the flight at 6,000 feet. He stated that he encountered visibilities of 2 to 3 miles throughout the flight because of haze. He also stated that the lowest visibility was over water, between Cape Cod,

Massachusetts, and eastern Long Island. He stated that he did not encounter any clouds below 6,000 feet.

A third pilot departed TEB about 20:30 destined for Groton, Connecticut, after a stopover at MVY. He stated that, after departure, he flew south of HPN and, remaining clear of the Class B airspace, he climbed to 7,500 feet. He also stated that, while enroute, he monitored several ATC frequencies, but did not transmit on any of them until he neared MVY. His route of flight took him over the north shore of Long Island to Montauk, New York. He stated that he then crossed over Block Island, Rhode Island, and proceeded directly to MVY.

He stated that the entire flight was conducted under VFR, with a visibility of 3 to 5 miles in haze. He stated that, over land, he could see lights on the ground when he looked directly down or slightly forward; however, he stated that, over water, there was no horizon to reference. He stated that he was not sure if he was on top of the haze layer at 7,500 feet and that, during the flight, he did not encounter any cloud layers or ground fog during climb or descent. He further stated that, between Block Island and MVY, there was still no horizon to reference. He recalled that he began to observe lights on Martha's Vineyard when he was in the vicinity of Gay Head. He stated that, before reaching MVY, he would have begun his descent from 7,500 feet and would have been between 3,000 and 5,000 feet over Gay Head (the pilot could not recall his exact altitudes). He did not recall seeing the Gay Head marine lighthouse. He was about 4 miles from MVY when he first observed the airport's rotating beacon. He stated that he had an uneventful landing at MVY about 21:45.

About 22:00, the pilot departed MVY as the controller announced that the tower was closing. After takeoff, he proceeded on a heading of 290 degrees, climbed to 6,500 feet, and proceeded directly to Groton. The pilot stated that, during the return flight, the visibility was the same as that which he had encountered during the flight to MVY, which was about 3 to 5 miles in haze.

Another pilot at CDW had stated to the news media that he cancelled his planned flight from CDW to MVY on the evening of the accident because of the "poor" weather. In a written statement he stated the following:

"From my own judgement visibility appeared to be approximately 4 miles-extremely hazy. Winds were fairly light. Based only on the current weather conditions at CDW, the fact that I could not get my friends to come with me, and the fact that I would not have to spend money on a hotel room in Martha's Vineyard, I made the decision to fly my airplane to Martha's Vineyard on Saturday."

Who are these pilots?

COMMUNICATIONS

No record exists of the pilot, or a pilot using the airplane's registration number, receiving a weather briefing or filing a flight plan with any FAA FSS for the accident flight. Further, no record exists of the pilot, or a pilot using the airplane's registration number, contacting any FSS or ATC tower or facility during the duration of the flight, except for those at CDW.

Not so, Steve Lagudi was an airport radio attendant at Long Island's Republic Airport the night of the crash. He heard John call the tower on Martha's Vineyard.

174

This is a contradiction. The report clearly states that the pilot or a representative received two separate weather briefings.

The MVY ATC tower tape revealed that, during the period of time from when the accident airplane departed CDW until the tower closed and the recorder was turned off (about 22:00), no contact was attempted by the pilot, the call sign of N9253N, or any unknown station.

ABOUT 2200? If the recorder was indeed functional this should be a precise time in such a report. Adam Budd, intern airport attendant at MVY that night innocently spoke with members of the press. He stated that there was a very strict hush order being levied by officials which later led to his termination as airport attendant.

Initial reports from the FAA to the USCG stated that John had indeed contacted Martha's Vineyard Tower. Channel 5 Boston covered it live. Newscasters were suspicious and very upset when the Official Story contradicted this fact after the entire recovery had been compartmentalized.

TRAFFIC ALERT AND COLLISION AVOIDANCE SYSTEM (TCAS) ALERT NEAR HPN

According to the Aeronautical Informational Manual (AIM), definitions for Class B and D airspace are as follows:

Class B Airspace: "Generally, that airspace from the surface to 10,000 feet MSL [mean sea level], surrounding the nation's busiest airports in terms of IFR operations or passenger enplanements...An ATC clearance is required for all aircraft to operate in the area, and all aircraft that are so cleared receive separation services within the airspace...Regardless of weather conditions, an ATC clearance is required prior to operating within Class B airspace..."

Class D Airspace: "Generally, that airspace from the surface to 2,500 feet above the airport elevation (charted in MSL) surrounding those airports that have an operational control tower...Two-way radio communication must be established with the ATC facility providing ATC services prior to entry and thereafter maintain those communications while in the Class D airspace...."

The following TCAS alert occurred during the approach of a commercial airplane to HPN, which was located within published Class D airspace and the New York Class B airspace. On July 16, 1999, about 20:49, American Airlines flight 1484, a Fokker 100, was inbound for landing at HPN. According to the transcripts of communications between flight 1484 and the New York approach controller, at 20:49:33, flight 1484 was level at 6,000 feet. At 20:49:48, the controller instructed flight 1484 to descend and maintain 3,000 feet, which flight 1484 acknowledged. At 20:50:32, the controller issued an approach clearance to flight 1484, which flight 1484 also acknowledged. The following is an excerpt of the communications transcript between flight 1484 and the controller regarding the TCAS:

20:52:22, the controller, "American fourteen eighty four traffic one o'clock and five miles eastbound two thousand four hundred, unverified, appears to be climbing."

20:52:29, flight 1484, "American fourteen eighty four we're looking."

20:52:56, the controller, "fourteen eighty four traffic one o'clock and uh three miles twenty eight hundred now, unverified."

20:53:02, flight 1484, "um yes we have uh (unintelligible) I think we have him here American fourteen eighty-four."

20:53:10, flight 1484, "I understand he's not in contact with you or anybody else." 20:53:14, the controller, "uh nope doesn't not talking to anybody."

20:53:27, flight 1484, "seems to be climbing through uh thirty-one hundred now we just got a traffic advisory here."

20:53:35, the controller, "uh that's what it looks like."
20:53:59, flight 1484, "uh we just had a."
20:54:12, the controller, "American fourteen eighty-four you can contact tower nineteen seven." 20:54:15, flight 1484, "nineteen seven uh we had a resolution advisory seemed to be a single engine piper or Comanche or something."
20:54:21, the controller, "roger."

The event occurred outside of the New York Class B and the HPN Class D airspace, and no corrective action was reported to have been taken by the controller or flight 1484. A review of the radar data correlated the unknown target with the track of N9253N.

This is total fluff. No bearing on John's flight.

AIRPORT INFORMATION

MVY had a field elevation of 68 feet. The hours of operation for the contract-operated tower were from 06:00 to 22:00. MVY had two runways. Runway 06/24 was asphalt-surfaced, 5,500 feet long, and 100 feet wide. Runway 15/33 was asphalt-surfaced, 3,297 feet long, and 75 feet wide. A VOR-distance measuring equipment (DME) navigation aid was located on the airport. The

VOR was listed with a normal anticipated interference-free service of 40 nm, up to 18,000 feet with DME. ILS, VOR, and GPS instrument approaches were published for the airport.

MVY was located about 10 miles east of Gay Head. Gay Head had a lighthouse for marine navigation at 41 degrees, 20.9 minutes north latitude; 70 degrees, 50.1 minutes west longitude. According to USCG personnel, the top of the lighthouse was 170 feet above mean low water and operated 24 hours-a-day. The rotating beacon ran on a 15-second cycle, 7.3 seconds white and 7.3 seconds red. The expected range of the white light was 24 miles, and the expected range of the red light was 20 miles.

FLIGHT RECORDERS

The airplane was equipped with a Flightcom Digital Voice Recorder Clock, DVR 300i. The unit contained a digital clock, was wired into the radio communications circuits, and could record conversations between the airplane and other radio sources, ground, or air. The unit was voice activated, and the continuous loop could record and retain a total of 5 minutes of data. The unit had a nonvolatile speech memory that required a 9-volt backup battery to preserve the speech data. When the unit was located in the wreckage, it was crushed, its backup battery was missing, and it had retained no data.

Sad and probably true, but very convenient.

WRECKAGE INFORMATION

On July 20, 1999, the airplane wreckage was located by U.S. Navy divers from the recovery ship, USS Grasp, at a depth of about 120 feet below the surface of the Atlantic Ocean. According to the divers, the recovered wreckage had been distributed in a debris field about 120 feet long and was oriented along a magnetic bearing of about 010/190 degrees. The main cabin area was found in the middle of the debris field.

A Safety Board investigator was present on the USS Grasp during the salvage operation. On July 21, 1999, the main cabin area was raised and placed aboard the USS Grasp. On July 22, 1999, the divers made five additional dives, and the wreckage retrieved from these dives was also placed aboard the USS Grasp. On July 23, 1999, about 2100, the wreckage was transferred from the USS Grasp to the Safety Board at a naval base in Newport, Rhode Island. The wreckage was then transported to the USCG Air Station at Otis Air Force Base, Cape Cod, Massachusetts, the evening of July 23, 1999. The wreckage was examined by Board investigators in a hangar at the USCG Air Station on July 24, 25, and 26, 1999. Follow-up examinations were conducted on August 1 and 2, 1999.

Page 14 of 28 NYC99MA178

According to the Airworthiness Group Chairman's Report, the engine was found separated from the engine mount truss. The structural tubing on the right side of the engine mount truss was missing. The engine mount truss was deformed to the right and fractured in numerous locations. The upper left engine mount ear and both lower mount ears were fractured. The upper right engine mount ear was bent. The engine and propeller were retained for additional examination.

About 75 percent of the fuselage structure was recovered. A section of the aft cabin roof, about 5 feet long by 3 1/2 feet wide, had separated from the fuselage; this section included the airframe-mounted hinge of the left-side cargo door and a partial frame of the left-side cabin door. The left side of this section exhibited accordion crush damage in the aft direction and contained multiple folds about 5 inches deep. <mark>No fuselage structure from the left or right side of the cabin area was recovered, except for a piece of skin, about 2 feet by 2 feet, located beneath the left-side passenger window frame.</mark>

We need to examine the evidence highlighted above in detail. The weaker parts of the airplane, windows, and doors have separated from the fuselage. The accordion crush damage, which has multiple 5-inch folds travels in the aft direction. This is inconsistent with damage incurred in a forward impact.

No fuselage structure from the left or right side of the cabin area was recovered. These panels were probably blown clear of the 120 ft. debris field as was Lauren's luggage. More evidence of explosive forces within the aircraft.

The belly skin and floor structure of the fuselage were intact aft of the wing spar box carry-through section. The recovered floor structure forward of this section was fragmented. Portions of five of the six seats were found inside the fuselage. The sixth seat was not recovered. Most of the fuselage structure aft of the cabin area was recovered.

About 60 percent of the right-wing structure was recovered, including the entire span of the main spar. The right wing had separated into multiple pieces and exhibited more damage than the left wing. The right wing main spar had separated into three pieces. The wing spar had fractured at its attachment to the main carry-through section. The upper spar cap fracture exhibited tension on its forward edge and compression on its aft edge. The spar web exhibited aft bending and tearing in this area.

The outboard portion of the wing leading edge exhibited rearward accordion crush damage and was separated from the remainder of the wing. No evidence of upward spar bending damage was found. No evidence of metal fatigue was found in any of the fracture surfaces.

The entire span of the right flap was recovered; it had separated into two sections (chordwise fracture), and both sections had separated from the right wing. Neither flap section exhibited bowing, bulging, or planar deformation. About 33 inches of the right aileron was recovered, and the leading edge of this section exhibited rearward crush deformation.

About 80 percent of the left wing structure was recovered, including the entire span of the main spar. The left wing main spar had separated into several pieces and exhibited less deformation than the right wing. The wing spar was fractured near the left edge of the main carry-through section. The upper and lower spar cap fractures in this area exhibited tension on the forward edges and compression on the aft edges. The spar web also exhibited aft bending and tearing in this area. No evidence of upward spar bending damage was found. No evidence of metal fatigue was found in any of the fracture surfaces.

Page 15 of 28 NYC99MA178

About 90 percent of the upper and lower wing skin between the main and rear spars was recovered. The upper skin near the left wing tip was flattened out. The leading-edge skin near the inboard portion of the left wing, near the stall warning port, exhibited damage consistent with uniform hydrodynamic deformation in the aft direction.

A 27-inch inboard section of the wing flap section was recovered, and the leading edge of this section exhibited aft accordion crush damage. The flap section did not exhibit any bowing, bulging, or planar deformation. The entire span of the left aileron was recovered; it had separated into two pieces. The outboard section of the aileron was curled downward.

The vertical stabilizer and rudder had separated from the aft fuselage. The stabilator had separated from the aft fuselage attach points and had fractured into five pieces. Two of the pieces consisted of left and right outboard sections, about 22 inches long, and exhibited symmetrical aft crush marks that were semicircular, with diameters of about 5 inches. The fracture surfaces of the left outboard section exhibited tearing in the aft direction. The fracture surfaces of the right outboard sections exhibited forward and upward tearing. The left inboard section of the stabilator was more intact than the right inboard section. The leading edge of the right stabilator section exhibited rearward uniform crush damage along its entire leading edge.

The lower portion of the rudder had separated from the vertical stabilizer fin structure and remained attached to the torque tube bellcrank assembly and fin aft spar. The rudder was folded over toward the right side of the airplane. The vertical stabilizer was also twisted, bent, and curled around toward the right. The structure surrounding the dorsal fin area was deformed symmetrically upward.

All three landing gear assemblies had separated from the airframe and were recovered. The retraction/extension actuating cylinders associated with the nose gear and the left main gear were found in the fully retracted position. The retraction/extension actuating cylinder for the right main gear was not recovered.

Examination of the aileron control cable circuit and associated hardware did not reveal any evidence of a preexisting jam or failure. Flight control cable continuity for the entire right aileron control circuit, including the entire balance cable that links the right aileron to the left aileron, was established. The control cable continuity for the left aileron could not be established because of impact damage and fragmentation. All of the ends of the separations of the aileron control cable circuits exhibited evidence of tensile overload. The stops for the ailerons were examined; no evidence of severe repetitive strike marks or deformations was noted.

Examination of the stabilator control cable circuit and associated hardware did not reveal any evidence of a preexisting jam or failure. Flight control cable continuity for the stabilator was established from the control surfaces to the cockpit controls. The stabilator balance weight had separated from the stabilator, and the fractures associated with the separation were consistent with tensile overload. The stops for the stabilator were examined; no evidence of severe repetitive strike marks or deformations was noted.

Examination of the stabilator trim control cable circuit and associated hardware did not reveal any evidence of a preexisting jam or failure. Control cable circuitry for the stabilator trim was

established from the control surfaces to the cockpit area. An examination of the stabilator trim barrel jackscrew revealed that one full thread was protruding out of the upper portion of the trim barrel assembly housing. The barrel assembly was free to rotate and had the trim control cable wrapped around it. The two cable ends were separated about 41 inches and 37 inches, respectively, from the barrel assembly winding. Examination of the separations revealed evidence consistent with tensile overload.

Examination of the rudder control cable circuit and associated hardware did not reveal any evidence of a preexisting jam or failure. Flight control cable continuity for the rudder was established from the control surfaces to the cockpit controls. The stops for the rudder were examined; no evidence of severe repetitive strike marks or deformations was noted.

The electrically driven wing flap jackscrew actuator was not recovered. The flap switch in the cockpit was destroyed. The throttle and propeller controls were found in the FULL- FORWARD position.

John did not have time to close the throttle. Impact forces not ruled out, but the propeller damage indicated a full power entry into the sea.

The mixture control was broken. The alternate air control was found in the CLOSED position. The key in the magneto switch was found in the BOTH position.

John didn't have time to turn the ignition off.

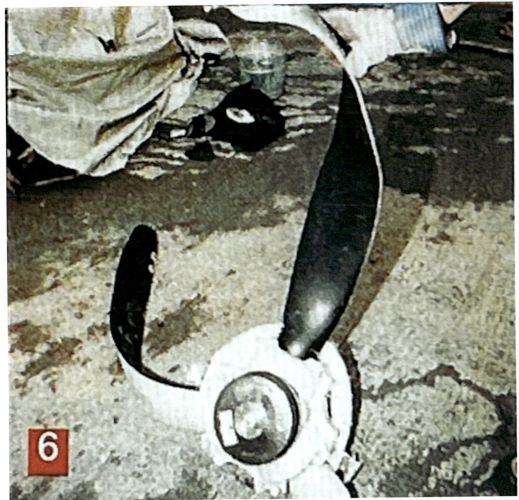

Propeller blades arcing rearward with a consistent radius from torque forces. Long proven evidence that the engine was operating at full power as it impacted the ocean.

==The tachometer needle was found intact, fixed in place, and pointed to 2,750 rpm. The red line on the tachometer began at 2,700 rpm.== The hour register inside the tachometer read 0663.5 hours. The manifold pressure gauge needle was found fixed in place and indicated 27 inches Hg. The fuel flow gauge needle was found slightly loose and indicated 22 gallons per hour. The exhaust gas temperature gauge needle was found loose and indicated 1,000 degrees Fahrenheit (F). The oil temperature gauge was found fixed and indicated 150 degrees F. The oil pressure gauge was found fixed and indicated about 17 pounds per square inch (psi). The cylinder temperature gauge needle was not found. The fuel quantity gauges were destroyed. The altimeter needle was found fixed and indicated 270 feet. The altimeter setting was found fixed at 30.09 Hg. The top of the VOR indicator heading card was found at the 097-degree bearing.

John was utilizing a navigational radio which was providing the exact bearing to the MVY.

Examination of all recovered electrical wiring and components did not reveal any evidence of arcing or fire. The circuit breaker panel was deformed and impact damaged. All of the breakers were found in the tripped position, except for the flap, transceiver, and DME. The circuit breaker that provided protection for the transponder, which provided the VFR code and altitude readout to radar facilities down to 1,100 feet, was also found tripped.

The fuel selector valve was recovered, and the bottom of the valve was missing. All three fuel line connections were broken off. The valve had separated from the fuselage attach points. The selector valve linkage was deformed, and the valve was found in the OFF position.

The position of the fuel valve has been the subject of much speculation. However, considering it has been established that the airplane engine was running under full power upon impact, the "Off Position" fuel selector valve had no bearing on failure of the aircraft. We explore the possibilities in chapter 14.

A liquid that had a similar color, odor, and texture as 100 low-lead aviation gasoline was found in the fuel selector valve sump. The electrically driven fuel boost pump was able to function when electrical power was applied to it.

The airplane had been equipped with six seats. The seats had been configured in a "club style" arrangement, with two forward-facing seats in row 1 (including the pilot's seat), two aft-facing seats in row 2, and two front-facing seats in row 3. The five recovered seats had separated from the floor structure. Examination of the aluminum backs of both aft-facing seats revealed that they were deformed (bulged) in the forward direction.

The left and right front seats were equipped with lap belts and shoulder harnesses. None of the belts for these seats could be identified in the wreckage. The four seats in rows 2 and 3 were also equipped with lap belts and shoulder harnesses. Both sections of the lap belt for the left-

side aft-facing seat were found and exhibited evidence of stretching. The inboard section of the lap belt for the right-side aft-facing seat in row 2 had been cleanly cut about 3 inches from the male-end of the latch, and the outboard section of lap belt for this seat exhibited evidence of stretching. All of the lap belt sections for the seats in row 3 were identified and none exhibited evidence of stretching. The shoulder harnesses for the rear seats could not be identified in the wreckage.

MEDICAL AND PATHOLOGICAL INFORMATION

On July 21, 1999, examinations were performed on the pilot and passengers by Dr. James Weiner, Office of the Chief Medical

Examiner, Commonwealth of Massachusetts. The results indicated that the pilot and passengers died from multiple injuries as a result of an airplane accident.

Toxicological testing was conducted by the FAA Toxicology Accident Research Laboratory, Oklahoma City, Oklahoma. The toxicological tests were negative for alcohol and drugs of abuse.

Medical Information

According to medical records, on June 1, 1999, the pilot fractured his left ankle in a "hang gliding" accident, and on June 2, 1999, he underwent surgical "open reduction internal fixation of left ankle fracture." On June 23, 1999, the pilot's leg was removed from a cast and placed in a "Cam-Walker." On July 15, 1999, the pilot's Cam-Walker was removed, and on July 16, 1999, he was given a "straight cane and instructed in cane usage." The medical records noted that the pilot was "full weight bearing with mild antalgic gait."

During interviews, the pilot's physical therapist stated that the pilot did not have full dorsiflexion (bending upward of the foot) and that he could not determine whether the pilot's gait was caused by his slight limitation of motion or by mild pain. The pilot's orthopedic surgeon stated that he felt that, at the time of the accident, the pilot would have been able to apply the type of pressure with the left foot that would normally be required by emergency brake application with the right foot in an automobile.

This is more than enough pressure to operate the rudder and brake pedal on the Piper Saratoga.

According to 14 CFR Section 61.53, "Prohibition On Operations During Medical Deficiency," in operations that required a medical certificate, a person shall not act as a pilot-in-command while that

188

person, "(1) Knows or has reason to know of any medical condition that would make the person unable to meet the requirements for the medical certificate necessary for the pilot operation."

According to an FAA medical doctor, a pilot with the type of ankle injury that the accident pilot had at the time of the accident would not normally be expected to visit and receive approval from an FAA Medical Examiner before resuming flying activities.

This is an arbitrary statement. Who is the doctor? John's own Orthopedic surgeon states John could operate an emergency brake in an automobile. This is sufficient pressure to operate the rudder pedals of the plane. The ankle is a non-issue.

TESTS AND RESEARCH
Engine and Propeller Examinations

On July 26, 1999, the engine was examined at the Textron-Lycoming Facility, Williamsport, Pennsylvania, under the supervision of a Safety Board powerplants investigator. On July 28, 1999, the propeller hub and blades were examined at the Hartzell Propeller Facility, Piqua, Ohio, under the supervision of a Safety Board powerplants investigator. Parties to the investigation were present during both examinations.

Page 18 of 28 NYC99MA178

According to the Powerplants Group Chairman's Factual Report, the examinations of the engine and propeller did not reveal evidence of any preexisting failures or conditions that would have prevented engine operation. The report further stated that "the investigation team found impact marks on one of the propeller blades and the top of the engine, witness marks inside the

189

propeller, and the engine controls and instruments in the cockpit that indicated high engine power output."

The airplane entered the water under full power conditions.

Autopilot Operation

The airplane was equipped with a Bendix/King 150 Series Automatic Flight Control System (AFCS), which was approved for use in Piper PA-32R-301 model airplanes by the FAA on November 1, 1982. The AFCS provided two-axis control for pitch and roll. It also had an electric pitch trim system, which provided auto trim during autopilot operation and manual electric trim for the pilot during manual operation.

The AFCS installed on the accident airplane had an altitude hold mode that, when selected, allowed the airplane to maintain the altitude that it had when the altitude hold was selected. The AFCS did not have the option of allowing the pilot to preselect an altitude so that the autopilot could fly to and maintain the preselected altitude as it climbed or descended from another altitude. The AFCS had a vertical trim rocker switch installed so that the pilot could change the airplane's pitch up or down without disconnecting the autopilot. The rocker switch allowed the pilot to make small corrections in the selected altitude while in the altitude hold mode or allowed the pitch attitude to be adjusted at a rate of about 0.9 degree per second when not in altitude hold mode.

The AFCS incorporated a flight director, which had to be activated before the autopilot would engage. Once activated, the flight director could provide commands to the flight command indicator to maintain wings level and the pitch attitude. To satisfy the command, the pilot could manually fly the airplane by referencing the guidance received in the flight command indicator, or the pilot could engage the autopilot and let it satisfy the commands by maneuvering the aircraft in a similar manner via the autopilot servos.

The AFCS incorporated a navigation mode that could provide guidance to the pilot, or the autopilot, about intercepting and tracking VOR and GPS courses. While engaged in this mode, the AFCS could receive input signals from either the selected VOR frequency and course or from GPS course data selected for presentation on the pictorial navigation indicator. The flight command indicator could then command the bank required to maintain the selected VOR or GPS course with automatic crosswind compensation, and the autopilot, if engaged, would satisfy those commands.

The AFCS incorporated a heading select mode that allowed the pilot to select a heading by moving a "bug" on the outer ring of the pictorial navigation indicator. Once the bug was moved to the desired heading with the heading select button engaged, the autopilot could command the airplane to that heading at a bank angle of about 22 degrees.

The AFCS had a control wheel steering (CWS) button mounted on the control yoke that allowed the pilot to maneuver the aircraft in pitch and roll without disengaging the autopilot. According to AlliedSignal, when the CWS button was released, the autopilot would resume control of the aircraft at the heading and altitude that had been selected at the time the CWS button was released.

According to the FAA and Bendix/King, the trim system was designed to withstand any single in-flight malfunction. Trim faults were visually and aurally annunciated in the cockpit. Through the use of monitor circuits, aircraft control would automatically be returned to the pilot when a fault was detected.

After the AFCS had been preflight tested, it could be engaged and disengaged either manually or automatically. The following conditions would cause the autopilot to automatically disengage power failure, internal flight control system failure, loss of a valid compass signal, roll rates greater than 14 degrees per second, and pitch rates greater than 8 degrees per second.

The AFCS could have been altered or more exactly tampered with to produce the flight maneuver deviations experienced during John's approach to the island.

Avionics Examinations

On July 29 and 30, 1999, the avionics were examined at the AlliedSignal/King Radios Facility, Olathe, Kansas, under the supervision of a Safety Board investigator. On October 13 and 14, 1999, a follow-up examination of the navigation and communications transceivers and all three autopilot servos was also performed at the AlliedSignal/King Radios Facility under the supervision of a Safety Board investigator. Parties to the investigation were present during both examinations.

The accident airplane's AFCS was examined. Examination and functional testing of the AFCS pitch, pitch trim, and roll servos did not reveal any evidence of a preimpact malfunction or jam.

The accident airplane was equipped with a GPS receiver, Bendix/King model KLN-90B. The GPS was capable of presenting moving map displays; bearings and distances to programmable destinations, such as airports and waypoints; airport information;

ground speed; and other information. The GPS was also capable of interfacing with the AFCS and the pictorial navigation indicator.

Examination of the GPS unit revealed that it was crushed vertically. The display in the front face of the unit was destroyed. The ON/OFF switch was found in the ON position. The navigation database indicated that it was effective on October 8, 1998, and that it expired on November 4, 1998. A wire that connected the circuitry of a 3.6-volt lithium battery was separated. According to AlliedSignal, the lithium battery provided electrical power to retain the nonvolatile memory of the GPS receiver and required a minimum of 2.5 volts to retain memory. The battery voltage was measured to be 0.2 volt, and it was determined that the memory had not been retained.

Examination of the Bendix/King model KR-87, automatic direction finder, revealed that the receiver's primary frequency was set at 400 kilohertz (kHz) and the secondary frequency was set at 200 kHz.

Both of the airplane's communication/navigation transceivers received severe impact damage and could not be powered up. The nonvolatile memory circuit chips were extracted from the transceivers, placed in a test unit, and powered up. The following information was noted about each of the transceivers:

Transceiver No. 1, KX-165

The in-use communication frequency was set at 132.02, which was the same frequency as the TEB automatic terminal information service (ATIS).

The standby communication frequency was set at 135.25; the CDW ATIS had a frequency of 135.5.

The in-use navigation frequency was set at 109.80, which was the same frequency as the New

Haven, Connecticut, VOR.

The standby navigation frequency was set at 113.10, which was the same frequency as the LaGuardia Airport, New York, VOR.

Transceiver No. 2, KX-165

The in-use communication frequency was set at 121.40, which was the same frequency as the MVY tower.

Evidence proves that John either contacted the tower or intended to. This is major evidence. A nighttime pilot who is running late and has relatives waiting at the airport would have typically contacted the tower by the 10 mile out mark. This is not mandatory but is more frequently done than not. Keep in mind John was unable to call a mayday or ask for help.

The standby communication frequency was set at 127.25; the MVY ATIS had a frequency of 126.25.

The in-use navigation frequency was set at 108.80, which was the same frequency as the BDR VOR.

The standby navigation frequency was set at 110.00, which was the same frequency as the Norwich, Connecticut, VOR.

Safety Board Materials Laboratory Examinations

An examination of the accident airplane's components was conducted in the Safety Board Materials Laboratory in Washington, D.C.

The flight command indicator (Bendix/King model KI-256) was deformed, and its glass faceplate was missing. The center portion of the pictorial display was partially embedded in the side of the housing in a position that indicated a right turn with a bank angle of about 125 degrees and a nose-down pitch attitude of about 30 degrees. The air-driven gyro housing inside of the flight command indicator was corroded but not deformed. Disassembly and inspection of the gyro did not reveal any scoring marks on the spinning mass gyro and mating housing. The turn coordinator was deformed, and its glass was missing. The display was captured in a position indicating a steep right turn. The electrically driven gyro assembly inside of the instrument was removed and found free to rotate with no binding or case interference. No scoring marks were found on either the spinning mass gyro or mating housing.

The pictorial navigation indicator (Bendix/King model KI-525A) was deformed, and its glass faceplate was missing. The heading indicator was pointing to 339 degrees. The center navigational display needle was oriented along the 300/120-degree bearing. The heading flag was displayed. The heading bug was located at the 095-degree mark. The slaved gyro assembly was partially separated from its mounting, and its case exhibited minor deformation. The gyro housing and internal rotor were disassembled. The interior surface of the case and the exterior surface of the spinning mass rotor did not exhibit any deformation, impact marks, or rotational scoring.

The engine-driven vacuum pump drive shear shaft was intact. The drive end was removed to expose the internal rotor and vanes. The rotor showed several cracks between the bottom of the vane slots and the center of the rotor. All six vanes were removed intact. The rotor was removed in several pieces, and the housing was examined. Examination revealed no evidence of scoring or rotational damage. A metal straight-edge was placed along the long ends of each vane, and no warping or wear was noted.

The electrically driven vacuum pump drive shear shaft was intact. The pump was opened from the motor drive end to expose the rotor and internal vanes. Several cracks were noted in the

rotor between the vane slots and the center shaft area. Five of the six vanes were removed and found intact with no fractures or edge chipping. The sixth vane was found wedged and stuck in the rotor, which was stuck inside the housing. Approximately half of the rotor was removed, and examination of its housing revealed no evidence of scoring or rotational damage. A metal straight-edge was placed along the long ends of the removed vanes, and no warping or wear was noted. Disassembly and examination of the vacuum system filter did not reveal any evidence of contaminants or blockages.

The airspeed indicator was damaged, and its glass faceplate was missing. The needle position was found off-scale near the right edge of the density altitude adjustment window; it could be moved, however, when released, it spring-loaded to its as-found position. Magnified examination of marks on the instrument face revealed an outline similar to the size and shape of the needle. This mark was located about two needle widths above the 210-knot marking, which was the maximum marking on the indicator. The location of the needle mark on the airspeed indicator was consistent with the maximum mechanical needle travel position for the airspeed indicator design.

The VSI needle was missing. Magnified examination of marks on the instrument face revealed an outline similar to the size and shape of a needle. This needle mark was pointed at the down-limit position of 2,000 fpm descent.

Microscopic examination of the AFCS light bulbs on the front face of the unit was performed. None of the light bulbs exhibited evidence of filament stretch, including the autopilot engage, flight director, or trim failure light bulbs. An examination of all recovered light bulbs from the airplane's main and landing gear annunciator panels revealed no evidence of filament stretch.

Aircraft Performance Study

An aircraft performance study was performed by a Safety Board specialist using the Board's computer simulation program. According to the specialist's report, airplane performance data for the final portion of the flight were calculated using radar, aircraft, and weather data. Performance parameters were then computed for the final 7 minutes of the flight.

The calculated parameters showed the airplane initially descending from 5,500 feet at descent rates varying between 400 and 800 fpm, at 21:33:40. At 21:37:20, the airplane attained a steady descent rate of close to 600 fpm as the airplane passed through 3,000 feet. During the entire descent from 5,500 feet, the calculated airspeed remained near 160 KIAS, and the flightpath angle remained close to -2 degrees. About 21:38, the airplane started to bank in a right-wing-down (RWD) direction toward a southerly direction. Calculated parameters indicated an almost constant roll angle of 13 degrees RWD and a vertical acceleration of 1.09 G's while executing the turn. About 30 seconds after the turn was initiated, at an altitude of 2,200 feet, the airplane stopped descending. The airplane then climbed for the next 30 seconds, attaining a maximum climb rate of 600 fpm. During the ascent, the airplane finished the turn to a southeasterly direction, reduced speed slightly to 153 KIAS, and returned to a wings-level attitude by 21:38:50. By 21:39, the airplane leveled at 2,500 feet and then flew in a southeasterly direction with wings level while increasing airspeed back to 160 KIAS.

At 21:39:50, the airplane entered a left turn, while slightly increasing altitude to 2,600 feet. The airplane reached a maximum bank angle of 28 degrees left-wing-down (LWD) and a maximum vertical acceleration of 1.2 G's in this turn. When the maximum LWD bank angle was obtained, the altitude started to decrease at a descent rate close to 900 fpm. The LWD attitude was

Page 22 of 28 NYC99MA178

maintained for approximately 15 seconds until the airplane was heading towards the east. At 21:40:07, the airplane bank angle returned to wings level. At 21:40:15, with the airplane continuing towards the east, it reestablished a descent close to 900 fpm and then started to increase its bank angle in a RWD direction at nearly a constant rate. As the airplane bank angle increased, the rate of descent increased, and the airspeed started to increase. By 21:40:25, the bank angle exceeded 45 degrees, the vertical acceleration was 1.2 G's, the airspeed increased through 180 knots, and the flightpath angle was close to 5 degrees airplane nose down. After 21:40:25, the airplane's airspeed, vertical acceleration, bank, and dive angle continued to increase, and the right turn tightened until water impact, about 21:41.

This is the extremely suspicious maneuvering which occurred very close to the island. The climbs and turns are only a

ADDITIONAL INFORMATION Cell Phones

The cell phone records for the three occupants of the airplane reflected one out-going call, about 20:25. No calls were listed as being made from, or received by, the cell phones from the time of the takeoff through the estimated time of the accident.

Preflight Briefing

The AIM, published by the FAA, is the official guide to basic flight information and ATC procedures. Under the Section, "Preflight Briefing," it states that FSSs are the primary source for obtaining preflight briefings and in-flight weather information. The AIM states that a standard briefing should be requested any time a pilot is planning a flight and has not received a previous briefing or has not received preliminary information through mass dissemination media. The standard briefing should include the following information:

Adverse Conditions: Significant meteorological and aeronautical information that might influence the pilot to alter the proposed flight.

VFR Flight Not Recommended: When VFR flight is proposed and sky conditions or visibilities are present or forecast, surface or aloft, that in the briefer's judgment would make flight under VFR doubtful, the briefer will describe the conditions, affected locations, and use the phrase "VFR flight not recommended."

Current Conditions: Reported weather conditions applicable to the flight will be summarized from all available sources.

Enroute Forecast: Forecast enroute conditions for the proposed route are summarized in logical order (for example, departure/climb out, enroute, and descent).

Destination Forecast: The destination forecast for the planned estimated time of arrival. Any significant changes within 1 hour before and after the planned arrival are included.

Winds Aloft: Forecast winds aloft will be provided using degrees of the compass. The briefer will interpolate wind directions and speeds between levels and stations as necessary to provide expected conditions at planned altitudes.

The AIM also states that a standard briefing should include synopsis, notices to airmen, and ATC delays.

John performed the preflight briefings.

Spatial Disorientation

A review of 14 CFR Part 61, "Certification: Pilots, Flight Instructors, and Ground Instructors," revealed that no specific training requirements exist regarding spatial disorientation.

Page 23 of 28 NYC99MA178

According to the FAA Practical Test Standards, an applicant for a private pilot rating must exhibit knowledge of spatial disorientation. In addition, the publication states that "the examiner shall also emphasize stall/spin awareness, spatial disorientation..."

A review of training records from FSI revealed that while the pilot was preparing for his private pilot certificate, he received instruction on the symptoms, causes, and effects of spatial disorientation and the correct action to take if it occurred. In addition, <mark>the pilot received unusual attitude training while attending the private pilot and instrument training courses at FSI.</mark>

According to an FAA Instrument Flying Handbook, Advisory Circular 61-27C (AC) (Section II, "Instrument Flying: Coping with Illusions in Flight"), one purpose for instrument training and maintaining instrument proficiency is to prevent a pilot from being misled by several types of hazardous illusions that are peculiar to flight. The AC states that an illusion or false impression occurs when information provided by sensory organs is misinterpreted or inadequate and that many illusions in flight could be created by complex motions and certain visual scenes encountered under adverse weather conditions and at night. It also states that some illusions may lead to spatial disorientation or the inability to determine accurately the attitude or motion of the aircraft in relation to the earth's surface. The AC also states that spatial disorientation as a result of continued VFR flight into adverse weather conditions is regularly near the top of the cause/factor list in annual statistics on fatal aircraft accidents.

The AC further states that the most hazardous illusions that lead to spatial disorientation are created by information received from motion sensing systems, which are located in each inner ear. The AC also states that the sensory organs in these systems detect angular acceleration in the pitch, yaw, and roll axes, and a sensory organ detects gravity and linear acceleration and that, in flight, the motion sensing system may be stimulated by motion of the aircraft alone or in combination with head and body movement. The AC lists some of the major illusions leading to spatial disorientation as follows:

"The leans - A banked attitude, to the left for example, may be entered too slowly to set in motion the fluid in the 'roll' semicircular tubes. An abrupt correction of this attitude can now set the fluid in motion and so create the illusion of a banked attitude to the right. The disoriented pilot may make the error of rolling the aircraft back into the original left-banked attitude or, if level flight is maintained, will feel compelled to lean to the left until this illusion subsides.

Coriolis illusion - An abrupt head movement made during a prolonged constant-rate turn may set the fluid in more than one semicircular tube in motion, creating the strong illusion of turning or accelerating, in an entirely different axis. The disoriented pilot may maneuver the aircraft into a dangerous attitude in an attempt to correct this illusory movement....

Graveyard spiral - In a prolonged coordinated, constant-rate turn, the fluid in the semicircular tubes in the axis of the turn will cease its movement...An observed loss altitude in the aircraft instruments and the absence of any sensation of turning may create the illusion of being in a descent with the wings level. The disoriented pilot may pull back on the controls, tightening the spiral and increasing the loss of altitude....

Inversion illusion - An abrupt change from climb to straight-and-level flight can excessively stimulate the sensory organs for gravity and linear acceleration, creating the illusion of

tumbling backwards. The disoriented pilot may push the aircraft abruptly into a nose-low attitude, possibly intensifying this illusion.

Elevator illusion - An abrupt upward vertical acceleration, as can occur in a helicopter or an updraft, can shift vision downwards (visual scene moves upwards) through excessive stimulation of the sensory organs for gravity and linear acceleration, creating the illusion of being in a climb. The disoriented pilot may push the aircraft into a nose low attitude. An abrupt downward vertical acceleration, usually in a downdraft, has the opposite effect, with the disoriented pilot pulling the aircraft into a nose-up attitude....

Autokinesis - In the dark, a stationary light will appear to move about when stared at for many seconds. The disoriented pilot could lose control of the aircraft in attempting to align it with the false movements of this light."

The AC also states that these undesirable sensations cannot be completely prevented but that they can be ignored or sufficiently suppressed by pilots' developing an "absolute" reliance upon what the flight instruments are reporting about the attitude of their aircraft. The AC further states that practice and experience in instrument flying are necessary to aid pilots in discounting or overcoming false sensations.

Further, the FAA Airplane Flying Handbook, FAA-H-8083-3, chapter 10, states the following about night flying and its affect on spatial orientation:

"Night flying requires that pilots be aware of, and operate within, their abilities and limitations. Although careful planning of any flight is essential, night flying demands more attention to the details of preflight preparation and planning. Preparation for a night flight should include a thorough review of the available weather reports and forecasts with particular attention given to temperature/dewpoint spread. A narrow temperature/dewpoint spread may indicate the possibility of ground fog. Emphasis should also be placed on wind direction and speed, since its effect on the airplane cannot be as easily detected at night as during the day...Night flying is very different from day flying and demands more attention of the pilot. The most noticeable difference is the limited availability of outside visual references. Therefore, flight instruments should be used to a greater degree in controlling the airplane...Under no circumstances should a VFR night-flight be made during poor or marginal weather conditions unless both the pilot and aircraft are certificated and equipped for flight under...IFR...Crossing large bodies of water at night in single-engine airplanes could be potentially hazardous, not only from the standpoint of landing (ditching) in the water, but also because with little or no lighting the horizon blends with the water, in which case, depth perception and orientation become difficult. During poor visibility conditions over water, the horizon will become obscure, and may result in a loss of orientation. Even on clear nights, the stars may be reflected on the water surface, which could appear as a continuous array of lights, thus making the horizon difficult to identify."

According to AC 60-4A, "Pilot's Spatial Disorientation," tests conducted with qualified instrument pilots indicated that it can take as long as 35 seconds to establish full control by instruments after a loss of visual reference of the earth's surface. AC 60-4A further states that surface references and the natural horizon may become obscured even though visibility may be above VFR minimums and that an inability to perceive the natural horizon or surface references is common during flights over water, at night, in sparsely populated areas, and in low-visibility conditions.

Page 25 of 28 NYC99MA178

A book titled, Night Flying, by Richard Haines and Courtney Flatau, provides some additional information concerning vertigo and disorientation. It states the following:

"Vestibular disorientation refers to the general feeling that one's flight path isn't correct in some way. By calling this effect vestibular, it emphasizes the role played by the middle ear's balance organ. Flying an uncoordinated turn produces this effect as does excessive head turning during a turn in flight. Vestibular disorientation is often subtle in its onset, yet it is the most disabling and dangerous of all disorientation."

The previous five pages are all practical flying rubbish and filler that have little bearing on John's case. It is clearly inserted here to support the "Official Story".

Pilot's Operating Handbook (POH)

According to the POH and a photo of the accident airplane's cockpit, the fuel selector control was located below the center of the instrument panel, on the sloping face of the control tunnel, on the cockpit floor. In the "Normal Procedures" section of the POH, under "Cruising," it states, "In order to keep the airplane in best lateral trim during cruise flight, the fuel should be used alternately from each tank at one-hour intervals." Also, in the "Normal Procedures" section, under the "Approach and Landing" checklist, the first item listed is "Fuel selector - proper tank."

The NTSB starving for reasons to explain the final critical pitch and bank changes which occurred just before the final plunge.

Wreckage Release

On August 5, 1999, the main airplane wreckage was released to a representative of the accident pilot's insurance company. On November 17, 1999, the remainder of the retained parts were released and shipped to the insurance company's storage facility.

Additional Persons Participating in the Investigation:
Richard I. Bunker - Massachusetts Aeronautics Commission,

Boston, Massachusetts Tom McCreary - Hartzell Propeller Inc., Piqua, Ohio

Pilot Information

Certificate: Private **Age:** 38, Male

Airplane Rating(s): Single-engine Land **Seat Occupied:** Left

Other Aircraft Rating(s): None **Restraint Used:** Seatbelt

Instrument Rating(s): None **Second Pilot Present:** No

Instructor Rating(s): None **Toxicology Performed:** Yes

Medical Certification: Class 2 Valid Medical--no **Last FAA Medical Exam:** 12/27/1997 waivers/lim.

Occupational Pilot: Last Flight Review or Equivalent:

Flight Time: 310 hours (Total, all aircraft), 36 hours (Total, this make and model), 212 hours (Pilot In Command, all aircraft), 45 hours (Last 90 days, all aircraft), 18 hours (Last 30 days, all aircraft)

Aircraft and Owner/Operator Information

Aircraft Make: Piper **Registration:** N9253N

Model/Series: PA-32R-301 PA-32R-301 **Aircraft Category:** Airplane

Year of Manufacture: Amateur Built: No

Airworthiness Certificate: Normal **Serial Number:** 32-13100

Landing Gear Type: Retractable - Tricycle **Seats:** 6

Date/Type of Last Inspection: 06/25/1999, Annual **Certified Max Gross Wt.:** 3600 lbs.

Time Since Last Inspection: 41 Hours **Engines:** 1 Reciprocating

Airframe Total Time: 664 Hours **Engine Manufacturer:** Lycoming

ELT: Installed, not activated **Engine Model/Series:** IO-540-K1G5

Registered Owner: JOHN F. KENNEDY JR. **Rated Power:** 300 hp

Operator: JOHN F. KENNEDY JR. **Operating Certificate(s)** None **Held:**

Operator Does Business As: RANDOM VENTURES **Operator Designator Code:**

Meteorological Information and Flight Plan

Conditions at Accident Site: Visual Conditions **Condition of Light:** Night/Dark

Observation Facility, Elevation: MVY, 68 ft msl **Distance from Accident Site:** 15 Nautical Miles	
Observation Time: 2153 EDT **Direction from Accident Site:** 95°	
Lowest Cloud Condition: Clear / 0 ft agl **Visibility** 10 Miles	
Lowest Ceiling: None / 0 ft agl **Visibility (RVR):** 0 ft	
Wind Speed/Gusts: 10 knots / 15 knots **Turbulence Type / Forecast/Actual:**	
Wind Direction: 240° **Turbulence Severity / Forecast/Actual:**	
Altimeter Setting: 30 inches Hg **Temperature/Dew Point:** 75°C / 64°C	
Precipitation and Obscuration:	
Departure Point: CALDWELL, NJ (CDW) **Type of Flight Plan Filed:** None	
Destination: , MA (MVY) **Type of Clearance:** None	
Departure Time: 2039 EDT **Type of Airspace:** Class G	

Wreckage and Impact Information

Crew Injuries: 1 Fatal **Aircraft Damage:** Destroyed	
Passenger Injuries: 2 Fatal **Aircraft Fire:** None	
Ground Injuries: N/A **Aircraft Explosion:** None	
Total Injuries: 3 Fatal **Latitude, Longitude:**	

Administrative Information

Investigator In Charge (IIC): ROBERT L PEARCE **Adopted Date:** 07/06/2000	
Additional Participating Persons: TONY JAMES; WASHINGTON, DC PAUL LEHMAN; VERO BEACH, FL GREGORY A ERIKSON; WILLIAMSPORT, PA JAY WICKIM; MATTITUCK, NY	
Publish Date:	
Investigation Docket: NTSB accident and incident dockets serve as permanent archival information for the NTSB's investigations. Dockets released prior to June 1, 2009 are publicly available from the NTSB's Record Management Division at pubinq@ntsb.gov, or at 800-877-6799. Dockets released after this date are available at http://dms.ntsb.gov/pubdms/.	

The National Transportation Safety Board (NTSB), established in 1967, is an independent federal agency mandated by Congress through the Independent Safety Board Act of 1974 to investigate transportation accidents, determine the probable causes of the accidents, issue safety recommendations, study transportation safety issues, and evaluate the safety effectiveness of government agencies involved in transportation. The NTSB makes public its actions and decisions through accident reports, safety studies, special investigation reports, safety recommendations, and statistical reviews.

The Independent Safety Board Act, as codified at 49 U.S.C. Section 1154(b), precludes the admission into evidence or use of any part of an NTSB report related to an incident or accident in a civil action for damages resulting from a matter mentioned in the report.

Twelve

<u>The Smoking Guns</u>

One of the most disturbing and puzzling aspects of John Kennedy's flight was his (reported) failure to call Air Traffic Control. This element of the flight is one of the strongest 'smoking guns' supporting the scenario of aircraft sabotage. From their first hours of instruction all pilots are trained to call for help if something goes awry during the flight.

The NTSB report and The FAA both state that there was no communication with John's flight after he departed Caldwell. However, there is evidence to the contrary.

Steve Lagudi, 23 at the time, was a radio station attendant at Long Island's Republic airport the night of July 16, 1999. Lagudi heard radio transmissions from an aircraft "calling for Martha's Vineyard."

Steve Lagudi (undated photo)

Quoting Steve from his statement to Star Magazine's 20th anniversary issue of John's death; "We hear those kinds of calls all the time, pilots turn back because of the haze and other weather conditions. They find somewhere else to land. I figured this guy would too. The next morning, I learned to my shock that JFK Jr.'s plane was missing, and I knew right away that I had been listening to him. His voice still haunts me. I don't think I will ever forget it." Lagudi was contacted for comment but did not respond to messages.

SUBJECT: NYC99MA178, Piper, PA32R-300, Marthas Vineyard, Massachusetts

Mr. Lagudi is employed at Republic Airport, Farmingdale, New York. He preferred not to release his employer's name. On the night of the accident, approximately 2120 Eastern Daylight Time, he was monitoring the Unicom frequency, 122.95 Mhz.

During that time, Mr. Lagudi heard several transmissions from a pilot, but he could not remember the call sign of the airplane. During a period of approximately 10 minutes, the pilot attempted to contact "someone at Marthas Vineyard," and "anyone monitoring at Marthas Vineyard." Mr. Lagudi further stated that the pilot's voice sounded increasingly anxious and frustrated as the transmissions continued. Toward the end of the transmissions, someone responded to the pilot. The pilot stated "Well, if there is nobody on the ground, were not going to make Marthas Vineyard. Mr. Lagudi did not know who responded to the pilot.

Testimony from Steve Lagudi for CNN's 'How it Really Happened.'

John's arrival at the island coincides with the time field operations are shutting down. This pilot if it was indeed John sounds like he needs fuel. John's late arrival may have compromised his fuel needs before departing to Hyannis. This is not a distress call, this is a pilot deciding to land at an alternate airport.

Mr. Lagudi's statement requires some analysis and scrutiny. It is a massive smoking gun relating to whether John made contact with the Martha's Vineyard Control Tower. The Star article goes on to say that Martha's Vineyard uses an ATIS (Automatic Terminal Information Service). All Controlled airports utilize an ATIS. The ATIS employs a recorded message which informs arriving and departing pilots of various conditions at the field, such as ceiling, visibility, altimeter setting, wind characteristics, and active runway, all factors a pilot would expect to hear while listening to the ATIS report. The ATIS frequency does not facilitate communications from pilot to facility, it is only a recording. ATIS information is usually updated several times a day. All recordings are tagged using the phonetic alphabet. The recording will open by saying this is information Alpha, Bravo, Charlie, and etc.

The pilot typically listens to the information before calling the Tower or Ground control. He informs them by name that he has the most current ATIS.

to release his employer's name. On the night of the accident, between 2100 and 2230 Eastern Daylight Time, he was monitoring the Unicom frequency, 122.95 Mhz.

During that time, Mr. Perez heard several transmissions from a pilot that used a call sign similar to N9253N. During a period of several minutes, the pilot attempted to contact "Skipple". Mr. Perez believes this may be a fixed based operator at Marthas Vineyard, Massachusetts. The pilot received one response that was unintelligible to Mr. Perez. Then, the pilot responded "I'm not trying to speak with you, I'm trying to contact the facility." One last transmission was heard. The pilot stated "We're not going to make it if we don't get a hold of the facility." Mr. Perez believes that the pilot may have been attempting to arrange ground transportation or fuel services.

Additionally, Mr. Perez stated that his coworker also witnessed the transmissions. At this point, he preferred not to release his coworker's name, but would give him the option of contacting the National Transportation Safety Board.

Mr. Perez testimony for CNN's 'How it Really Happened,' program.

Mr. Perez's testimony is highly supportive of the scenario outlined in Lagudi's testimony. "The Facility" is almost certainly the fuel vendor. He may have called the tower or unicom by mistake.

To summarize: An approaching aircraft would dial in the appropriate frequency, listen to the field information provided by the ATIS, then contact the Tower stating the pilot has information Bravo, Charlie or whatever. This procedure lessens the Tower operator's workload and prevents him from having to unnecessarily repeat the same information.

The procedure outlined here has been standard fare for the 50 years author Ise has been flying. Nothing has changed in its format or procedure.

John's Saratoga employed two NAV/COM radios; most aircraft do. The left displays are used for communication, the right displays are for navigation. The radios are usually located one above another in the center of the instrument panel.

The above illustration is a triple stack. The pilot can load frequencies into the displays ahead of time and change the active transmitter at will. This provides for organized sequencing when a pilot is handed off from one controller to the other. The redundancy in having the triple stack lends safeguards to the pilot in case of a radio failure, if one goes bad he's got two more.

Discussed below is information from John's radios, as recovered and documented in the NTSB report:

Transceiver 1 was programmed with all the information necessary to depart Caldwell and transition through New York.

Transceiver 2 displays some very interesting evidence indicating John had tried to contact the Tower. Quoting the NTSB report:

"The in-use communication frequency was set at 121.40 which was the same frequency of the MVY Tower."

"The standby communication frequency was set at 127.25: The MVY ATIS had a frequency of 126.25."

The single digit inconsistency may have been a result of impact forces changing the frequency slightly. It is also possible that this was the frequency used by the fuel vendor at the time. Attempts to determine that frequency have been fruitless. The last frequency John used before the crash was indeed the frequency designated to Martha's Vineyard Tower. VHF radios are subject to line-of-sight transmission. Steve Lagudi was able to hear John's call to the Tower because John was at altitude. Conversely, Steve would not have heard a reply from MVY Tower because of the line-of-sight rule. Both airports are nearly at sea level. Considering the evidence, it appears that John did indeed contact the Tower on Martha's Vineyard and Steve Lagudi was correct about who he heard call.

The NTSB report's official findings conclude that Kennedy died from the result of inadvertently entering a 'graveyard spiral,' a condition which sets up slowly and escalates into catastrophe. Had John Kennedy become slowly disoriented, considering his level of flight experience, he would have undoubtedly had the time to radio ATC for assistance.

Had he experienced a control failure he would absolutely have issued a 'Mayday' distress call to Vineyard Tower. Had he experienced any type of progressive failure of his aircraft he would have had the time to contact ATC. The lack of recorded contact with ATC is of great concern to author/pilot Ise. John was meticulous and thorough about his flying. When it comes to his communications with ATC that night, the silence is deafening!

Sherman Skolnick

In 2005, Sherman Skolnick obtained a secret FBI report on the recovery of JFK, Jr.'s Piper Saratoga aircraft. Details are listed here:

- **1. No declassification until 7/22/2029.**

- **2. This is in deference to the wishes of a senior member of the Kennedy family.**

- **3. Also in deference to the order of the national government and in respect to certain foreign intelligence agencies having reciprocal agreements with the U.S.**

- **4. POTUS order and national security findings attached.**

- **5. The recovered aircraft shows evidence of an explosive device having been glued or affixed within the tail luggage compartment.**

- **6. Device was apparently actuated by a barometric trigger. Radio signals not ruled out.**

- **7. Tail of aircraft was dismembered from the plane making it front heavy.**

- **8. Study of radar shows the plane fell in excess of 6,000 feet per minute up to radar cutoff.**

- **9. Satellite images supplied by the National Reconnaissance Office record an out-bursting flash** from the aircraft just prior to it going into perpendicular descent.

- 10. Tail structure was dismembered just prior to descent.

- 11. Recovery of a piece of luggage from beyond the flight path of the aircraft correlates with it being hurtled out of the tail luggage compartment at outburst.

- 12. Preliminary examination of the aircraft shows residue of an explosive device the Laboratory identifies as being the type used by certain foreign intelligence agencies. Refer to POTUS order and findings.

- 13. Study of Air Traffic Control and other radio signals shows no Mayday report from the aircraft, explained by rapidity of descent.

- 14. Investigation and examination has been strictly compartmentalized.

- 15. A short, perfunctory examination of the recovered bodies was completed. Examination revealed that Carolyn Bessette Kennedy was in third trimester pregnant, the fetus a boy. The four bodies were transferred to a senior member of the Kennedy family. The Bureau was not informed whether the bodies were actually cremated. Indirect advisories report that the bodies may have been shipped in

untagged containers to foreign destinations. Reliable assets are to submit reports.

There are several noticeable inconsistencies in the report, as discussed below.

13—Study of Air Traffic Control and other radio signals shows no Mayday report from the aircraft, explained by rapidity of descent. These circumstances can only lead to one conclusion:

Something immediate and catastrophic occurred onboard his aircraft that rendered him unconscious. This occurrence was sudden, stunning, shocking, and quite possibly incapacitating.

An explosion in the aft end of the aircraft could cause the airplane to career into the water and totally immobilize its occupants instantly and simultaneously.

5—The recovered aircraft shows evidence of an explosive device having been glued or affixed within the tail luggage compartment.

Tarping the tail. The empennage or tail end of the aircraft would be the area most likely targeted by a saboteur. It is an ideal location to deploy an aneroid incendiary device, which is simply a bomb or thermite charge which is activated and detonated by changes in atmospheric pressure. The traditional aneroid detonator could easily be built by using an aircraft altimeter wired as a switch to the explosive charge. Modern detonators have evolved with the digital age, being more compact and reliable.

6—Device was apparently actuated by a barometric trigger. Radio signals not ruled out.

The FBI Report allows for the possibility that the explosive charge may have been remotely detonated.

Two things would be accomplished: The tail control surfaces would be rendered useless, and the Emergency Locator Transmitter (ELT) would probably be destroyed. Without a structural tail the airplane would nosedive straight into the water just as the flight profile indicated.

10—Tail structure was dismembered just prior to descent.

7—Tail of aircraft was dismembered from the plane making it front heavy.

This indicates that the tail section was planted with a bomb that either exploded due to atmospheric pressure or was predetermined to explode once it reached a certain altitude upon descent.

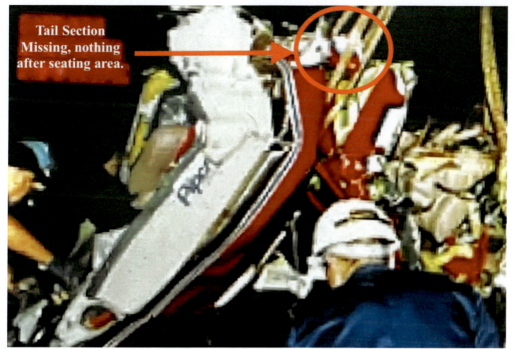

Tail Section Missing, nothing after seating area.

Remnants of JFK Jr.'s Piper Saratoga. Note: No tail section recovered.

9—Satellite images supplied by the National Reconnaissance Office record an out-bursting flash from the aircraft just prior to it going into perpendicular descent.

11—Recovery of a piece of luggage from beyond the flight path of the aircraft correlates with it being hurtled out of the tail luggage compartment at outburst.

The use of the word, 'out-bursting' presents further evidence of explosive forces tearing off the aircraft's tail.

Fortunately, three eyewitnesses surfaced after the midair explosion of John's airplane seven miles southwest of Philbin Beach on the night of July 16th.

3—Also in deference to the order of the national government and in respect to certain foreign intelligence agencies having reciprocal agreements with the U.S.

National government and certain foreign intelligence agencies? If this is allegedly just a pilot with spatial disorientation, why would there be a need for government and foreign intelligence agencies to have protection from this report? This could however explain why members of Mossad were seen with the aircraft the day before the fatal flight.

A reporter for the Vineyard Gazette newspaper told WCBV-TV in Boston that he was out walking Friday night about the time of the crash and saw "a big white flash in the sky" off Philbin Beach. (1) Author Ise exchanged emails with WCBV-TV reporter Steve Sbraccia a few years ago, and he volunteered that something didn't seem 'right' to him about the JFK Jr. plane crash. He also verified that he'd spoken to the Hyannis Port Gazette reporter, and he was definitely a real person. None of the early investigators were ever able to track down this elusive reporter. Unfortunately, Sbraccia has not responded to further emails. (2)

Several researchers have tried unsuccessfully to determine exactly who this reporter was. When contacting the Gazette, there were told the reporter was a part time, student employee. The receptionist provided no further assistance and nervously suggested that the sighting was a 'mistake.' She cited fireworks show in Falmouth as being the source of the flash. Her explanation lacks credibility since Falmouth is about ten miles due North of the Vineyard as opposed to 7 miles to the South and

West. To be completely accurate the crash site was much more westerly than southerly.

Another witness, Victor Pribanic, distinctly and clearly heard the explosion and knows that it was much closer than the seventeen miles out to sea where the official investigators have said the plane went down. In fact, the position and location of the explosion heard by Pribanic was more in line with the ten miles from shore that Kennedy himself noted as his location when he radioed the airport at 9:39 p.m., as reported by UPI, WCVB-TV Boston, and ABC News.

To quote directly from the article in the Martha's Vineyard Times: Mr. Pribanic said, "he was concerned when he learned that the search area was 17 miles west of the Vineyard." He continued, "I was convinced from the sound I heard that the area was much closer and within a short distance of Nomans Land," a small island off the southwest coast of the Vineyard used for artillery practice until a few years ago. (3)

Eyewitness & Pittsburgh Lawyer, Victor Pribanic.

The following article appeared in the Martha's Vineyard Times immediately after the crash.

Fisherman at Squibnocket Friday Heard 'Loud Crash' toward Nomans Land. By Nelson Sigelman.

"A fisherman standing on Squibnocket Point in Chilmark Friday night heard a 'loud explosion-like sound' from the direction of Nomans Land, where the search for the plane containing John Kennedy Jr., his wife, Carolyn Bessette Kennedy, and sister-in-law, Lauren Bessette, is now concentrated.

Victor Pribanic, 45, of Pittsburgh, spoke with local and state police Saturday morning after learning of the disappearance of the plane piloted by Mr. Kennedy. That information was passed on immediately to Federal Aviation Administration officials and the United States Coast Guard. State Police Sgt. Jeff Stone said the beach to the west of where Mr. Pribanic was fishing "was the area where some of the items washed up." Sergeant Stone said police were aware of several reports from people who reported low-flying planes or unusual noises that night. On Sunday, West Tisbury Police Chief, Beth Toomey, took Mr. Pribanic to meet with police up-island so he could describe where he was fishing and what he heard. But other than meeting with local and state police officials, he'd not been contacted by any other investigators."

Attempts to learn whether officials with the National Transportation Safety Board (NTSB), which was now handling the investigation, or whether the Coast Guard had adjusted the search recovery effort based on any of the reports, or why they did not speak with Mr. Pribanic, were unsuccessful. Mr. Pribanic

Wooden wall that conceals JFK Jr. plane wreckage.

runs a very successful law practice in Pittsburgh. Author Ise has made several attempts to contact Mr. Pribanic for comment in the last two years. Three detailed messages were left on his voicemail, and a detailed message was left with his answering service. As of this publication, Mr. Pribanic has not responded.

A guest at the Kennedy wedding and another eyewitness were nearby at the same time. Both saw and heard the same explosion. This guest was mentioned repeatedly by Shepherd Smith of FOX News on live broadcasts Saturday morning, July 17, who identified the witness as a friend of the show's producer. (4)

Oddly, a photograph of the aircraft's remains on the deck of the recovery vessel clearly show a blue tarp covering a large portion of the empennage (tail) which seems to be more intact than the rest of the plane. Why was this particular section hidden from the cameras? Although this image is no longer available, further verification was provided by 'The National Enquirer' displaying a cover photo which shows the wreckage without the tail section visible.

National Enquirer cover July 2014 depicting plane with no tail section.

Aircraft Sabotage; the Ultimate Assassination Tool:

Testimony of Mr. Sherman Skolnick
Background:

Since 1958, he has been a court reformer. Since 1963 he has been the founder/chairman, of Citizen's Committee to Clean Up the Courts, a public interest group researching and disclosing certain instances of judicial bribery and political murders. In 1973, Mr. Skolnick wrote a book, 'The Secret History of Airplane Sabotage,' a heavily documented book dealing, among other things, with the sabotaged plane crash on December 8, 1972, in Chicago, one month after Nixon was re-elected President. Twelve Watergate figures died when the United Air Lines plane pancaked just short of Midway airport. Dead in the crash were Mrs. E. Howard Hunt, wife of Watergate burglar and others linked to the Watergate Affair. She had in her possession over $2 million in valuables obtained by blackmailing Nixon for his role in the 1963 political assassination of President John F. Kennedy. Skolnick's group 'liberated' the entire unpublished file of the National Transportation Safety Board, 1,300 pages of documented reports and pictures indicating sabotage.

Skolnick brought a suit against the NTSB contending sabotage and cover-up. The NTSB re-opened their public hearings on the crash but continued to contend it was caused by 'pilot error.'

Skolnick was the star witness at the re-opened hearings and demanded that the NTSB panel disqualify themselves since most were financially tied to the airline industry and the Rockefellers, owners of all three News Networks, and a major owner of United Air Lines., who wanted the matter censored. The NTSB panel

United Airlines Flight 553 crash site near Midway Airport.

refused to disqualify themselves and entered a whitewashed report, condemning Skolnick and his associates. Thereafter, Rockefeller's lawyers harassed the publisher such that Skolnick's book was stopped in the printing cycle and no copies are currently available.

Over the years, federal crash investigators have covered up several sabotaged plane crashes, among them TWA Flight 800 and American Airlines Flight 587. AA Flight 587 departed from JFK Airport on November 12, 2001 and crashed shortly after take-off, the second deadliest crash in U.S. history.

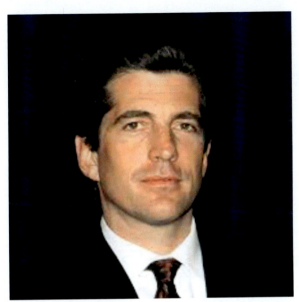
John F. Kennedy Jr.

The FBI covered up the bombing of JFK Jr.'s plane. Sections of the secret FBI Report (on pages 215-217) are listed in this book, which were not to have been disclosed until July 22, 2039. The file is located on the FBI website (Golden Boy on our website, Part 4). Once the FBI knew we had their secret report, within 48 hours they mysteriously announced without explanation that henceforth no Public visitors would be allowed into the Bureau's headquarters in Washington D.C., claiming that unspecified 'terrorists' were threatening them. Skolnick and TV show assistant Joseph Andreuccetti were placed on an 'enemy's list' by Hillary Clinton, and falsely labeled as 'domestic terrorists.' A nefarious federal judge in Chicago dismissed the case without legal formality.

Around August 1, 1999, JFK Jr. had planned to announce he was running for President, either as a traditional Democrat or as an independent on a third-party ticket, a nod to his distrust of both major political parties. He made one grave mistake. He trusted Al Gore, Jr.'s campaign officials regarding his plans. This

227

VP Al Gore with TX Gov. George W. Bush.

interfered with Gore's plans along with those of George W. Bush, the Governor of Texas. The Gore campaign reportedly promised total secrecy, a pledge they never kept.

JFK Jr. originally planned to run against Hillary Clinton for the U.S. Senate seat from New York but decided instead to focus on the Presidency. The secret was somehow leaked. George W. Bush would have preferred that JFK, Jr. didn't exist, and may have had an interest in the demise of JFK Jr. About three days before John's plane exploded in mid-air, Michael Harari and another Mossad agent (allegedly Mossad General Rafael Eitan) were seen with former President George H.W. Bush and his son, George W. Bush at the same Essex County, New Jersey airport

American Airlines Flight 587, Queens, New York.

where JFK Jr. kept his plane. This was confirmed by separate U.S. intelligence sources who were willing to testify before a grand jury. All four individuals were positively identified by an aircraft mechanic and a maintenance worker.

Was this a coincidence? JFK Jr. was a captivating speaker and unlike other members of his family was untouched by scandal. He would have most likely swept the field of Presidential candidates. Conservatives and Liberals, both would join together to support him.

John F. Kennedy Jr. was murdered before his planned announcement to run for the Presidency. Had he lived and been elected, he would have turned 40 shortly after the 2000 election, which would have made him the youngest President to ever be elected. The youngest elected before him? His Father, John F. Kennedy, aged 43. It is tragic that these two young American icons, with so much to offer, so much promise and so much to give had their lives cut short with surreptitious cunning and cruelty by their enemies within the Government that both men sought to serve.

Thirteen

<u>Beginnings of a Cover-up</u>

This graphic of a 'Graveyard Spiral' was derived from a Wikipedia resource. It bears no similarity to the N Tap Radar summary listed below first graphic.

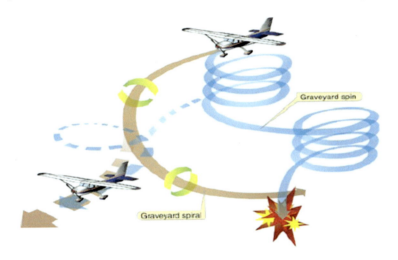

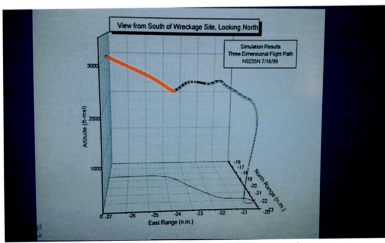

N Tap Radar summary of JFK Jr. plane crash.

The 'Graveyard Spiral' that supposedly doomed JFK, Jr.'s flight is listed repeatedly by the Media and Government Agencies as the official cause of the crash. The term 'Graveyard Spiral' is a contradictory or paradoxical phrase used carelessly in aviation circles. Author Ise's impressive experience as a seasoned flight instructor questions the use of this term. Ise notes, "If the Graveyard Spiral were such a potentially treacherous condition of flight, why in all of my training and flight time has no one ever said to me, "Beware of the Graveyard Spiral." The FAA itself makes no mention of the Graveyard Spiral in its brochure, which explicitly describes the maneuvers and performance standards required of the pilot candidate by the FAA Certified Flight Examiner.

The term Graveyard Spiral implies that the pilot becomes slowly and progressively disoriented. The assumption is that the pilot has inadvertently lost his horizon by accidentally flying into instrument flight conditions created by fog, haze, or the like. The pilot then enters a diving turn with a severe angle of bank. He aggravates this flight configuration trying to gain altitude by raising the nose of the aircraft. With the bank angle continuing to increase the airplane enters what is called an accelerated stall. Essentially, the lower wing in the turn fails to produce lift while the high wing continues to fly. It is speculated that once the stall occurs the airplane spins uncontrollably into the ground or the sea.

Curiously, within days of John's death, the media unanimously reported that he had entered a deadly 'graveyard spiral' causing the crash of the airplane and the deaths of the occupants. This information was released to the press long before the NTSB report was completed. It is highly unlikely that Kennedy lost his life per the flight scenario described. (pg. 231)

Let us examine the ambiguity, generality, and inaccuracy of the terminology. A spiral is a perfectly coordinated flight maneuver designed to bleed off altitude in the event of a forced landing. The pilot is mandated by law to always be aware of potential landing sites in case of emergency. The steep spiral allows the pilot to maintain a position over a given point while descending to an altitude that allows him to execute a normal traffic pattern over the emergency landing sight.

The flight path of the spiral is similar to descending a spiral staircase. When trimmed properly, the airplane assumes a slightly nose-down attitude and maintains 60 degrees of bank. The bank angle is varied slightly during the 360 degrees of turn to compensate for wind direction and speed. The lowered wing is in no danger of stalling during the spiral. Airspeed and lift coefficients remain constant. The airplane is easily flown hands off by a skilled pilot.

Recovery from unusual attitudes is a primary training focus of all flight schools. FAA regulations mandate that a pilot is trained in recovery from unusual attitudes. From his first five hours of training, the student pilot is repeatedly drilled in 'Critical Attitude Recovery.' The trainee is fitted with a blinding hood which limits the range of his vision to the aircraft's instrument panel. The trainee is asked to lower his head so that he can only see his lap. The instructor then initiates the unusual attitude which is typically a nose high, or nose low situation augmented by a considerable bank angle. Once the critical attitude is established the student or trainee is instructed to recover from that attitude using nothing except instrument references.

As the trainee develops proficiency with his recoveries, the instructor complicates the situation by placing a shade such as a piece of paper over some of the instruments. The trainee is then taught recovery techniques based upon certain instrument failure. The blinding of certain primary instruments is commonly referred to as recovery using 'partial panel.' Practice in critical attitude recovery using both full and partial panel is commonplace in any pilot's aviation career.

All pilots are required to fly a biennial flight review with an instructor who examines his level of proficiency in recovering from critical attitudes. Critical attitude recovery, both full and partial panel, are normally included in the pilot's competency check. The flight examiner is mandated by law to assess the pilot's skill at critical attitude recovery. The examiner may not eliminate any required component of the flight test. It needs to be noted again: the pilot candidate must perform all of the maneuvers mandated by the FAA. If a candidate fails any of the required maneuvers, he flunks the test. He must then be re-trained in the deficient areas. He must have his logbook endorsed by a CFI, then be re-recommended for a second flight test. At his discretion the examiner may choose to only review the deficient areas.

There is no room whatsoever for error in the examination environment. The pilot executes everything correctly or busts in-flight school terminology. Instructors take failures seriously since a formal rejection goes on record with the FAA. An instructor with an inordinate number of student failures will most undoubtedly be reviewed by the controlling agency and if found incompetent will lose his instructor privileges until he proves he deserves to have them reinstated.

Taking these factors into consideration, how could it be that the 'Graveyard Spiral' is never even mentioned in formal aviation terminology? Nor is it ever mentioned in the thousands of pages of procedural and legal protocol outlined in the FAR's or in the Airman's Information Manual. To an experienced flight instructor, it seems nearly inconceivable that JFK Jr. would inadvertently get himself into a critical attitude situation. John's final rate of descent exceeded 4,500 feet per minute. This speed produces a force equivalent to smashing a beer can into solid concrete at 60 mph. It is inconceivable that JFK Jr. was in a spiral of any sort. The airplane entered the water at an angle of five degrees relative to vertical. The N tap flight analysis proves that after several shallow banking turns and a minor altitude correction JFK Jr.'s airplane entered the water at a high rate of speed completely atypical to the conditions present during the coordinated flight of a steep spiral.

So, why the misnomer of the 'Graveyard spiral?' Why would the NTSB, the AOPA (Aircraft Owners & Pilot Association) and numerous other aviation sources support a theory that has no basis in real physics? Why did so many news agencies misrepresent the circumstances surrounding John's final 2 minutes alive? The Coast Guard was rightfully the first official spokesman for the search. Someone obviously and purposely leaked a juicy story about ATC contact with John's airplane to Channel 5 Boston. Reporters covered the incident extensively and should be interviewed if they are still alive.

The Pentagon

Everything suddenly went 'hush' and the Pentagon took command of the Search and Rescue operation, a brazen, totally unprecedented statement of unequivocal authority. If this display of power took place in the early hours of July 17, 1999, doesn't it stand to reason President Clinton would have been notified beforehand? He was not advised of the accident until 5:00 a.m. the next morning. Rats in the woodpile?

The Air Force

The Air Force took over the search, and an Air Force official became the official spokesperson for the Pentagon. They denied that John ever contacted the ATC tower, a deliberate, obvious lie. They conducted a search and rescue effort 100 miles in the wrong direction on a fake ELT transmission east of Montauk. They abruptly and illegally cut off all communication with reporters from Channel 5 in Boston. And where was Bill Clinton, the titular head of all these government agencies?

The Logbook

Damon Selicson recovered Lauren Bessette's suitcase on Philbin Beach, Martha's Vineyard, Massachusetts. He told CNN Boston affiliate WBZ that, "the case contained a hair dryer and other personal items, as well as a business card with her name on it." He continued, "I dragged (the suitcase) out of the water. Everyone was very, very upset. We pulled it up, we put it where we were sitting, and we called the police." Another witness, Gordon Campbell, said he saw police take away three pieces of luggage; an aqua green duffle bag, an attaché case, and a small black bag, all of which appeared to be intact. (1)

The aqua green duffle bag absconded from the beach by officials probably contained John's logbook. If the logbook was available, there would be fewer questions and assumptions about his flight training and qualifications. Of particular interest:

236

According to official records, John Kennedy Jr. received an inordinate amount of dual instruction compared to his solo time as pilot in command. Although it is possible, it is highly unlikely that these numbers reflect his actual Pilot in Command Time. Few flight schools would support such a disproportionate amount of solo time. It would be considered unsatisfactory to allow such an imbalance.

Dispelling the Myths:
Missing Instructor or Manchurian CFI.

In support of the theory: Recovery teams are extremely thorough and efficient. A seat is a very large piece of equipment anchored to the center section of the aircraft, the backbone of the airplane. In lower velocity crashes this section is recovered as a unit.

There was speculation that a 'Manchurian Candidate' flight instructor was programmed for the task of crashing the airplane. The still unrecovered right front passenger seat anchored to the center section of the airplane raises suspicions that a flight instructor was on board the aircraft. Certain research sources suggest that the instructor's body was secreted from the wreckage prior to recovery. Although this theory is possible, it is highly improbable.

(1) John Kennedy was an advanced pilot who had received endorsements (certification) in both Complex (Retractable Landing Gear and Constant Speed Propeller) and High-Performance Aircraft. Under VFR (Visual Flight Rules) he did not need an Instructor on board to make this flight.

(2)   Hankey stated, "John never flew his new airplane without a flight instructor on board." Not so, according to the official NTSB Report. His estimated flight time in the new aircraft was about 36 hours, of which 9.4 hours were flown at night. Approximately 3 hours of that flight time was without a CFI on board, and another 0.8 hours of that time was flown at night, including a night landing. In the 15 months before the accident, John had flown about 35 flight legs either to or from the Essex County, Teterboro, New Jersey area and the Martha's Vineyard, Hyannis, Massachusetts area. He flew more than 17 of these legs without a CFI on board, including at least 5 at night. The pilot's last known flight without a CFI on board was May 28, 1999. (2)

John had been actively working to earn his instrument rating. He flew a typical VFR (Visual Flight Rules) flight to the island. Considering that he was working on his instrument rating, if a CFI had been on board, they would have filed and flown an IFR (Instrument Flight Rules) flight plan. A training hood, or blinder would have been used so that John could not make visual references outside the aircraft. Any time logged during the flight would be credited to his instrument rating requirements. Instructors and students normally take advantage of every opportunity to further the pilot's level of experience. Even for the wealthy, flight training means total commitment of time and energy, along with considerable expense. There are few 'joy rides' in the world of aviation training.

Fuel Selector Valve

In his documentary, Hankey focused on the plane's fuel selector valve. Allegedly the valve was recovered in the OFF position. This would have cut fuel supply to the engine. This is not as mysterious as it might seem. According to the NTSB report, the engine was running when the plane hit the water. The valve could easily have been altered once the plane was recovered, thereby lending credence to the suggestion of pilot error.

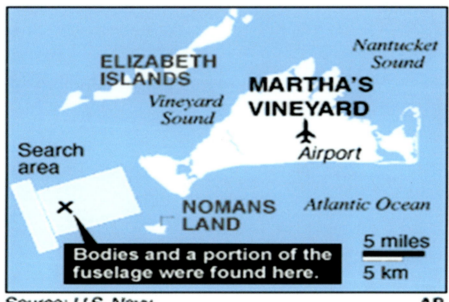

Source: U.S. Navy   AP

The New York Times Metro Edition published on Sunday, July 18, 1999 stated that at about 5:00 a.m., Air Force investigators were provided with a radar track of a plane that had followed Kennedy's assumed route and time of flight. Officials said the plane was tracked until it flew too low to be picked up by radar. "It looked like a normal flight to me," said Colonel Roark, who studied the track of the plane. He continued, "It looked like it was on its descent. I didn't see anything unusual." Colonel Roark, official spokesman for the Air Force had these N Tap results in his hands at 5:00 a.m. The results clearly illustrate the crash site and clearly indicate a catastrophic rate and angle of descent in the final 45 seconds of flight. Yet according to Roark, the flight path was normal.

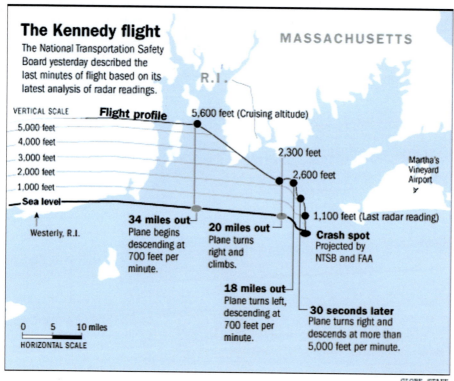

The Kennedy flight

The National Transportation Safety Board yesterday described the last minutes of flight based on its latest analysis of radar readings.

MASSACHUSETTS

R.I.

VERTICAL SCALE   **Flight profile**   5,600 feet (Cruising altitude)

5,000 feet
4,000 feet
3,000 feet   2,300 feet
2,000 feet   2,600 feet
1,000 feet
Sea level

Martha's Vineyard Airport

Westerly, R.I.

34 miles out
Plane begins descending at 700 feet per minute.

20 miles out
Plane turns right and climbs.

1,100 feet (Last radar reading)

Crash spot
Projected by NTSB and FAA

18 miles out
Plane turns left, descending at 700 feet per minute.

30 seconds later
Plane turns right and descends at more than 5,000 feet per minute.

0   5   10 miles
HORIZONTAL SCALE

GLOBE STAFF

The Air Force search efforts continued to be focused off Horton Point, Long Island. Aware of the N Tap results, the news media grilled Colonel Roark, wondering why the search wasn't focused on the aircraft's last known location. Was there a reason the search was focused elsewhere? Roark sheepishly stated that the search effort would continue over the entire area and that the

N Tap results merely suggested a 'possible final location.' He also made lame comments suggesting that no one was certain the flight path of the airplane in question was indeed the Kennedy airplane. One frustrated female reporter persisted in broaching the issue with Roark. Her call was cut off in the middle of her question. No response from Roark, no follow up with the press.

Fourteen

Autopsies and Further Deception

Richard J. Evans, Chief Medical Examiner, performed the autopsies on John, Carolyn and Lauren. He said, "All three victims were probably alive when the plane hit but died instantly." After an examination that lasted less than four hours, Evans reported that all three died from 'multiple traumatic injuries.' His office came under fire in the years afterwards, plagued by a case backlog and accusations of shoddy work. The autopsy of anyone who is a victim in a plane crash is usually less complex than that of a murder victim, the deaths were accidental and the autopsies were not conducted as a possible murder case. Each body was examined for approximately 45 minutes. A routine autopsy takes 2-4 hours and lab tests results on samples of body fluids and tissues often take a few weeks to be returned. The cause of death is generally known, and the bodies do not always lead investigators closer to the cause of the wreck.

The autopsies in the Kennedy case were curiously abbreviated, according to pathologists. The Medical Examiner's office and the Cape and Islands District Attorney's Office reported that the remains were taken to Bournewood Hospital around 7:15 p.m. on Wednesday night and released to the victim's families at 11:00 p.m. according to the Medical Examiner's office and the Cape and Islands District Attorney's Office. "Many jurisdictions refuse to perform autopsies at night," said Robert Kirschner, a former deputy chief medical examiner for Cook County, IL. The haste in this case, he said, could lead to questions about the investigation's thoroughness.

The Commonwealth of Massachusetts
STANDARD CERTIFICATE OF DEATH
REGISTRY OF VITAL RECORDS AND STATISTICS

REGISTERED NUMBER 321

STATE USE ONLY

DECEDENT - NAME FIRST: John MIDDLE: Fitzgerald LAST: Kennedy, Jr. SEX: Male DATE OF DEATH: July 16, 1999

PLACE OF DEATH (City/Town): Falmouth COUNTY OF DEATH: Barnstable HOSPITAL OR OTHER INSTITUTION: United States Coast Guard Station

PLACE OF DEATH: ☐ Inpatient ☐ ER/Outpatient ☐ DOA OTHER: Coast Guard Station ☐ Nursing Home ☐ Residence ☒ Other

SOCIAL SECURITY NUMBER: 119-36-5900

US WAR VETERAN SPECIFY WAR: No

WAS DECEDENT OF HISPANIC ORIGIN: ☒ NO ☐ YES Specify RACE: White DECEDENT'S EDUCATION: 6

AGE - Last Birthday: 38 DATE OF BIRTH: Nov. 25, 1960 BIRTHPLACE: Washington, D.C.

MARRIED: Married LAST SPOUSE: Carolyn Bessette USUAL OCCUPATION: Publisher KIND OF BUSINESS OR INDUSTRY: Magazine

RESIDENCE: 20 North Moore Street, New York, New York, New York ZIP CODE: 10013

FATHER - FULL NAME: John F. Kennedy, Sr. STATE OF BIRTH: MA MOTHER - NAME MAIDEN: Jacqueline Bouvier STATE OF BIRTH: NY

INFORMANT'S NAME: Caroline Schlossberg MAILING ADDRESS: 888 Park Ave., New York, NY 10021 RELATIONSHIP: Sister

METHOD OF DISPOSITION: ☐ BURIAL ☒ CREMATION ☐ ENTOMBMENT ☐ REMOVAL FROM STATE ☐ DONATION ☐ OTHER FUNERAL SERVICE LICENSEE OR THEIR DESIGNEE: Robert L. Studley LICENSE #: 5024

PLACE OF DISPOSITION: Duxbury Crematory LOCATION: Duxbury, Massachusetts

DATE OF DISPOSITION: July 21, 1999 NAME AND ADDRESS OF FACILITY OR OTHER DESIGNEE: Doane, Beal & Ames, Inc., 160 W. Main St., Hyannis, MA 02601

IMMEDIATE CAUSE: Multiple traumatic injuries. APPROXIMATE INTERVAL: Instant

WAS AUTOPSY PERFORMED: Yes WERE AUTOPSY FINDINGS AVAILABLE PRIOR TO COMPLETION OF CAUSE OF DEATH: Yes

WAS CASE REFERRED TO M.E.: Yes

MANNER OF DEATH: ☐ NATURAL ☐ HOMICIDE ☐ COULD NOT BE DETERMINED ☒ ACCIDENT ☐ SUICIDE ☐ PENDING INVESTIGATION

DATE OF INJURY: July 16, 1999 TIME OF INJURY: on or about 9:41 p.m. INJURY AT WORK: No

DESCRIBE HOW INJURY OCCURRED: Plane crash victim. PLACE OF INJURY: Ocean LOCATION: waters off of Martha's Vineyard, MA

DATE SIGNED: July 21, 1999 HOUR OF DEATH: on or about 9:41 p.

PRONOUNCED DEAD: July 21, 1999 5:30 p.

NAME AND ADDRESS OF CERTIFYING PHYSICIAN OR MEDICAL EXAMINER: Richard J. Evans, M.D., 870 County Road, Pocasset, MA 02559 LICENSE # OF CERTIFIER: 58622

WAS THERE A PRONOUNCEMENT POINT: No ☐ M.D. ☐ P.A.

DATE OF BURIAL PERMIT: July 21, 1999 SIGNATURE OF HEALTH AGENT: Robert Carrigan

RECEIVED IN THE CITY/TOWN OF: Falmouth CLERK'S SIGNATURE: Carol S. Martin DATE OF RECORD: July 27, 1999

I, the undersigned, as the Clerk of the Town of Falmouth, Barnstable County in the Commonwealth of Massachusetts, have custody of all the records on DEATHS recorded in my office; and as such I certify that the above is a TRUE COPY from said records.

Carol S. Martin

CAROL S. MARTIN
FALMOUTH TOWN CLERK

John F. Kennedy Jr. Death Certificate.

In a high-profile case, he said, the pressures are high, and so are the risks of carelessness. Kirschner pointed to other autopsies associated with the Kennedy family, case in point the investigation that followed President John F. Kennedy's assassination and the questions surrounding the death of Mary Jo Kopechne 30 years prior, in the Martha's Vineyard car crash on Chappaquiddick.

"You can't let those kinds of pressures alter your routines," Kirschner said. He continued, "If you alter your procedure and do things differently, then you're always going to run into problems. You can't possibly do three investigations in four hours." (1)

On Thursday, July 22nd, the Cape Cod Times reported that the Kennedy family had asked that no photographs be taken during John's autopsy because they could end up being published in tabloids or on the internet. Such photographs are routinely taken during autopsies. Authorities would not confirm the report, saying only that the wishes of the family were "appropriately expressed" where it was possible. Senator Ted Kennedy had requested a burial at sea, saying it was his nephew's wish to be cremated and have his ashes spread on the waves. The request was approved by Defense Secretary William Cohen. "The family of the Bessette sisters requested that the two women be buried in the same ceremony," the Pentagon said. John Jr., like his father, the late President John F. Kennedy, had a love of the sea. He spent many summers sailing and kayaking the waters where his plane crashed. Pentagon officials told CNN there were two grounds for granting permission for a naval burial at sea.

(1) There is a provision allowing for such burials for people providing 'notable service or outstanding contributions to the United States.'

(2) Protocol allows sea burials for the children of decorated Navy veterans. President Kennedy was a naval officer wounded and cited for heroism in World War II. (2)

The Floodgates of Disinformation Burst Open

Several days after the crash of John Kennedy Jr., author Ise was contacted by a reporter from the Providence Journal. A mutual friend had advised him of Ise's considerable experience flying in and out of the Vineyard. The reporter asked Ise for his opinion as to the cause of the crash, which was published as a featured article on July 25, 1999 in The Providence Sunday Journal. At that time, Ise believed the published reports, that John had flown into fog and became disoriented. Ise gave a casual, unresearched and rather cavalier statement about "Having to be on top of your game" as a pilot, because the fog and haze can roll in rapidly under the right conditions. Several other pilots were also quoted, including Dr. Robert 'Bob' Arnot, medical and aviation correspondent for NBC News.

Years passed and Ise never gave the incident thought. Then he began researching the deaths of the Kennedy brothers and re-read the Providence Journal article for the first time in ten years. He realized his opinion was flawed - he had never bothered to check the weather conditions the evening of the crash. He researched the hourly field observations from that evening and discovered that the weather conditions were far better than reported. (See chapter on Hourly Field Observations).

During his review of the article, he came across the Dr. Arnot quote. Arnot's opinion was viewed by millions of Americans on "Dateline" via NBC News. Ise read the quote with a professional scrutiny had failed to exercise when initially asked for his opinion many years before. Immediately, he identified several issues that appear to have been contrived, exaggerated and grossly inaccurate.

Dr. Robert 'Bob' Arnot, aviation consultant, NBC News.

Arnot was a former military pilot, and official aviation consultant for NBC News. The public comments he made on NBC were picked up by The Associated Press. Preposterously, he claimed he had been flying (via VFR) to Nantucket at the same time that JFK Jr. was on his way to the Vineyard. He gave the press a laughable, obviously canned statement that sounded thoroughly rehearsed and quoted as follows.

"Dr. Bob Arnot, a pilot, and a medical correspondent for NBC, was among those who taxied into the flight line

to soar out of Fairfield on that Friday Night. Arnot was bound for Nantucket Island, due east of Martha's Vineyard. Arnot flew past Martha's Vineyard at about the same time Kennedy was descending toward the island. Arnot peered to his left when he was three miles south of the Vineyard. He knew that the island was out there, but he could not see it. The sky over the island that night was, "dark, black, inky air," Arnot said on Dateline NBC. "I said to myself at the time, Boy, if there's someone out here who does not have an instrument license, who is not really proficient, I bet they run into trouble." (3)

First, Nantucket is not due east of Martha's Vineyard, it is exactly 26 nautical miles due Southeast. This may seem like a minor discrepancy, but it is not when one considers how fog banks and haze normally develop from the south and slowly overtake landmass in a northerly flow.

Secondly, it is unclear whether Arnot was flying VFR (Visual Flight Rules) or IFR (Instrument Flight Rules). If the Vineyard had been truly obscured and Arnot's flight path took him three miles south of the Vineyard as he passed, one would have to assume he was experiencing instrument conditions. A pilot may not fly in instrument conditions without having filed an IFR Flight Plan. Qualified instrument pilots are sequentially handed off from controller to controller and constantly monitored by radar until reaching their destination airport and completing a successful landing. It is required that IFR flights are conducted along 'Victor Airways' which are essentially the low altitude (below 10,000 feet) highways of the sky. They are clearly marked on all sectional charts as straight blue lines labeled with the I.D. Codes such as V-374, which stands for Victor 374, much like automobile drivers might follow I-95 or I-80.

Arnot stated the sky was, 'dark, black, inky air' and that he could not see the island. His statement strongly suggests he was flying in instrument conditions. He also stated he was three miles south of the Vineyard at that time. This location is closer to the source region of fog and haze, and further substantiates the argument that if he couldn't see the Vineyard three miles due north of him, he would most assuredly be flying in IFR conditions.

From a professional pilot's perspective Arnot's whole story sounds contrived. Pilots with his credentials would invariably fly the coastline up from Fairfield at night, intercept Victor 374 at Point Judith, fly directly to Martha's Vineyard and then proceed to Nantucket via Victor 146. In any aircraft, flights over open ocean are risky business, especially in the event of a forced landing. Flights at night exacerbate any problems even the most experienced pilot might encounter. This is precisely why JFK Jr. navigated the Connecticut and Rhode Island coastlines before turning southeast to intersect the Vineyard. The NTSB accident report stated, "After passing Pt. Judith, Rhode Island, the target continued over the Rhode Island Sound." (4) John Kennedy was tracing the coastline and using the Elizabethan Islands as steppingstones to the Vineyard.

Every airplane has a 'built in' Glide Ratio. In the event of engine failure, airplanes glide to the ground, they do not career out of the sky. Usually, the heavier the airplane, the steeper the glide ratio. John Kennedy was an accomplished hang glider and ultralight aircraft pilot. Glide Ratio was always his primary concern when flying aircraft. If the Piper Saratoga had a glide ration of 6:1, the aircraft would be able to fly six miles horizontally for each mile of altitude. A well-trained pilot never takes his aircraft beyond 'power off' gliding distance from shore. Staying within gliding distance of land ensures a greater level of safety in the event of a forced landing. Putting an airplane onto a highway or beach at night is still a long shot, but it's far safer than ditching the aircraft in water and having to swim to safety.

Bob Arnot's reported position three miles south of the Vineyard on a 'black and inky night' claiming he can't see the Vineyard makes no sense whatsoever. The automated field observations taken during the time in question at Martha's Vineyard read: "Clear at or below 12,000 feet, visibility 8 miles, winds 250 degrees at 7 kts." (5) Nantucket reported: "Clear at or below 12,000 feet, visibility 4 miles, mist." (6)

Any pilot who values his life and the life of his passengers would fly the coastline all the way to the Vineyard. Bob Arnot's reported location in the article is three miles south of the Vineyard, not even close to hugging the coastline. He never specified his altitude, or which plane he was flying at the time. It is impossible to determine if he was within safe gliding distance of the island.

All of this suggests that with all of his military and civilian flight experience, Arnot finished his work week, readied his airplane, and flew off to relax on Nantucket. He then deviates from a safe, expeditious and logical flight path at 9:00 p.m. and just happens to take a joy ride three miles out over open water, south of Martha's Vineyard into marginally instrument conditions, while flying under VFR rules. He looks out his window to find the Vineyard is no longer visible and conjures up this fabricated statement: "I said to myself at the time, Boy, if there's someone out here who does not have an instrument license, who is not really proficient, I bet they run into trouble. (7) Arnot's story borderlines on absurdity.

The following article, titled 'Parting Shots' was written by Joe Hagan and appeared in the New York Observer on February 16, 2004:

"Bob Arnot, the medical doctor turned foreign correspondent for MSNBC and NBC News, the onetime chief medical correspondent, 'Dr. Bob' on NBC News, who has been filing prickly, Geraldo-like dispatches from Iraq has been conspicuously absent from TV lately. Dr. Arnot's contract was up at NBC in December 2003 and according to the network, won't be renewed in the foreseeable future. Dr. Arnot did not leave willingly. Although personal, his departure has also exposed the divides over TV coverage of the war in Iraq.

In a 1,300-word email to NBC News President Neal Shapiro, written in December 2003 and obtained by NYTV, Dr. Arnot called NBC News' coverage of Iraq biased. He argued that keeping him in Iraq and on NBC could go far in rectifying that. Dr. Arnot told Mr. Shapiro that NBC had alienated the Coalition Provisional Authority in Baghdad since it shot and then aired footage of correspondent Jim Miklaszewski at the scene of the November bombing of the Al Rashid Hotel, in which a CPA staffer was shown injured. That incident, he wrote, 'earned the undying enmity of the CPA.'

We've been at a significant disadvantage given NBC's reputation in Iraq, Dr. Arnot wrote Mr. Shapiro. He argued that due to his excellent relationships with military and CPA personnel, NBC News could repair its standing with government authorities by airing more of his material. "I'm uniquely positioned to report the story," he wrote. **"NBC Nightly News routinely takes the stories that I shoot and uses the footage, even to lead the broadcast, but refuses to allow the story to be told by the reporter on the scene."**

In other words, he suggested NBC News did not like putting him on the air. Dr. Arnot included excerpts from an email from Jim Keelor, President of Liberty Broadcasting, which owns eight NBC stations throughout the South. Mr. Keelor had written NBC, stating that, "the networks are pretty much ignoring" the good-news stories in Iraq. "The definition of news would incorporate some of these stories," he wrote. Hence, the FOX News surge.

Reached for comment, Mr. Keelor said that he was, "not lambasting anyone" and that NBC News, "indicated they were sensitive to the issues." He added, "Of course it's political. Journalism and news are what unusual (events) happened that day. And if the schools are operating, they can say that's usual. My response to that is, 'The Hell it is.' My concern there is that almost everything that has occurred in Iraq since the war started is unexpected."

That pretty much summed up Dr. Arnot's attitude as well. In his letter to Mr. Shapiro, he wondered why the network wasn't reporting stories of progress in Iraq, a frequently heard complaint of the Bush Administration. "As you know, I have regularly pitched most of these stories contained in the note to Nightly, Today and directly to you," he wrote. "Every single story has been rejected."

Contacted at his home in Vermont, Dr. Arnot said Mr. Shapiro was no longer interested in his kind of coverage. He said, "On the MSNBC side, they've been very generous, and they want me back." He continued, "But from the NBC vantage point, Neal neglected to put any money into the pot, and that's the reason I'm not back in Baghdad." Did Mr. Shapiro respond to his email? Arnot said, "That particular email, I didn't get any response," he continued, "There was an earlier email and the response said, 'We're just too strapped. We don't have the money to be able to afford the editorial oversight."

Dr. Arnot said he knew "for a fact" that Mr. Shapiro's problem with his reporting was that "it was just very positive." Mr. Shapiro responded by email saying that NBC News had re-evaluated its coverage for 2004, determined that, "we were in the post-war period in Iraq" and shifted its resources to political coverage. Mr. Shapiro wrote, "Given that we were well covered in Iraq with regular correspondents, we explored other options with Bob, which to this point have not resulted in a new agreement. Any implication that NBC News has been reluctant to cover the rebuilding story in Iraq is absolutely ridiculous," citing pieces on 'the reopening of schools' and on how the 101st Airborne 'reorganized the north and has very good relations there.' Mr. Shapiro added that the Center for Media and Public Affairs found NBC News to be the most balanced among the networks. Shapiro added, "I am proud of our coverage and feel absolutely comfortable with the way Bob Arnot's reporting was utilized by the network."

Several high-ranking military officials contacted by NYTV complimented Dr. Arnot's superior reporting skills, especially in light of what they perceived as the chronically negative war reporting on TV in the United States. Larry DiRita, the Pentagon spokesman for Donald Rumsfeld, said that Dr. Arnot captured Iraq as he experienced it when he visited there himself. "It was complex and nuanced and uneven then, and you had to get around to see it that way—and he does." Mr. DiRita continued, "I think his coverage provided an aspect of daily Iraqi life that is being missed by a heck of a lot of coverage." Maj. Clark Taylor emailed NYTV from Baghdad to state that Dr. Arnot, "highlighted what is really happening over here. He generally reported positive things because generally, that is what is happening. Of course, there are occasional bad things...and he reported those as well. The fact was, he reported what he saw, which was positive."

Major General David Petraeus

Major General David Petraeus wrote in an email, "As you probably know, he is quite a renaissance man (doctor, athlete, TV journalist) and the 'Screaming Eagles' (the nickname for the 101st's soldiers) really took to him. Our soldiers and leaders were particularly pleased that he demonstrated so much interest in the nation-building endeavors that were carried out by our troopers and our many superb Iraqi partners." Another military official, Brg. Gen. Mark Hertling, said he and his colleagues had recently done an assessment of the 37 reporters they'd worked with, determining which ones they liked and which ones they didn't. "Thirty-seven different reporters we talked about, and we decided who we would really like to go to war with in the future, or who we would like to drink a beer with later on," General Hertling told NYTV. He continued, "I won't tell you that number," he added laughing, but he did say Dr. Arnot was at the top of the list.

In his email to Mr. Shapiro, Dr. Arnot argued that his relationships with the authorities earned him access to stories that other reporters couldn't get. "I was the only reporter to be shown the actual list of terrorists found in Saddam's briefcase," he wrote. "The military even let me witness the capture of one of the leaders of the insurgency, a major general in the Baathist military wing." Mr. Shapiro had several complimentary things to say about Dr. Arnot, but in the halls of NBC News, several insiders at the network said, Dr. Arnot was a cheerleader for the military and the CPA. Some questioned his accuracy as a reporter.

In 1998, Mr. Arnot's best-selling book, 'The Breast Cancer Prevention Diet,' came under intense scrutiny from medical watchdogs for its broad claims, so much so that both the American Cancer Society and Memorial-Sloan Kettering Cancer Center in New York City complained of inaccuracies and misstatements in Dr. Arnot's book. "In the end, there were no technical faults with the book," Arnot claimed.

In 2001, Dr. Arnot, then Chief Medical correspondent for NBC's Today Show and for Dateline NBC gave up his stethoscope and donned a flak jacket for some foreign adventures. Dr. Arnot's friendship with MSNBC President Erik Sorenson, a colleague from his days at CBS, helped transform him into a special foreign correspondent after the attacks of September 11, 2001. He made his way to dangerous locations like Sudan and Somalia, writing about his adventures for Men's Journal. In 2003, he went to Baghdad, assigned to cover the First Marine Expeditionary Force. "There was a lot of pressure to make sure that FOX News didn't win the war," said an NBC insider familiar with Dr. Arnot's work. But the insider also said, "NBC didn't have correspondents who wanted to fight that war." Dr. Arnot was willing and able. He said he had risked his life many times for MSNBC and NBC News, and he was very friendly with the military.

In his email, Dr. Arnot revealed what he had to offer NBC if they allowed him to stay. "At the end of the war I scrubbed in on an operation to save a young girl hit by a grenade. As a female surgeon closed her abdomen at the end of the operation, I asked if the child would survive." She said, "Yes she will, she is the future of Iraq." She also survived because a U.S. Army sergeant took the ticking grenade from her hand and turned away from her. The girl survived because of his heroism. At his request, the Army sent a Blackhawk helicopter to evacuate a four-and-a-half-year-old girl with 55% burns, under fire, and protected by two Apache gunships. These stories were never aired on NBC.

Arnot said, "What happens if NBC is wrong?" He wrote, "What happens if this is a historical mission that does succeed, that transforms the Middle East, that brings peace and security to America? What if NBC's role was like that of much of the media in general, allowing the terrorists to fight their war on the

American television screen, where their stories of death and destruction dominate rather than that of American heroes?"

Dr. Arnot became popular with military leaders in Iraq and with the CPA (Coalition Provisional Authority) in Baghdad. A high-ranking CPA official said Dr. Arnot, "was visible, he was active, he told a complete story," adding that NBC News had effectively stopped reporting on Iraq, leaving a single Pentagon reporter, Mr. Miklaszewski, in Baghdad. "NBC doesn't really cover the Iraq story," the official said. "They don't have serious resources on the ground. If they did, they would cover the release of the Zarqawi memo with a reporter on the ground," referring to a document that the U.S. military claimed was an Iraqi insurrection orchestrated by Abu Musab Zarqawi, a terrorist that the White House linked to Al Qaeda.

"It's been over six months since Brokaw has been here," the official added. "There are over 120,000 troops on the ground and there's no real NBC presence." Dr. Arnot told NYTV, "I've been attacked many times, once with guns, once with swords. Once he was at the al-Aike Hotel when it was blown up. There have been no journalists who have been intentionally attacked. The bomb was right under my window. We were attacked with swords down in Najaf. It was a ten second difference between being hacked down and just before Christmas, I was basically ambushed with assault weapons in Abu Ghraib in the middle of the night. That was a bad situation. It's a very dangerous thing. My Mother was saying, "I don't think it's the smart thing for you to be out there."

Dr. Arnot's email to Mr. Shapiro claimed that the September 25, 2003 bombing of the al-Aike Hotel in Baghdad, where NBC employees were stationed at the time was directly aimed at him.

"I've been targeted on several occasions," he wrote, recalling "a bomb placed directly under my window at the al-Aike hotel resulting in several shrapnel wounds."

Dr. Arnot's enthusiasm occasionally got the best of him, said NBC News staffers, noting that he claimed he knew how to speak Arabic. He was speaking with some Iraqi barbershop customers, asking them what they thought of a speech given by President Bush. "He's telling them what Bush is saying in Arabic and then translating their responses live on the air," said one co-worker who remarked that NBC translators "said he was talking gibberish." Arnot stated, "I was asking these guys yes or no questions, and this guy went on and on and on." He continued, "There are many kinds of Arabic. Am I good at understanding the Iraqi accent? No, I'm terrible."

NBC sources said that when the statue of Saddam Hussein was toppled in Baghdad, Nightly News anchor Tom Brokaw declined to put Dr. Arnot on the air, even though he was the sole NBC reporter on the scene. Instead, Mr. Brokaw interviewed a British reporter from a news agency called ITN. "They used ITN, their British affiliate rather than someone on the NBC payroll," said the NBC staffer. He continued, "They don't use his (Arnot) reporting because they don't trust his reporting."

In November, Dr. Arnot hosted a series for MSNBC's 'Hardball,' titled, "Iraq: The Real Story," an effort to find the so-called 'good news' stories that Ambassador L. Paul Bremer III and the CPA said the media was hesitant to report. The CPA was so distressed by network coverage that its senior media advisor, Dorrance Smith, created a separate government feed, an attempt to provide the kind of stories they wanted to disperse to local affiliates in the U.S.

Smith told NYTV that he had lobbied MSNBC to do the Hardball series. Dr. Arnot was not the first NBC employee to complain about coverage in Iraq. In fact, Noah Oppenheim, the producer of the Hardball series, a self-identified neoconservative and onetime producer for Scarborough Country, wrote an article for 'The Weekly Standard' upon his return from his three weeks in Iraq, asserting that reporters rarely got out of the so-called Green Zone in Baghdad, and that they cribbed wire reports. Mr. Oppenheim left MSNBC when Nightly News executive producer Steve Capus and anchor Tom Brokaw complained openly that the article was unseemly coming from an NBC-affiliated news producer.

Our observations of Dr. Arnot should not be taken lightly. We decided to publish them in their entirety so that the readers may come to their own conclusions about Dr. Arnot and whether his testimony is truly credible. Obvious viewpoints include but are not limited to:

Arnot seemed closely aligned with high-ranking military officials.

He was delusional about our invasion of Iraq.

His colleagues questioned his credibility.

The American Cancer Society raised objections to misstatements and inaccuracies in his book, 'The Breast Cancer Prevention Diet.'

The Myths are Perpetuated

On January 3, 2019, ABC aired a documentary entitled, 'The Last Days of JFK Jr.' This production was yet another extension of the misinformation we have been accustomed to hearing about John. The script was written in the style of tawdry supermarket tabloids. The program dishonored John, portraying him as an irresponsible daredevil who took chances with his own life and the lives of others. The segment lacked continuity, pieced into three-minute segments followed by five-minute commercial interruption. The presentation was abundant with personal opinion and irrelevant inflammatory and thoroughly false and misleading puffery about the lives of John and Carolyn.

The aviation-based material was a sterling example of status quo reporting. The same lies and misinformation regarding John's character and competency as a pilot were broadcast to millions of households across America. The program was completely devoid of any science that could have been used to explain the flight or its demise. The public was misled into believing that John's skills as a pilot were not sufficient to handle the Saratoga's newer technology. Alternate flight paths were drawn on the screen to insinuate that there were safer routes of flight to Martha's Vineyard via Hyannis that John could have taken. Remember, John was dropping Lauren Bessette off first on Martha's Vineyard and then continuing onto Hyannis for the wedding of Rory Kennedy.

The NTSB report is a bit vague but describes John as having flown the final leg of the flight over open ocean from Rhode Island sound to the Vineyard. Their account flies in the face of the care that John would have taken in choosing a responsible and safe flight route which traced beaches and landmass for its duration. Most experienced pilots would find it highly improbable that John would choose to fly straight from Narragansett Bay to the island. It is far more likely that John made the final turn toward the island from Horse Neck Beach in Massachusetts. This course would provide him with added safety by utilizing the Elizabethan Islands as steppingstones of sorts. Choosing this route would guarantee that the Saratoga would remain within gliding distance of land in the event of engine failure. We are only talking about four additional minutes of flight time between Rhode Island sound and Horse Neck Beach. We believe this to be the actual route flown by John on the night in question.

We should not have been surprised when Bob Arnot turned up as the aviation consultant of choice for the ABC docudrama. Yes, Bob is a thoroughly experienced military and civilian pilot with thousands of hours in many different types of aircraft. We try to refrain from being critical, but Bob continually regurgitates the same old rhetoric he used when consulted 20 years ago by The Associated Press, but his story changes a little. Recall that Bob said, "I said to myself at the time, Boy, if there's someone out here who does not have an instrument license, who is not really proficient, I bet they run into trouble." (9) Bob was supposedly South of the Vineyard looking in a northerly direction when he made this statement to himself.

In the documentary, Arnot now claims to have made this statement to his nephew who was riding with him in the passenger seat of the airplane. He also yammered on to describe and subscribe to the 'death spiral' theory supporting the NTSB findings. He then wrapped up with a very thin statement suggesting that may not have been able to handle the plane's autopilot. He never mentioned the Field observations listed in chapter 9. He never quoted the tower manager on Martha's

Vineyard. He never referred to the N Tap results which clearly indicate that John went from straight and level flight to a nearly vertical descent in a matter of seconds. Despite being positioned as a professional, investigative critic he never utilized the science available to analyze what happened on that evening in July of 1999. This seems very curious for a pilot of Bob's stature. Was he lackadaisical in his research? Perhaps. Was he in full acceptance of the 'official story' and simply providing boiler plate opinion? Was he willingly or unwittingly helping to cover up the murder of four innocent people? Only Bob Arnot knows for sure. Regretfully, the lie always pays better than the truth. What is abundantly clear is that John F. Kennedy Jr. did not meet his demise due to fog, disorientation or any sort of pilot error. This leads us to conclude the inevitable: this flight was taken down due to intentional malfeasance, perpetrated by some evil collective who were terrified enough to allow him to live.

Fifteen

Motive to Murder JFK Jr.

John has been proven to be an exemplary pilot. His airplane was meticulously maintained. The enroute weather conditions have been proven to be completely unsubstantiated. His route of flight was deliberately misrepresented several times by the authorities. The 'death spiral' theories which were perpetuated by the NTSB are completely negated by the N Tap radar report and by witness Victor Pribanic. The bogus search patterns executed by the U.S. Air Force are grossly suspicious. The secret FBI report expunged by Sherman Skolnick in the nick of time, states there were samples of explosives found onboard John's airplane. The tower manager at Martha's Vineyard is on record stating ten to fifteen miles visibility and his ability to observe airplanes at that distance. The 45-minute autopsies, and the immediate cremation of the bodies are very suspicious. These ten issues listed in this paragraph strongly suggests murder. Why are the authorities lying to us?

THE WATCH

During its tenure 'George' was the most widely read political magazine in the United States. In 2018, Christopher Fulton wrote his book, 'The Inheritance: Poisoned Fruit in the JFK Assassination.' Upon meeting JFK Jr., he said, "Mr. Kennedy, with all due respect, I knew I wanted to make this deal with you, that's why I'm here. But I'm not entirely sure about why you want to interview me?" JFK Jr. replied, "Because Christopher, you are a part of the chain of custody of material evidence in my

Father's assassination." 'The Inheritance' is the story of how Christopher Fulton came to own the watch JFK was wearing when he was assassinated and how owning the watch came to ruin Fulton's life because it was the last link to who actually killed the President. (1)

President Kennedy was gifted a Cartier watch shortly before his assassination. He was wearing the watch when he was murdered. The watch was then given to Bobby Kennedy along with other personal effects belonging to the President.

Bobby entrusted Evelyn Lincoln, the President's personal secretary, with the Cartier watch and a treasure trove of the President's personal items and files. She guarded them for many years until her death. Christopher Fulton claims to have acquired the watch through a second party during the distribution of Evelyn's estate.

The nefarious forces who were involved in the President's killing were aware of this exchange. Mr. Fulton claims his life was turned upside down by criminal events brought against him related to his possession of the watch.

The Cartier watch could very well be the last solid evidence that could destroy the credibility of the Warren Commission forever. The watch would have been contaminated with the President's DNA when he was assassinated and would also have held traces of mercury from the bullets that killed him. (Mercury is used in the manufacture of frangible, exploding bullets.)

Evelyn Lincoln with John Jr. & President Kennedy.

Had the watch been properly analyzed it might have created embarrassing and criminal inquiries into the President's murder. The fiction of Oswald being characterized as a lone nut assassin would be forever dispelled, and the official story of JFK's assassination and who was responsible would finally be recognized as a plethora of lies.

In his book, Mr. Fulton states the watch was sold to John Jr. through a private auction house and that John had possession of the watch when he was murdered. In support of Mr. Fulton's story, the following excerpt was taken from Fox Business News on the twentieth anniversary of John's death; "The gold Cartier watch was left to the Schlossberg's." In fact, John was in possession of the watch.

The Gemstone File

The Gemstone File is a conspiracy document attributed to Bruce Porter Roberts. In 1975, Stephanie Caruana published 'A Skeleton Key to the Gemstone File.' The 'Key' is purportedly a synopsis of Roberts' documents that presents a chronicle of interlocking conspiracies, including claims that world events since the 1950's were shaped by suppressed information, the names of JFK's supposed shooters, and the connections between a number of political assassinations which occurred within a relatively short time frame. Authors James McConnachie and Robin Tudge called Carauna's book "the original mega-conspiracy theory." (2)

Hollywood actor, political insider, and possible contract agent Bruce Roberts authored the Gemstone files along with his father over many years. The original manuscripts totaled more than 1,000 pages of 'Dark Side' American history. The final draft was then divided into many segments and distributed to various trusted individuals throughout the U.S. Originally distributed by hand and mail in photocopy form, the Gemstone File has appeared in slightly revised form in Hustler Magazine and on the internet. Roberts, known only to Stephanie Caurana and conspiracy theorist Mae Brussell, purportedly began gathering information in the file when Howard Hughes stole his invention for processing synthetic rubies, hence the title, 'Gemstone.' Gerald Carroll, author of "Project Seek: Onassis, Kennedy and the Gemstone thesis" states that Roberts was born in New York state on October 27, 1919 and died of lung cancer in San Francisco on July 16, 1976.

A look at JFK Jr.'s net worth and will, 20 years after his death

John F. Kennedy Jr. was ready to pursue politics, determined to save his marriage before plane crash, says pal

Historian Steven M. Gillon recalls his friendship with John F. Kennedy Jr. on the 20th anniversary of his fatal plane crash. The life of the late magazine publisher is being chronicled in a new A&E documentary titled 'Biography: JFK Jr — The Final Year,' as well as a book by Gillon titled 'America's Reluctant Prince.'

Tuesday marks 20 years since John F. Kennedy Jr., his wife, Carolyn and her sister, Lauren Bessette, died when the single-engine plane he piloted plunged into the Atlantic Ocean off Martha's Vineyard.

A young boy leaves flowers in front of the building where John F. Kennedy Jr. and his wife Carolyn Bessette lived at 20 North Moore Street in the Tribeca section of New York on July 19. People have left flowers, balloons, handwritten notes and drawin

Although a final number on his net worth varies, the 38-year-old was a multimillionaire when he died in 1999.

His fortune was estimated at $30 million-$100 million dollars, with the bulk of his personal estate going to the children of his older sister, Caroline.

His former assistant tells People magazine he would not want to be forgotten.

CLICK HERE TO GET THE FOX BUSINESS APP

Among other items they reportedly received were their uncle's clothing, furniture and
mementos from their grandfather, former President John F. Kennedy, including a
rocking chair, a PT-109 tie clip, gold Cartier watch and a silver money clip.

FILE PHOTO MAY 1997 - Caroline Kennedy Schlossberg and John F. Kennedy Jr.,
seen in this file photo at a May 1997 event at the John F. Kennedy Presidential Library
in Boston, released a letter through the Kennedy Library Foundation March 16 criticizi

Kennedy also apparently left cash to his sister and her children, cousins Timothy
Shriver, and Robert F. Kennedy Jr as well as his personal lawyer, assistant, his former
nanny and his mother's former assistant.

Two boats carrying Massachusetts State Police divers from the Underwater Recovery
Unit depart from Menemsha harbor on Martha's Vineyard Island, July 19, to search for
the wreckage of the single engine plane belonging to John F. Kennedy Jr. Kennedy's

The Bessette family, who has one surviving daughter today living in
Michigan, reportedly reached a $15 million dollar settlement with Kennedy's estate in
2001 in a wrongful-death suit.

According to Stephanie Caruana, author of 'Skeleton Key and Memoirs' which contains 250 pages of actual gemstone files, both Roberts and his father were murdered for authoring the volumes. Between 1976 – 2006, six books have been written based on the Skeleton Key.

'The Gemstone File: Sixty years of Corruption and Manipulation Within World Government Detailing the Events Surrounding the Assassination of JFK.' Richard Alan; (1992) This 400-page book consists of clippings from major publications which elucidate many details supporting the Gemstone File thesis.

'The Gemstone File,' Jim Keith, ed. (1992, IllumiNet Press, 214 pages) Includes the Skeleton Key, an interview with Stephanie Caruana, excerpts from Mae Brussell's two 1977-8 KLRB radio broadcasts on the Skeleton Key and Bruce Roberts' Gemstone File, Kiwi Gemstone and articles by Jonathan Vankin, Robert Anton Wilson, Kerry Wendell Thornley, Ben G. Price and others.

'Project Seek,' by Gerald A. Carroll (1994, Bridger House. 388 pages). Extended documentation of Skeleton Key. Includes Kiwi Gemstone, discussion on Robert F. Kennedy and Martin Luther King Jr., assassinations, interviews with an employee of Hughes, and etc.

'Inside the Gemstone File,' by Kenn Thomas (Steam Shovel Press) and David Hatcher Childress (1999, Adventures Unlimited Press, 250 pages). Explores connections between Ian Fleming's 'James Bond' novels and movies and the Skeleton Key. Includes Kiwi Gemstone, account of Danny Casolaro's mysterious death, Com-12 Briefing Documents, interview with Stephanie Caruana, and etc.

'**The Opal File,**' also known as 'The Kiwi Gemstone,' is a paper written by Anthony Pollock that links the Skeleton Key to the politics of Australia and New Zealand. This paper has been included in several of the books on Gemstone listed here.

'**The Gemstone File: A Memoir,**' by Stephanie Caruana (2006, Trafford Press, 480 pages). Contains an updated, expanded 'Skeleton Key 2', related articles by Stephanie Caruana and Mae Brussell, 220 edited pages from Bruce Roberts' original handwritten Gemstone File letters; the Kiwi Gemstone, and other items.

Stephanie Caruana

Mae Brussells

Aristotle Onassis exercised more control over American history than has ever been disclosed. While kidnapping Howard Hughes he stole ruby rod technology from Hughes Tool, working with insider and former FBI informant, Robert Maheu.

The Testimony of Mr. Truly Ott

Mr. Ott inadvertently came into possession of a key Gemstone file. The following is an account, in his own words given to author and Videographer John Hankey on September 12, 2007.

While examining "The Las Vegas Files" in 1995, Ott happened upon a sealed, manila envelope that a financial planning client had placed in his trust a decade earlier. Ott had completely forgotten about it and decided to call his client. Upon doing so, Ott learned that his client had suffered a stroke a year earlier, was in his seventies, confined to a nursing home and in very poor health. His wife knew nothing of the file and suggested Ott dispose of it.

Initially, Ott threw the envelope away, but his curiosity got the best of him. Recovering and then reading the contents, he was stunned at what he discovered. It was 'file #5' of a group of 7 files called the 'Gemstone' files. He didn't know what the other six files contained, but this file shocked and alarmed him like nothing he had ever read. It described in full detail how the CIA planned and executed John Fitzgerald Kennedy, President of the United States. The file was very thorough, and contained items such as photostats of canceled checks, travel vouchers, orders on CIA letterhead, lists of participants, disposition of witnesses and evidence, and etc. To his amazement, Ott recognized the names of many of the key men who participated in the assassination, as well as the massive cover-up that followed.

The file was extremely damning towards George H.W. Bush, who in 1963 was the unofficial head of the CIA in Dallas. The obvious involvement of the FBI and Dallas PD, and their subsequent squelching of information as outlined in the file made Ott physically ill. There was no person in Federal Law Enforcement he could trust with this information, assuming it was even legitimate! He thought the file might be fiction, and every aspect of his reasoning, instinct, learning, and research supported that conclusion. But he wondered why his client even had such a file, and why – if he died suspiciously – he would want the file sent to Beverly Hills, CA and to Hank Greenspan of The Las Vegas Sun newspaper. Ott realized the conundrum facing him. If true, this document would shake the foundations of American government. He was inclined to shred its contents but couldn't bring himself to do so. Instead he kept the file hidden until a chance meeting with an editor from 'George' Magazine.

During the summer of 1998, Ott was involved in actively protesting the expansion of Circle 4 Farms gigantic hog factory farm into Iron County. His grass-roots citizen's organization, Citizens for Responsible and Sustainable Agriculture, (CRSA) had received a bit of notoriety, with several AP wire stories circulating their story nationally. One such story caught the eye of a publication called, 'George' Magazine. The editor and staff contacted Ott and scheduled an appointment to meet and review his story.

The editor of 'George' Magazine flew into Cedar City in his private plane to meet Ott and shoot a photo spread. They spent all of Saturday together. At the end of the day, at a local steak house, they sat down for dinner. Over salad, Ott confessed that he had never heard of 'George' magazine. The editor reached into his briefcase and handed him a copy. Ott was surprised to see that it was owned and founded by John F. Kennedy Jr. Ott asked him about John and his politics and was told that John was a real 'champion of the underdog' which was why they were producing the story on CRSA. Ott replied, "I believe that my image of John is like most Americans. The enduring image of little 'John-John' courageously stepping forward and giving his best salute as the caisson carrying his father's body slowly rolled by. Tell me, does John accept the 'official Warren Commission' account of the assassination or does he think there was more to it? At this late date, does it even matter?"

The editor nodded and said, "Of course he doesn't accept the Warren Commission, but there is not a lot he, or anyone else can do about it! I guarantee you, it does indeed matter, at least to him. It is one of his major goals in life to find out the truth!" Ott replied, "Has he ever heard of something called the 'Gemstone Files?" With that, the air became electrified. The editor laid down his salad fork and said, "What do you know about the Gemstone?" Ott answered, "Oh, it just might be that I have a copy of file #5. Does that interest you?" He almost screamed, "You can't be serious! Are you serious? Don't kid me about something like that! Where did you get it?"

The dinner was immediately over, even though their steaks were just coming from the kitchen. They had them placed into containers to take out. The editor had to see the infamous Gemstone immediately. He couldn't wait until the meal was finished. It was late on a Saturday night in Cedar City, Utah. Ott handed him the file and he offered to compensate him for it. Ott refused, asking only one thing in return; if the information proved out to be genuine, he wanted to know. He wanted justice to be served, and the guilty parties prosecuted.

Ott was awakened the next morning at 5:00 a.m. John's editor explained that he had been up all night reading the file. He had called John directly and was instructed to fly it back immediately for John. John again offered to compensate Ott up to $10,000 for the information. He felt it was that good. Ott politely refused and gently reminded him of his earlier request. For him, that would be payment enough.

The rest of 1998 went by quickly. The national political stage was being set. George W. Bush was seeking to secure the nomination to run against Vice President Al Gore. On July 5, 1999, Ott's home phone rang. His wife, Joan, answered it and said, "True, it's for you." As he answered, a very polite masculine voice on the other end said, "Hello True Ott, do you have a moment to speak? This is John Kennedy calling!" Ott immediately asked him to hold and went to the privacy of his home office to take the call. After a few minutes of small talk, he told Ott, "Well, I understand that you want to know what I think of your file. I want you to know that I have spent over six figures in private investigators to verify its contents. I can say to you without hesitation that its contents are indeed factual. As a matter of fact, because of this file, a federal grand jury with be convening within the next few weeks. It is my opinion, as well as my attorneys', that this federal grand jury will pass down an indictment against George Herbert Walker Bush for conspiracy to commit murder against my father and will also indict others as the evidence unfolds. If George W. thinks he can run for dogcatcher after this grand jury convenes and his father is indicted, he is sorely mistaken."

Ott was thrilled, yet deeply saddened by John's disclosures. He asked John how he felt about making this information public. Did he understand that it would shake American politics, especially the Republican Party to its very foundation? JFK Jr. replied, "Yes, I do realize the gravity of the story and my accusations, but the guilty must be brought to justice." Ott pressed, "But, Mr. Kennedy, how do you feel?" The phone went silent for a minute or two. Then John replied, "I feel like a mighty weight has been lifted from my shoulders. For the first time in my life, I feel empowered. I feel my Father's spirit beside me on this, and finally, I can exorcise a few demons from my life." He was emotional, and very close to tears. Ott was as well. He would forever be a part of American history. He had helped a brother's search for truth.

He warned John to be careful, suggesting that such actions were potentially very dangerous. John agreed and said that he was taking every precaution. Then, in a quiet voice, he asked Ott for his banking information, wanting to wire $50,000 to Ott's account. Ott declined, saying "Give it to charity. I don't think it is right to accept money for such terrible information. I am totally satisfied knowing the file went to the very person that needed it the very most! Above all, John, please BE CAREFUL!" John thanked Ott profusely and said that he wished there were more people in America like True Ott. He said that someday, he would somehow return the favor. Ott liked that. It was good to have made a friend such as John Kennedy Jr.

A little over two weeks later, on July 16, 1999, John Kennedy Jr., along with his wife and her sister, were killed in a plane crash enroute to Hyannis Port for a family wedding. Ott's new friend was gone, and the guilty involved in both murders have still not been punished. There is no doubt whatsoever why John was killed. Unequivocally, it was not an accident. Ott was informed that the original Gemstone file was lost with John's plane.

USA Today cover, July 19, 1999.

Wisely, Ott had sent a copy of the file to his attorney in Washington, D.C. Fearing for himself and his family, he has not made the file available to anyone since that time. (giving it to others would violate the 'détente' agreement.) Columnist Jack Anderson evidently saw the file several years ago and has declined to discuss it with anyone. Best to let sleeping dogs lie. The sobering truth is that the criminal cartel running the United States is simply too big and too powerful for the common man to fight. (3)

George Herbert Walker Bush

George H.W. Bush is on record stating he couldn't remember where he was when President Kennedy was assassinated. Apparently, he and E. Howard Hunt were the only two people on the planet over the age of five who didn't know where they were at 12:30 p.m. on November 22, 1963. Ask any number of people who were alive at the time, and they can tell you exactly where they were the day our President was murdered. The memorandum (page 279) was provided to the FBI in Houston shortly after JFK was assassinated. Curiously, it was sent by George Bush of Zapata Oil.

Note: There is no reference to George H.W. Bush in any official capacity. He was just a private citizen who heard some gossip about a potential assassin named Mr. James Parrott. It turns out Mr. Parrott was nothing more than an individual who painted campaign signs for the local Republican headquarters. Assassination was not even in this man's realm of consciousness.

George H.W. Bush needed to go on record regarding his whereabouts the morning of the Kennedy killing. Parrott was the perfect stooge, local Republican headquarters the perfect stage. Bush could control everything.

Although Bush claimed he couldn't remember where he was, researchers have been able to locate his whereabouts that day. The image on page 280 shows the entrance to the Texas School Book Depository Building shortly after the assassination of President John F. Kennedy. Many researchers believe the man standing on the extreme left of the photograph in the narrow tie is George H.W. Bush. On page 280 is an extreme enlargement of the image of this mysterious man in Dealey Plaza alongside a known image of George H.W. Bush during the same era. Neither George H.W. Bush nor E. Howard Hunt could remember where they were on November 22, 1963. Ironically, two photos of E. Howard Hunt were also found, showing him in Dealey Plaza on November 22, 1963.

Additional evidence of George H.W. Bush being in Dallas and more importantly, proof of his intelligence background with the Central Intelligence Agency was disclosed one week after the JFK assassination pursuant to a document released by J. Edgar Hoover.

UNITED STATES GOVERNMENT

Memorandum

TO : SAC, HOUSTON

DATE: 11-22-63

FROM : SA GRAHAM W. KITCHEL

SUBJECT: UNKNOWN SUBJECT;
ASSASSINATION OF PRESIDENT
JOHN F. KENNEDY

At 1:45 p.m. Mr. GEORGE H. W. BUSH, President
of the Zapata Off-shore Drilling Company, Houston, Texas,
residence 5525 Briar, Houston, telephonically furnished
the following information to writer by long distance
telephone call from Tyler, Texas.

BUSH stated that he wanted to be kept confidential
but wanted to furnish hearsay that he recalled hearing in
recent weeks, the day and source unknown. He stated that
one JAMES PARROTT has been talking of killing the President
when he comes to Houston.

BUSH stated that PARROTT is possibly a student
at the University of Houston and is active in political
matters in this area. He stated that he felt Mrs. FAWLEY,
telephone number SU 2-5239, or ARLINE SMITH, telephone
number JA 9-9194 of the Harris County Republican Party
Headquarters would be able to furnish additional information regarding the identity of PARROTT.

BUSH stated that he was proceeding to Dallas, Texas,
would remain in the Sheraton-Dallas Hotel and return to his
residence on 11-23-63. His office telephone number is
CA 2-0395.

ALL INFORMATION CONTAINED
HEREIN IS UNCLASSIFIED
DATE 10-15-93 BY 9803 ADD/KSR
(JFK)

GWK:djw
(2)

Schmidt —

Jackson —

62-2115-6

SEARCHED_____ INDEXED____
SERIALIZED 224 FILED 224
NOV 28 1963
FBI - HOUSTON

Letter from George H.W. Bush warning of JFK assassination attempt.

279

Is this George H.W. Bush standing in Dealey Plaza on November 22, 1963?

Mystery man in Dealey Plaza and known image of George H.W. Bush (R).

Possibly E. Howard Hunt (red arrow) on Houston Street.

E. Howard Hunt crossing Elm Street moments after assassination of JFK.

This document surfaced in 1988 while George H. W. Bush was running for President. He was asked to comment since it implicated he had an intelligence background with the CIA. The 41st President said, "It must be another George H.W. Bush in the CIA."

Although difficult to read, the last paragraph on the preceding memorandum (page 283) from J. Edgar Hoover says,

"The substance of the forgoing information was orally furnished to Mr. George Bush of the Central Intelligence Agency and Captain William Edwards of the Defense Intelligence Agency on November 23, 1963, by Mr. V.T. Forsyth of this Bureau."

On November 21, 1963, on the front page of the Houston Chronicle, below a picture of JFK and Lyndon Johnson is an article headlined, 'First Family Jets Toward Houston,' a brief article appeared entitled, "Harris GOP Chief Urges Cordiality,' with the kicker, 'FOR PRESIDENT.' The article quotes George H.W. Bush as saying that he hoped Houstonians, including Republicans, would offer the Kennedy's and their party a 'warm and cordial welcome befitting his high office.' The article continued, 'Bush said he hopes there will be no picketing or demonstrating against the President.' "I would strongly condemn this," he said, "It would be a disgrace to the President and the high office he holds. There may be some nuts around who might do something, but they won't be Republicans." The day after the assassination Houston Police Chief H. (Buddy) McGill admitted "I was scared to death something like this might happen here. I never really stopped shaking the whole time he (JFK) was here."

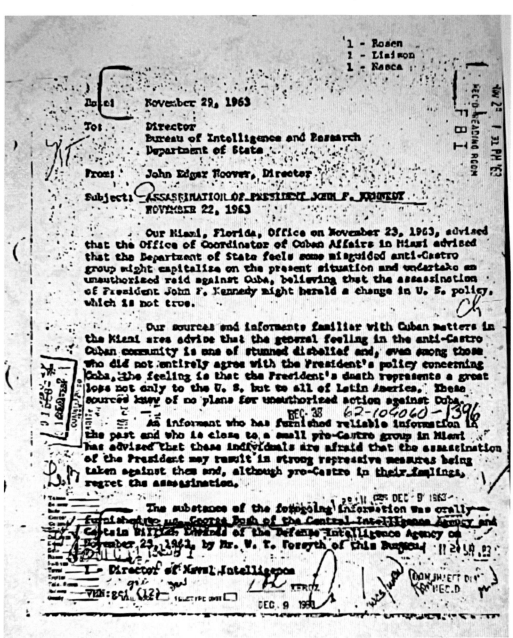

Date: November 29, 1963

To: Director
         Bureau of Intelligence and Research
         Department of State

From: John Edgar Hoover, Director

Subject: ASSASSINATION OF PRESIDENT JOHN F. KENNEDY
         NOVEMBER 22, 1963

         Our Miami, Florida, Office on November 23, 1963, advised
that the Office of Coordinator of Cuban Affairs in Miami advised
that the Department of State feels some misguided anti-Castro
group might capitalize on the present situation and undertake an
unauthorized raid against Cuba, believing that the assassination
of President John F. Kennedy might herald a change in U. S. policy,
which is not true.

         Our sources and informants familiar with Cuban matters in
the Miami area advise that the general feeling in the anti-Castro
Cuban community is one of stunned disbelief and, even among those
who did not entirely agree with the President's policy concerning
Cuba, the feeling is that the President's death represents a great
loss not only to the U. S. but to all of Latin America. These
sources knew of no plans for unauthorized action against Cuba.

         An informant who has furnished reliable information in
the past and who is close to a small pro-Castro group in Miami
has advised that these individuals are afraid that the assassination
of the President may result in strong repressive measures being
taken against them and, although pro-Castro in their feelings,
regret the assassination.

         The substance of the foregoing information was orally
furnished to Mr. George Bush of the Central Intelligence Agency and
Captain William Edwards of the Defense Intelligence Agency on
November 23, 1963, by Mr. W. T. Forsyth of this Bureau.

         Director of Naval Intelligence

REC-38   62-104060-1396

Letter from J. Edgar Hoover regarding information on JFK assassination
dated 11/29/63.

The following was from the March 1997 'George' Magazine article, 'Assassination of Rabin.' It lists the following:

The Gemstone Files

Aristotle Onassis exercised more control over American history than we were aware of. He stole ruby rod technology from Hughes Tool while kidnapping Howard Hughes and working with insider and former FBI informant, Robert Maheu.

Clinton Complacency

President William Clinton claimed not to have been notified about the loss of JFK Jr. or the debauched search and rescue efforts until 5:00 a.m., July 17, 1999. The thought is purely inconceivable. Approaching the end of two terms in the White House, the Clinton's began preparing for their political future. They focused their attention on developing Hillary as a politician (even though she had no actual experience) and selling influence while they still had it...buy now, pay later...payable to what would become 'The Clinton Foundation.' Hillary suggested the purchase of a home in New York which would allow her to run for the Senate in the upcoming election. There was just one obstacle. JFK Jr. had entered the political scene. New York was electric with the word of JFK Jr. reclaiming his father's legacy. A piece of Camelot was still alive in America, and donors began to line up. Hillary knew she could never defeat the son of JFK in the Northeast. "I'm not going back to Arkansas!" (4)

Assassination research often involves scanning the field for likely suspects who aren't visible. The CIA is the specter in the legacy of John Jr.

The following six pages are excerpts from an incredibly well written and substantiated article written by Dr. Michael Salla for EXONEWS April 10, 2018:

"If the Clintons were involved in the death of JFK Jr., it would be ironic since Bill Clinton sought to find out who killed President Kennedy just before his inauguration in January 1993, presumably to avoid a similar fate. The answers he received later helped Hillary Clinton launch her political career.

Only months before the crash, Hillary Clinton had declared her candidacy for the Senate seat, but was running into criticism for being a carpetbagger since she and Bill Clinton were not New York residents.

According to a New York Daily News story published on July 20, 1999, JFK, Jr., was secretly planning to run for the Senate seat despite Hillary having already declared her candidacy. Given that the private poll showing that "John F. Kennedy Jr. was by far the state's most popular democrat, it is likely that he would have been victorious."

Kennedy's entry into the Senate seat race would have denied Hillary the start she was seeking to her political career just before Bill's impending Presidential retirement.

There is a Memorandum containing a set of eight policy directives drafted by Dulles on behalf of a mysterious committee called Majestic 12 (MJ-12) in charge of advanced aerospace programs. One of the eight directives, Project Environment, gave cryptic authorization for the assassination of any public official that threatened Majestic Twelve operations.

JFK JR. MULLED RUN FOR SENATE IN 2000

BY JOEL SIEGEL ✔ FOLLOW

NEW YORK DAILY NEWS   Tuesday, July 20, 1999, 12:00 AM

A private poll in 1997 found that John F. Kennedy Jr. was by far the state's most popular Democrat, and two friends said yesterday they believed he would have run for office some day. Earlier this year, in one of the best-kept secrets in state politics, Kennedy considered seeking the seat of retiring Sen. Daniel Moynihan (D-N.

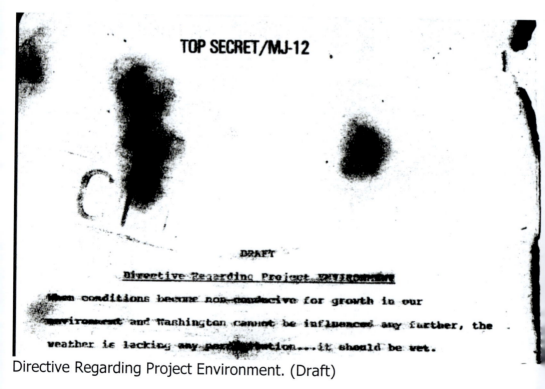

Directive Regarding Project Environment. (Draft)

Draft – Directive Regarding Project Environment – When conditions become non-conducive for growth in our environment and Washington cannot be influenced any further, the weather is lacking any precipitation ... it should be wet.

Dr. Robert Wood, who is the foremost expert in analyzing MJ-12 documents using forensic methods, has concluded that the partially burned document is an assassination directive. In an interview discussing the burned document, he pointed out that the cryptic phrase "it should be wet" originates from Russia, where the phrase "wet works" or "wet affairs" denotes someone who had been killed and is drenched with blood.

In the book, 'Kennedy's Last Stand,' I analyzed the testimonies, circumstances and documents supporting the conclusion that Dulles had arranged for the MJ-12 directives to be applied to the Kennedy administration in general, and to President Kennedy in particular.

The CIA's Counterintelligence chief, James Jesus Angleton, was given the authority to carry out the MJ-12 directives, as documented in a leaked November 12, 1963 Memorandum released only 10 days before Kennedy's assassination.

The Top-Secret Memorandum instructed then Director of the CIA, John McCone, to share all classified UFO information with NASA, in order to fulfill its requirement as outlined in National Security Action Memorandum (NSAM) 271. Its requirement as outlined in National Security Action Memorandum (NSAM) 271.

TOP SECRET

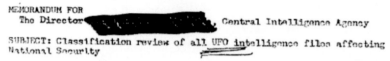

November 12, 1963

MEMORANDUM FOR
The Director ▓▓▓▓▓▓▓▓▓▓▓▓, Central Intelligence Agency

SUBJECT: Classification review of all UFO intelligence files affecting National Security

As I had discussed with you previously, I have initiated ▓▓▓▓▓▓▓▓▓ and have instructed James Webb to develop a program with the Soviet Union in joint space and lunar exploration. It would be very helpful if you would have the high threat cases reviewed with the purpose of identification of bona fide as opposed to classified CIA and USAF sources. It is important that we make a clear distinction between the knowns and unknowns in the event the Soviets try to mistake our extended cooperation as a cover for intelligence gathering of their defence and space programs.

When this data has been sorted out, I would like you to arrange a program of data sharing with NASA where Unknowns are a factor. This will help NASA mission directors in their defensive responsibilities.

I would like an interim report on the data review no later than February 1, 1964.

/S/ John F. Kennedy

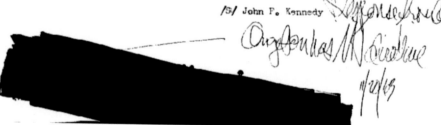

Letter to CIA Director John McCone from JFK dated November 12, 1963.

In short, the two memoranda Kennedy issued on November 12, 1963 would ensure that access to classified UFO files would be extended to more government agencies, ultimately resulting in direct Presidential access.

Such direct access had been denied to President Kennedy by McCone's predecessor, Allen Dulles, who retired as CIA Director in November 1961, but likely continued on in his other position as head of the MJ-12 Committee as suggested in the eight MJ-12 Policy Directives.

It's feasible that the MJ-12 Directives drafted by Dulles and approved by the MJ-12 Committee were used not only for the 1963 assassination of President Kennedy, but also for the removal of his son, 36 years later.

There have been many questions raised about Kennedy's plane crash and whether or not it was simply due to his inexperience as a pilot, compounded by marital and financial problems, as suggested in an official report by the National Transportation Safety Board. Was the report a cover up for the plane being shot down or sabotaged in a targeted assassination conducted by the CIA?

So why would the CIA want to help Hillary Clinton attain public office, and was this related in any way to Dulles' mysterious MJ-12 Directives? To get an answer, we can begin with the Clintons involvement in a CIA drug operation run out of Mena, Arkansas during Bill's governorship. There have been multiple witnesses and documents showing how then Governor Clinton was protecting and facilitating the CIA operation in Mena.

In late 2017, the movie, 'American Made,' based on real events was released, showing how a former TWA airline pilot, Barry Seal, was recruited by the CIA to manage a covert operation out of Mena, Arkansas, involving illegal arms and drug running, and how Governor Clinton protected the entire operation.

The drug money was used by the CIA to finance MJ-12 operations secretly conducted throughout the U.S. in the development of advanced aerospace programs.

Having shown his usefulness in the CIA drug running operation at a state level, the MJ-12 group cleared the path for Clinton to become President so he could do the same at a national level.

By the end of Bill's Presidency, the CIA's "unofficial" black budget was estimated to be as much as one trillion dollars annually, which was more than double the Pentagon's budget at the time.

The Clintons had become a critical part of the CIA/MJ-12 operations at both state and national levels during Bill's political career. As Bill's Presidency wound down, Hillary's political career offered another opportunity for a compliant and heavily compromised political leader who would support the CIA's illicit fund raising for secret MJ-12 operations.

Secret deals were subsequently struck, and the CIA/MJ-12 (aka Deep State) supported Hillary's rise to political power, and the New York Senate Seat was intended to be her launching pad for high political office.

Consequently, when JFK Jr. was on the verge of publicly declaring that he was going to run for the Senate seat, not only did he threaten Hillary's nascent political career, but he also threatened the carefully crafted plans for future CIA funding of MJ-12 operations. Therefore, the same or a similar policy directive to Project Environment, which had been used to assassinate President Kennedy, could now be used against JFK Jr. for his threat to MJ-12 operations."

Linking JFK Jr.'s 1999 plane crash with Hillary Clinton and the CIA is certainly controversial. Close examination of the history of the Clintons and CIA secret Deep State actors such as MJ-12 provides a powerful rationale for why JFK Jr. was perceived as a threat and assassinated in a plane crash made to look like an accident. The conspiracy group QAnon also believed this theory. The authors of this book do not believe in QAnon theories.

Sixteen

<u>'Delbert' and CIA Division 4</u>

The following article was written and posted on www.TomFlocco.com on August 31, 2005. In the article, a CIA Division 4 team member who went by the codename 'Delbert,' was interviewed regarding JFK Jr.'s death. It is very startling and names individuals in high Washington, D.C. positions as the primary planners of the murder of JFK Jr.

"I know I'm risking my life in allowing you to interview me; but I'm aware there is an operational grand jury and indictments regarding the White House, so now is the time. I'm tired of knowing all the details and perpetrators of the murder of an innocent and good man without seeing justice. John's death has caused tremendous trauma throughout the Kennedy family," said a (40'ish) ex-operative who consented to discuss the investigation and his part in writing the JFK Jr. plane crash preliminary and final reports by the FBI. "Just refer to me as 'Delbert.' That's good enough," he said, adding, "If they will kill 'John-John,' they'll kill anybody."

"One of my family members was related to JFK Jr.'s grandmother, and although it was not a blood relationship, I had at least a half dozen lengthy conversations with John during the years before he died. We liked each other and hit it off; so, this was why John opened up to me and seemed to trust me regarding his future plans to run against either Hillary Clinton for the Senate or George W. Bush for the Presidency in 2000. John had many conversations with my relative; and he gave her permission to discuss his political aspirations with friends, so this was not a closely held secret. But what was interesting was that John told me he was pretty sure he could win either of those races."

The long time Special Forces and Division 4 operative's explosive evidence, witness testimony and his team's suppressed and classified final report naming former President's Bill Clinton and George H.W. Bush, current President George W. Bush and Senator Hillary Clinton among others as being involved in orchestrating the assassination of John F. Kennedy Jr. will require U.S. Special Prosecutor Patrick Fitzgerald to hear testimony to investigate John Jr.'s death as part of his ongoing grand jury probe involving White House crime families.

U.S. Special Prosecutor Patrick Fitzgerald.

During three exclusive interviews with TomFlocco.com, the ex-operative told us the final classified report specifically said, "JFK Jr.'s plane broke in half just aft of the cabin. The damage was caused by a plastique (C-4) shape charge which was formed along the bottom of the fuselage and up along both sides of the walls. The charge was caused to be set off or exploded with a large spark generated by a barometric switch device triggered by the altitude of the plane. In other words, the assassins chose the altitude for the explosion of the plane—a standard procedure to make the target's murder look like an accident."

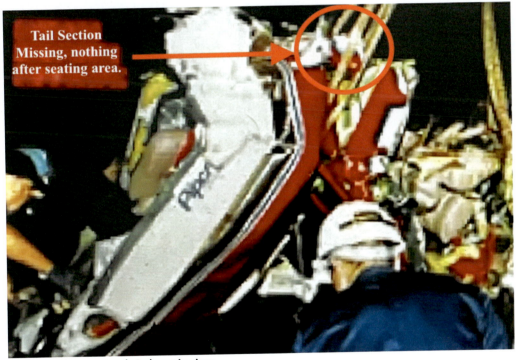

Tail section completely missing.

Delbert said his team and their witnesses and families have been in physical jeopardy since 1999, "because the media did not report the truth about what happened" and that all involved are now placing their lives in the hands of Fitzgerald and his deputies to prosecute the evidence—charges that will serve to mitigate compromised media outlets now protecting the White House with spin and insinuations that Fitzgerald is using the "perjury trap" to manufacture crimes instead of genuinely seeking evidence.

Sources close to one grand jury indicate the spin will not work this time. The U.S. intelligence community is monitoring the work of all the prosecutors and grand juries. Serious crimes with supporting evidence involving three branches of government and the media have already threatened the long-term survival of the Republic.

We learned that scores of witnesses were interviewed by Division 4:

(a) At the scene of the explosion off Martha's Vineyard in Massachusetts.
(b) When the plane and bodies were recovered.
(c) In the White House regarding the assassination plot prior to the crash, and
(d) At the airport concerning what witnesses saw three days before Kennedy's plane took off.

Collectively, they tell a different story than the media—one that might ultimately rival the political intrigue surrounding ancient Rome's ruling Caesars.

The Decision to Come Forward

After observing that the Interpol JFK Jr. preliminary report (filed three days after the crash, but later leaked within the intelligence community for a number of years) had remained online for the last six months, contact was made with stewwebb.com where we first saw the document. Webb had already faxed the document to more than 300 top electronic and print media outlets which collectively ignored it.

We inquired whether it would be possible to interview one of the active or retired Division 4 members who conducted the actual investigation and wrote the reports, given the rapidly gathering swirl of secret grand juries.

A former member of the Division 4 International Murder Investigative team named Delbert, who helped write the reports and interview witnesses, was asked to come forward by Stewart Webb and was subsequently contacted by TomFlocco.com, consenting to several interviews to discuss his findings in the leaked preliminary report and reveal specific names and evidence details contained in the final classified report which has been withheld from the American people.

Delbert told us today that he cringes when he reads the report and thinks about it being in 'general' circulation: "It was NEVER meant for general dissemination and consumption; and frankly, I'm somewhat appalled when I think of it being 'out there.' The final report was cleaned up grammatically and the actual facts presented in a much clearer, concise manner leaving out any speculation. But I regret this report ever getting out."

Grand jury activity notwithstanding, what piqued our initial interest was a feeling that the Division 4 team, with experience tracking murderers across the globe and placed on loan to assist an overwhelmed FBI for the JFK Jr. probe—had apparently conducted an investigation far more complete than what the mainstream media was telling its trusted viewers and readers.

Denver Field Office
July 19, 1999
Location On-Site: Long Island, New York

Subject: Aircraft Crash And Apparent Death Of John F. Kennedy Jr.
Requesting Agency: FBI

Status: Open – subject to final review – management and General Assembly. Nature – Suspect.
Repeat – Suspect. Case review – Final – non-withstanding review. Request open
Status pending Final. Eyes Only – Chief Bureaus.

Subject, John F. Kennedy, Jr., left Essex County Airport, Caldwell, N.J., at 8:38 P.M.
Friday, July 16, 1999 in a Piper Saratoga II TC. Aircraft was built in 1995, purchased last
year by subject. It has been reported to have been in excellent condition – simple and
comfortable to fly. Subject did NOT file a flight plan (?) and it is suspected he altered his
route. We strongly (suspect) this to be true. Visibility was eight (8) miles – I say again –
visibility was eight (8) miles. Media reports of "hazy" or "foggy" conditions are untrue.
Subject's flight path took him over the Connecticut shore, after passing over the south-
Western tip of Rhode Island. Aircraft banked and began its approach to Martha's
Airport at 9:26 P.M. Subject was expected at Martha's Vineyard Airport by no later than 10:00
P.M. At 9:39 P.M. JFK radioed the Martha's Vineyard Airport giving his location. Subject was
completely calm, giving no indication of any difficulties, stating that he was making his final
approach, no more than 10 miles from the shore, and 13 miles from the airport. Subject then began
his (final) descent. Subject was at 5,600 feet when he headed out over the ocean. When he
radioed at 9:39 P.M., 17-18 miles West of Martha's Vineyard, he was at 2,500 feet. When
detected on radar 29 seconds later, he was at 1,800 feet, 16 miles West of Martha's Vineyard.
He was then lost off radar. No MAYDAY was ever heard. Tower personnel at Martha's Vineyard
Airport verified previous data.

Within app. 10 seconds of this final radio contact at 9:39 P.M., an aircraft fitting
the description of the subjects (aircraft) and in that same general location was identified
on Radar by both Military personnel and Martha's Vineyard Airport tower personnel
as descending 1,200 feet in 12 seconds – a full, head-long dive, in other words. A reporter
for the Vineyard Gazette newspaper told WCVB-TV in Boston that he was out walking

298

Friday night about the time of the crash and saw a "big white flash in the sky" just off Philbin Beach. Luggage, a tire, Plexiglas, pieces of the cowling have all washed up on Philbin Beach. Said reported has now partially recanted his story by stating that "perhaps It was a bright light from an explosion, but he just cannot be sure". Reporter has been "gotten to", compromised. Unknown as to who, at this time. Several local news reports initially (reported) that several people SAW and Heard an explosion in the air over the ocean South of Martha's Vineyard towards Eastern Long Island, at the same time that subject's plane "went missing". We have confirmed these reports by speaking with 4 of the witnesses whom have asked to remain anonymous. Detected definite fear on their part. All evidence at this time indicates that aircraft was in a fiery, head-long crash dive within Seconds after the 9:39 radio transmission. Aircraft was equipped with a radar transponder That transmit a 4-digit ID code and the altitude. Aircraft contained a 406 MHz satellite Distress beacon which would have notified the FAA of exact lat.&long. Device was NOT Activated. Believe reason as aircraft disintegrated instantly. Coast Guard claims of an Emergency beacon thought to belong to this aircraft being activated and heard, by the Coast Guard at 3:40 A.M., Saturday, in Long Island, New York, are as yet unsubstantiated. Subject has been reported by all interviewed, including 3 flight instructors, to be an Excellent pilot who did not take chances. Subject had logged many hours and had acquired An abnormal amount of expertise for an individual holding a pilots license for only 15 months. In fact, it has been reported that JFK, Jr. had logged enough hours, and acquired enough Expertise to qualify as a Commercial Pilot! He had passed instrument checks with no reported difficulties. Although subject did not like Flying at night, all information indicates he did so efficiently. Media's reports of "pilot error", "failed instrument test and checks" and "scared to fly at night" are patently untrue. Standard American Media disinformation.

When SK Alpha team began investigating weather anomalies and any possible phenomena, (weather), Radar images/data that have proven useful in such investigations, to include the observations of Electromagnetic/radio frequency phenomena, where discovered to be missing from the archives for the Eastern Long Island/Martha's Vineyard area during the two (2) critical hours in which JKF Jr's Plane apparently crashed/disappeared. This is/was more than suspect. After demanding said data from air control personnel, and receiving stammering, red-faced explanations as to it's whereabouts, team notes data has been intentionally "misplaced", or in fact lost. This indicates that the subject's aircraft was indeed "shot out of the sky", with either a C4 charge, placed aft the cabin, a bomb, activated on descent by a barometric switch or a Particle Beam Laser, fired from Montauk Point. Agency is quite familiar with the evil legacy of Montauk Point. Technology reputed to be null and void is in fact known to be in existence there, and being employed against the American public. This includes not only this Laser, but (Mkultra) mind-control, Remote Viewing, the infamous "Montauk chair", and so on. We strongly suspect one of the latter two technologies was used against subject's aircraft. Currently, evidence points to the Laser, although this cannot be completely substantiated. Intrigue Assessment is based on following facts;

(1) A bright light, or explosion was observed by app. 10 people in the area of the aircraft's disappearance.,

(2) The headrest, steering yoke, pieces of the cowling, Plexiglas and carpeting where literally torn apart from/off the plane, floating up on Gay Head Beach. This indicates a mid-air explosion not a stall and crash. Debris from the crash have also been washing up on the West end of Martha's Vineyard, creating a very wide spread area of destruction (in other words, the remains of the aircraft are spread out over a very large area of space on the Ocean, indicating a mid-air explosion, not a stall and crash).

(3) Recorded conversations with air traffic control all indicate a calm, relaxed pilot in full command of the flight, with no difficulties in the final approach. Seconds after the last transmission, the explosion was observed and contact was lost with subject's plane.

(4) Previously mentioned weather and electromagnetic/radio frequency data has been lost, or misplaced. Since this typical NEVER happens, a cover-up of some sort is strongly indicated.

(5) The wings of the aircraft where NOT torn off, which they would have been had subject's Plane gone into uncontrollable dive, as being reported by the American press.

(6) If aircraft had had engine trouble, as reported, it should/could have simply gone into a slow glide and made a soft-water landing.

(7) No MAYDAY was ever heard, indicating catastrophic occurrence. No satellite distress beacon was activated, indicating pilot did not have time to do so.

(8) Forensics and physical evidence thus far in regards to suitcases, pieces of the aircraft, etc., indicate a violent explosion of some sort, but not that of a C4 type device.

(9) The aircraft plummeted from the sky at Terminal Velocity.

(10) All reports from subjects flight instructors indicate a very good pilot, who did not take Unnecessary chances or risks. Qualified for all aspects of flight for the particular aircraft being flown. The chances of him loosing control and plummeting in the manner now being described by the mass media or almost impossible.

(11) We have learned that subject was preparing to either run against Hillary Clinton in the New York Primary, or for the Presidency in 2000 (which we believe he would have won). Knowing Clinton's methods of political intrigue, and the app. 300 murders he and his wife are guilty of, it is possible this is three more to add to the tally. Also, knowing the saga of the Kennedy bloodline, and the Illuminati's obsession with this bloodline issue, the Kennedy's certainly being a member of this organization, it is entirely possible that these murders where ordered by (the Illuminati) because of a reported feud between the Kennedy's and the Rockefellers or the Cameron's. The Kennedy's have long been very unhappy with the (Illuminati) due to the murder of JFK, Sr. having been threatened and blackmailed into silence. Every indicator points towards JFK, Jr. having "had enough" of this humiliation and planning on turning his magazine "George" into a true political vehicle for change. For the American public, not for the New World Order. In fact, he had already begun this process by publish factual exposes on George Wallace and the Rabin assassination. This alone is enough to have gotten him killed.

(12) Subject had begun looking into to his Fathers murder, and had developed plans to slowly expose those involved (in his magazine).

(13) Subjects wife may have been pregnant. Again, the bloodline obsession of the Illuminati, not wanting to risk another JFK (for the people) and his offspring, had them killed instead. There has long been rumors from this evil entity that it was considered a mistake that when in 1963 JFK, Sr. was killed, that the remaining family was allowed to live. Perhaps they decided to "rectify that mistake".

(14) The American Press/mass media are now releasing news reports that are far from factual. In fact, they can be considered, at best, to be (classic) disinformation, if not outright lies. In the initial reports that where released, the essential truth of the situation, the facts where (being released). However, what is now being reported is (essentialy) leaving out the essence of truth and simply glossing over what actually occurred. Again, what we regard as standard American Press procedures, disinformation at best. This strongly indicates a cover-up, else the truth would still be reported.

(15) Although request onsite by Federal agencies, team has been coherced to "back off", albeit subtly and quietly. This particular tactic speaks well for itself. We have not "backed off", nor well we.

(16) Kennedy family will NOT comment, other than a prepared speech by Caroline. End of Prepared statement definitely indicates full knowledge and awareness of event surrounding JFK Jr's murder.

Conclusion:

Subject was a qualified pilot, in control of his flight, flying a reasonably new aircraft, in excellent condition. Visibility was 8 miles. Wind, calm. All indication from Forensics and Physical evidence investigations lend themselves to a violent explosion, either from a altitude or barometric pressure device, or from a Particle Beam Laser. Aircraft "broke up" in mid-air, as evidenced by wide-spread-debris gathered from the ocean and several different beaches. This can only be caused by an onboard explosion, or an attack by a missile or Laser.

Considering the nature of current political leanings of subject, and today's political atmosphere in America, and the before mentioned facts, there is little doubt that subject was assassinated. In fact, team considers this a Political Assassination of the highest order. It was meant to eleviate a potential threat to the ruling elite. And it succeeded.

Request final authorization – return file copy.

Not unexpectedly, the team was told to "back off," since its leaked preliminary report written by Delbert and another team member revealed specific contradictory evidence, calling JFK Jr.'s death to be a "political assassination of the highest order."

Division 4 investigative team's past exploits can currently be seen on the Discovery Channel in 'The Hunt for the Serpent,' about a serial killer they chased through Nepal, India, Pakistan, and China; but the team also became well-known for a chase through the Hudson Valley into Canada before capturing the Green Valley killer who had murdered 43 young prostitutes. As part of this international version of the FBI, the team specializes in tracking serial killers and pedophiles across foreign boundaries.

The 'Phoenix Project' and Assassinations

Years prior to serving on this team for three years, Delbert said he was a member of the U.S. Army Special Forces, attached to the Phoenix Project/Operation, on orders to "destabilize targeted governments by murdering government officials, elites, professionals, bankers, military leaders, teachers, professors and medical professionals."

"This started in Vietnam and then moved to Central America," said Delbert, adding "I was part of what we called the Bush-Clinton New World Order takeover to place in power selected individuals who received their marching orders directly from the U.S. government. Plain and simple, Project Phoenix required Americans to kill off innocent people to place in power those selected by the U.S. ruling elite; but I left, finding it very objectionable."

"These activities are still going on today," said the intelligence insider. "America now uses FBI Division 5, CIA Division 4, and elements from within the Department of Defense (DOD) and Defense Intelligence Agency (DIA) for its dirty work. Five-man Delta teams made up of nationals from Mexico and Ecuador are being trained for house-to-house extraction and murder of American citizens—when the day comes that Martial Law is declared and what little is left of our Constitution is scrapped."

"These (elements) are counter-intelligence goon squads of trained assassins which engage in covert operations both inside and outside the United States—with or without the knowledge of Congress which is supposed to be restraining them from actions against our own citizens. They're out of control—just a marvelous group of human beings," said the former intelligence veteran.

With a measure of insight into Delbert's background and credibility, we asked him to talk about Division 4's JFK Jr. findings, the specific content of the team's written accounts and the details of the assassination plot.

The Preliminary and Final Reports

The preliminary report and our three interviews with Delbert provide an open window template through which to view previous evidence that could point to prosecutable obstruction of justice by a grand jury regarding past FBI probes of major political figures who also died in plane crashes or in another manner. Ample evidence indicates that Congress has permitted the Bureau to serve as a private taxpayer-funded political cover-up arm for each White House administration.

A grand jury itself presents what amounts to a citizen-controlled fourth branch of government, set aside by founding fathers as a necessary precaution against corruption, obstruction of justice and/or treason on the part of the Supreme Court, White House and Congress—acting separately or in concert. Individuals talking to sources close to the grand jury told us that citizen panelists are currently reviewing powerful evidence with explosive documents and are dead-serious about cleansing the government.

A case in point for a grand jury to become operational would occur if, for example, Fitzgerald had witnesses who could corroborate that members of the Supreme Court received financial bribes in 2000 to install George W. Bush in the White House, or if Florida's elected officials destroyed voter ballots to prevent Al Gore from becoming the duly elected President for the same reason. In short, evidence would be collected, and the grand jury would hear testimony.

While John Fitzgerald Kennedy, Jr. was reported to have died in an accidental plane crash on July 16, 1999, Division 4's preliminary report reveals careful details dissimilar to those reported by news outlets, indicating what the team described in its report as "classic media disinformation, if not outright lies" pertaining to suspect circumstances surrounding the death of the only son of President John F. Kennedy who was himself assassinated on November 22, 1963 under a similar investigative cloud.

Most families of well-known politicians killed in "accidental" plane crashes were not afforded the opportunity of having a separate outside agency like Division 4 to investigate the evidence of their loved one's death as in the case of the son of an assassinated President. The preliminary report summary is revealing:

"Subject was a qualified pilot, in control of his flight, flying a reasonably new aircraft, in excellent condition. Visibility was eight miles. Wind, calm. All indication from Forensics and Physical evidence investigations lends themselves to a violent explosion, either from an altitude or barometric pressure device, or from a Particle Beam laser. (Delbert said Particle Beam laser was left out of final classified report). Aircraft 'broke up' in mid-air, as evidenced by widespread debris gathered from the ocean and several different beaches. This can only be caused by an onboard explosion, or an attack by a missile or Laser. (Delbert said missile and Laser were left out of final report) Considering the nature of current political leanings of subject and today's political atmosphere in America, and the before-mentioned facts, there is little doubt that subject was assassinated. In fact, team (Interpol Serial Killer Alpha Team) considers this a Political Assassination of the highest order. It was meant to alleviate a potential threat to the ruling elite...and it succeeded." (From the JFK Jr. preliminary report, filed on July 19, 1999. This document has been authenticated by several intelligence agents; and we were told copies have been passed around the intelligence community for several years.)

Four team members and two from another U.S. law enforcement agency who jointly participated in producing the final classified report, filed on August 5, 1999, revealed startling evidence which will prevent a continued cover-up.

The six members of the Division 4 team and others will have to be protected and then subpoenaed for sealed testimony, and the grand jury will also need to hear the testimony of scores of the team's interviewed citizen witnesses who have thus far remained understandably silent about what they saw and heard regarding JFK Jr.'s tragic death.

Delbert said the team's probe was rigorous. We found it staggering:

    (a)   30-40 witnesses were thoroughly interviewed.
    (b)   Ten individuals said they actually saw JFK Jr.'s plane explode in mid-air.

(c) Two witnesses told the team they saw George H.W. Bush and George W. Bush at the Essex County, New Jersey airport with Israeli Mossad agent Michael Harari and another Mossad agent who were both seen standing next to JFK Jr.'s Piper Saratoga—all four were at the airport just two days before the doomed plane took off with JFK Jr., his pregnant wife, and her sister.

(d) Several witnesses testified they overheard the murder plot being discussed in the White House Oval Office.

(e) One 'company' (CIA) witness at the scene saw the bodies and the damaged plane and told the team a mid-air explosion caused the crash.

(f) Approximately 150 witnesses gave individual depositions and signed statements for the final report.

(g) Three flight instructors who worked with JFK Jr. testified he was an excellent pilot and had logged a huge number of flying hours since being licensed—he loved to fly and was that good.

Delbert told us, "At the end of July, 1999, during the final phase of our investigation, we talked to several individual sources in the White House who consented to be interviewed as witnesses."

"We included their testimony in the final draft of the report which was classified until 2025—not currently available to any living individual," said the former operative.

"Since concrete evidence of a plot involving three Presidents and a Senator in the assassination of John F. Kennedy's son—who the report said they perceived as a political threat and future rival—would not exactly inspire public confidence in the government, it's probably that the American people will never see our final un-redacted report," said Delbert, "unless there are grand jury murder indictments and a public trial."

The Players

"The White House sources we interviewed overheard conversations involving individuals who made the decision to murder JFK Jr.," said Delbert, who joined three Division 4 fellow operatives and two other federal agency officials in alleging the following names in the final classified report as having participated in planning the murder of John Fitzgerald Kennedy, Jr. after the team had interviewed all the witnesses involved in the case:

The Division 4 team member told us, "The meeting to discuss the murder occurred in the White House Oval Office. The subjects named in the report who participated in ordering the murder of John Fitzgerald Kennedy, Jr. were President Clinton and his wife, Hillary—both in the room, former Attorney General Janet Reno—also in the room and who JFK Jr. had publicly called to task for her role in Waco and Ruby Ridge operations. FBI Director Louis Freeh—in the room, and former President George H.W. Bush, (now deceased) Lawrence Rockefeller (now deceased), and three Inner Circle Council of Thirteen members who were all teleconferenced into the Oval Office discussion via secure White House phone lines."

Quietly taken aback by the revelations, we asked Delbert to summarize the content of the alleged Oval Office murder plot overheard by the team's interviewed witness sources, including witnesses assigned to White House domestic security:

(a) "Conversation about JFK Jr.'s magazine, 'George' becoming a political vehicle which could threaten ruling elite families and expose past White House crimes.

(b) Discussions about blowing up his Piper Saratoga, John Jr.'s vulnerability and even carelessness about his plane's security when warned that suspicious individuals had previously been seen lurking around his plane at the airport.

(c) Attorney General Janet Reno's problems with JFK Jr. criticizing Waco and Ruby Ridge.

(d) Speculation about who John Jr. would pick to run against in 2000—Hillary Clinton or George W. Bush.

(e) Discussion about political family factions and relationships between federal law enforcement, national security, and intelligence agencies.

(f) Discussion about how the assassination would take place, starting at the airport—with specific Mossad agents named by the subject conspirators without mentioning the actual Israeli agency.

(g) General agreement that John Jr., had become over-zealous in planning to employ 'George' to circuitously expose those who were behind the assassination of his father."

White House Controlled Foreign Assassination Teams in America

As we listened without comment, the Division 4 operative continued: "We were told by the same White House sources we interviewed that FBI Director Freeh left the Oval Office after the murder plot was discussed and met with Israeli Mossad agent Michael Harari who then met with his supervisor, General Rafael Eitan, considered to be one of the most dangerous Israeli agents who ever lived," stated Delbert.

Delbert explained that testimony by White House and airport witnesses and others will provide outrageous but credible grand jury evidence that three United States Presidents have their own private Israeli Mossad assassins—as well as assassins from several American federal government agencies—and will use them to commit treason and murder against other Americans perceived to post a political threat to their power, a fact surely to horrify Jewish-American and all U.S. citizens.

"I had heard that even our own FBI agents literally trembled at the fear of being assigned to watch General Eitan's movements, since collaborating congressional oversight allowed him to freely enter the United States at any time, using passports under a different name," the Division 4 special investigative team member said.

Delbert continued his shocking narrative, "About three days before John's plane took off and exploded in mid-air, Michael Harari, and another Mossad agent were seen with former President George H.W. Bush and his son Texas Governor George W. Bush at the Essex County, New Jersey airport where John Jr.

kept his plane." This fact was also confirmed by separate U.S. intelligence sources who are also willing to testify before a grand jury.

"All four were positively identified by an aircraft mechanic and a maintenance worker we interviewed for the final classified report; but we didn't include their names of the names of some other key witnesses so that there would be citizens left to testify in case the Clintons or Bushes started having people murdered," said the former Special Forces member.

Delbert's chilling words provided concrete and credible proof that congressional oversight over counterfeit immigration documents acquired by assassins and terrorists, wide-open U.S. borders and homeland 'security' is so seriously flawed, broken down and corrupted that Senate and House members are permitting known foreign murderers to move around America at will.

Given the state-side depletion of National Guard and Reserve troops which renders the U.S. more vulnerable to foreign enemies while pre-emptive war based on lies is being fought, the physical and economic security of the nation is problematic enough to assert that Senate and House members may literally be conspiring against their own constituents in favor of a clandestine world-wide agenda supported by assassination of 'troublemakers,' political or otherwise.

The American-French Alliance (AFA), a tightly-knit and hushed organization of active intelligence community patriots from both countries, is said to be waging an under-the-radar-screen war to stop rogue elements and assassins in the FBI, CIA, DOD, and DIA—supervised by the White House and directly linked to Al Qaeda and former CIA operative Tim Osman, also known as Osama Bin Laden (now supposedly deceased) but also British MI-6 agents from engaging in black operations throughout the United States.

According to intelligence sources who spoke with federal whistleblower Stewart Webb, the AFA reportedly killed General Eitan in October, 2004 for his role in stealing the U.S. atomic nuclear codes from the National Security Archives.

TomFlocco.com and other websites have previously reported circumstances surrounding an attempt by eight rogue British MI-6 agents to blow up the Chicago subway underneath the Everett Dirksen Federal Building where federal prosecutor Patrick Fitzgerald and a grand jury are investigating multiple crimes and treason linked to the White House.

The Physical Evidence

"The preliminary Division 4 team report was written with my partner who has retired and returned to his own country. We were joined by two others from our team and two more from another federal agency in putting together the final report," said Delbert.

"Our boss ordered us to re-write the final draft, but we refused. We wanted to tell the truth; so, they classified the (final report) until the year 2025 despite the fact that we had interviewed scores of witnesses who can corroborate all of our findings. This was August 5, 1999."

"The obstruction of justice by our 'upper management' and the FBI caused so much chaos that they dissolved our team, then they, quite possibly along with the Clinton White House, tried to have me murdered within ten weeks at the end of October, 1999 while working in Belfast, Ireland. I was supposed to be in a car with a friend who was blown apart in the explosion," said Delbert.

"That explosion was meant either as a warning or an assassination attempt, and cost the life of not only my associate, but a friend of his as well; so, I closed all my accounts, resigned from Division 4 and went underground by November 1999, for six months," he said—but not before devastating reports had been filed by a team of investigators experienced in tracking evidence and criminals all over the world.

"Every indicator point towards JFK Jr. having 'had enough' of this humiliation (report said threats and blackmailing of Kennedy family) and planned on turning his magazine, 'George' into a true political vehicle for change for the American public, not the New World Order. In fact, he had already begun this process by publishing factual exposes on George Wallace and the Rabin assassination. This alone is enough to have gotten him killed," said Delbert. He continued, "Subject (JFK Jr.) had begun looking into his father's murder and had developed plans to slowly expose those involved in future editions of 'George.'

"The American press/mass media are now releasing news report that are far from factual. In fact, they can be considered, at best, to be classic disinformation, if not outright lies. In the initial reports that were released, the essential truth of the situation, the facts were being released. However, what is now being reported is essentially leaving out the essence of truth and simply glossing over what actually occurred. Again, what we regard as standard American Press procedures, disinformation at best. This strongly indicates a cover-up, or else the truth would still be reported," said Delbert.

In previous chapters, we have discussed George H.W. Bushs' role in the CIA dating back to at least November 22, 1963. In reality, he was probably recruited during its inception in 1947 with his father's background in oil related business and his wartime experience.

In the book, 'The Immaculate Deception—The Bush Crime Family Exposed, retired U.S. Army Brigadier General Russell Bowen refers to a Freedom of Information Act (FOIA) memo unearthed in 1977-78, dated seven days after the assassination of JFK on November 29, 1963, describing the full briefing given to 'George Bush of the Central Intelligence Agency' on the day after the assassination. (1)

General Bowen was an original member of the Office of Strategic Services (OSS) during the 1940's with George H.W. Bush, Henry Kissinger, Allen Dulles, and others who became known as the secretive 'brown-shoe boys,' which later became the CIA. Bowen told Stewart Webb that Kissinger served as a dual spy for Germany and Russia during World War II before later becoming U.S. Secretary of State under President Nixon.

According to Army Brigadier General William Penn Jones, both George H.W. Bush and J. Edgar Hoover met with others (John McCone, Herman Brown, Lyndon Johnson, H.L. Hunt, and John J. McCloy to name the most influential) at Clint Murchison Jr.'s house in Dallas on the evening before JFK was assassinated in Dallas.

Since witnesses have connected George H.W. Bush to JFK Jr.'s airport and the White House assassination plot prior to his murder, Special Prosecutor Patrick Fitzgerald would be negligent if the grand jury did not also probe the Hoover FOIA lawsuit evidence linking the ex-President to events surrounding the assassination of John Jr.'s father, JFK.

All of this information raises serious grand jury questions:

(1) Why has George H.W. Bush denied being in the CIA on November 22, 1963?
(2) Why was George H.W. Bush, at the age of 39, fully briefed on JFK's assassination on the day after the event?
(3) What does he know about J. Edgar Hoover being at the Murchison home in Dallas the evening before JFK's assassination?
(4) What was discussed at this meeting?
(5) Why did Hoover specifically name George H.W. Bush in the memo dated November 29, 1963?

George H.W. Bush also denied being involved in Iran Contra. But according to General Bowen, "Investigators obtained copies of Colonel Oliver North's diaries which documented Bush's role as a CIA supervisor of the Contra supply network. In 1988, Bush issued false statements to Congress, testifying he knew nothing about the illegal supply flights until late November, 1986; yet North's diary shows Bush at the first planning meeting on August 6, 1985."

After considering the team's gathered physical evidence, written testimony, and our talks with 'Delbert,' who had interviewed most of the investigation witnesses involved, rhetorical questions could be posed regarding how the mainstream media could be so controlled and manipulated that it would be able to cover up the obvious.

How come the media saw things differently than the Division 4 team? Were key editors, reporters, and global media executives' co-participants in obstructing justice by glossing over a political assassination? The simple answer is...yes. With Bill Clinton signing the 1996 Telecommunications Act, all media is now controlled by six companies or individuals. (2)

Three U.S. Presidents and at least one Senator were having their own private teams of foreign assassins available to do their political bidding, the ball is now in Special Counsel Fitzgerald's 'court.' This while Congress looks the other way, knowing it needs to be held accountable for gross corruption.

Considering what historians already know about the September 11 attacks and previously the Oklahoma City bombing, thousands of government agents are prepared to block obstruction if 'deals are cut' or 'private payoffs' are attempted in order to prevent the wheels of justice from turning. It wouldn't matter. Fitzpatrick never issued any subpoenas or sequestered a grand jury for any of the possible suspects in JFK Jr.'s murder.

If approximately 150 witnesses and credible evidence is not enough to render proper justice in the assassination of the son of an assassinated U.S. President, then the American justice system is not worth the paper that the Constitution and the United States Code are written on. It is quite obvious that someone 'got to' Patrick Fitzgerald and are likely deserving of separate consequences. However, we now know that will not happen.

There is nothing noble about what U.S. government leaders have done to America since November 22, 1963. As a country we have learned to 'look the other way.' With the death of America's Prince, John Fitzgerald Kennedy Jr., we continue to deny true justice to the New World Order elitists which have been running the United States and the world since a bright sunny day on a street in a modern city where JFK was killed because he wanted peace in the United States and world.

In June 1992, while being interviewed by Sarah McClendon of the White House Press Corps, she asked, George Bush, "what will the people do if they ever find out the truth about Iraq-gate and Iran Contra?" George H.W. Bush replied, "Sarah, if the American people ever find out what we have done, they will chase us down the streets and lynch us."

It is too late for justice against George H.W. Bush's involvement for the crimes against humanity he committed, but it's not too late for others.

Seventeen

<u>The Demise of George</u>

Unfortunately, with the passing of John F. Kennedy Jr., his wife Carolyn, and his sister-in-law, Lauren, the magazine 'George' also died tragically. What began in September 1995 with its tagline, 'Not Just Politics As Usual,' ended January 2001, merely 17 months after the murder of JFK Jr.

The debut issue with Cindy Crawford dressed as George Washington was brilliant. This cover set the tone for what the magazine would become. It's easy to say, 'Not Just Politics As Usual,' but the magazine was more in the style of Rolling Stone, Esquire, or Vanity Fair. The consistent underlying theme was to marry the themes of celebrity and media with the subject of politics in such a way that the general public would find political news and discourse about politics more interesting to read. (1).

Notable contributors included:

- Paul Begala
- George Clooney
- Kellyanne Conway
- Ann Coulter
- Al D'Amato
- Roger Black
- Al Franken
- Stephen Glass
- Rush Limbaugh
- Norman Mailer

First Edition of 'George'

- Chris Matthews
- Steve Miller
- Cathy Scott
- W. Thomas Smith Jr.
- Jackie Stallone
- Naomi Wolf

When it first appeared, 'George' was extremely popular due to its founder, JFK Jr. After initial success, 'George' started losing money rather quickly, primarily because JFK Jr. refused to capitalize on his name or image. To boost sales, the magazine featured articles that were controversial. Among those was the 1997 issue wherein JFK Jr. lambasted his cousins Michael

Kennedy and Joe Kennedy II, whose marital scandals had recently made news, as 'poster boys for bad behavior.'

Critics of 'George' called the magazine, 'the political magazine for people who don't understand politics,' and 'stripping any and all discussion of political issues from its coverage of politics.' Spy Magazine was even more harsh stating, 'politics overlapped with Pop Culture in such a limited number of ways', and 'scrambling for celebrities Hollywood Starlets as often as possible to put on the cover and then trying to figure out what that person had to do with politics.'

After the murder of JFK Jr., Hachette Filipacchi Magazines purchased Kennedy's portion of the magazine from his estate and continued to publish for more than a year. Due to failing advertising, the magazine ceased publication in 2001, 17 months after JFK Jr.'s murder. Sadly, the last issue of 'George' featured JFK Jr. on the cover, an idea that he always refused in order to sell magazines. In fact, JFK Jr. even refused to have photos of himself in his own magazine, despite the fact that he had interviewed numerous guests for the publication.

Despite all the controversy over 'George' covers, in the 24 years since his murder, JFK Jr.'s instincts have been proven correct. Politics and pop culture have become so intertwined that candidates now spend nearly as much time courting voters on late-night talk shows as they do on the Sunday morning talk circuit. Politicians are now revered by the media as if they were celebrities, while celebrities seek out a voice on politics. Donald Trump was largely a product of reality television, and his predecessor recently signed a production deal with Netflix. In

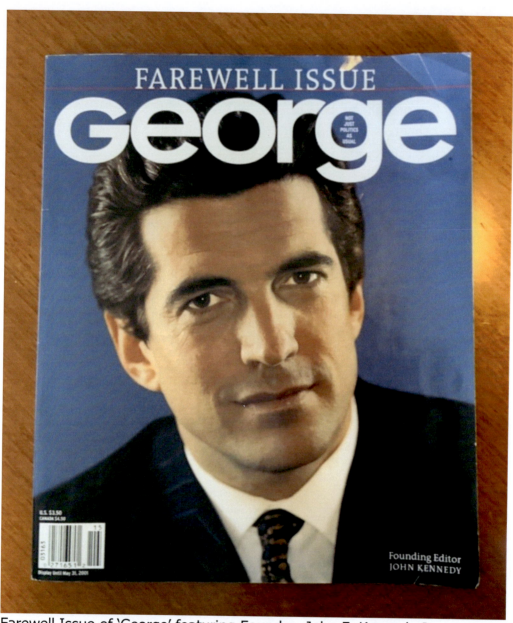

Farewell Issue of 'George' featuring Founder, John F. Kennedy Jr.

2022, Oprah Winfrey has been seriously touted as a potential Presidential candidate for the 2024 Presidential election. Why do celebrities think they have a better answer for America than anyone else? As the son of the 35th President and an elegant First Lady-turned-book editor, JFK Jr. was uniquely positioned to cover and promote the marriage of politics and pop culture, because he lived it. The four years he was editor for 'George' was designed to prep him for his family's business, politics.

JFK Jr.'s plan was to build the magazine to a successful status so it would survive without his name in the event he pursued a political career. He had built a fiercely loyal team at 'George' and created a new paradigm to think about politics. The problem facing John was separating the personal from the professional. He was a professional in editing, but it was personal because of his family's history. It was the Kennedy name that persuaded publishers, advertisers, and readers to take a chance on him, but at the same time, it was his family's legacy that complicated his role as an editor and led to conflicts both inside and outside the magazine. Frank Lalli, the editor who replaced Kennedy said, "John died before his time...and this magazine died before its time."

Matt Berman, 'George's' creative director worked with JFK Jr. into the spring of 1994. It was John Kennedy's salesmanship that persuaded Berman into selling his firm and going into business with John. They brought along Berman's former employee, Rose Marie Terenzio as their assistant. The internet was in its infantile stages. The early 1990's were a golden age for glossy magazines. People magazine had a subscription rate of 3.1 million readers a week in 1994. Being on the cover of People, LIFE, Vanity Fair or Rolling Stone could make a semi-famous celebrity a household name.

Demi Moore was photographed nude and pregnant by Annie Liebovitz for the cover of Vanity Fair. Rolling Stone called the grunge band, 'Nirvana' the new faces of rock. However, Berman and Kennedy were finding it difficult to obtain financing to start their magazine, even with JFK Jr.'s famous name. The idea of a political magazine interwoven with celebrities was risky. Besides, who would want to advertise in such a magazine?

Kennedy pitched the idea of 'George' to publishing giant Hearst, which owned Esquire and Cosmopolitan. Samir Husni, who consulted with Hearst in the mid-nineties said, "They (Hearst) thought it was too political, too hot of a potato to handle." He continued, "They didn't see a business model that would sustain the magazine, even with Kennedy's name."

In early 1994, a most unusual investing partner, David Pecker, President of Hachette Filipacchi Magazines agreed to fund 'George.' Hachette Filipacchi was known for producing Elle, Car and Driver, and Woman's Day magazines. Pecker is more recently known for his friendship with Donald Trump and his current company, American Media Inc, who publish the National Enquirer. Pecker is also famous for squelching negative stories about candidate Donald Trump in 2016. Pecker agreed to invest $20 million over a five-year period for 'George' Magazine giving the nascent publication its birthrights. Pecker discussed the early days of 'George' which he wanted to change the name to 'CrissCross.' He said, "John had shopped the idea for 'George' to all the major publishers, many of whom, like Jann Wenner, were personal friends. One by one they turned him down, usually with the excuse that a magazine connecting politics and pop culture would never work."

With the initial issue, JFK Jr. knew the importance of the first cover establishing the magazine on its own merits and not as the 'John Kennedy Magazine.' While brainstorming cover subjects, he invited photographer Herb Ritts, a friend of John's and Berman's over to his TriBeca loft. Sipping on Rolling Rock beer with girlfriend Carolyn Bessette, John suggested Bill Clinton for the first cover.

Ritts suggested supermodel Cindy Crawford, who at the time was the face of Pepsi Cola. Bessette jumped up, "Cindy Crawford's perfect!" She continued, "She's all-American, a self-made woman, sexy, strong, and smart." Ritts suggested dressing Crawford as George Washington, a cheeky play on politics and pop culture. They all agreed and Kennedy himself called Cindy asking her to adorn the first cover.

JFK Jr., Michael Berman, and David Pecker at the unveiling of 'George.'

"He called me directly at my hotel," said Crawford. "Who's going to say no to John F. Kennedy Jr.?" After talking with him and photographer Ritts, Crawford said, "I'm going to do what? Dress like George Washington with a wig and everything?"

On September 7, 1995, JFK Jr. specifically chose Federal Hall, where George Washington took his Presidential oath, for the first press conference on his newest venture. He began his speech jokingly, "I don't think I've seen as many of you in one place since they announced the results of my first bar exam." He talked about the purpose of his magazine, and when asked what his mother would think about his new venture, JFK Jr. said, "I think she'd be mildly amused, glad she wasn't standing here, and very proud."

'George' did not shy away from political issues. One of the biggest stories of the 1990's was President Clinton's relationship with intern Monica Lewinsky. A Hollywood script could not have provided a better story. Even Kenneth Starr's September 1998 report revealed that Lewinsky tried to get a job at 'George' after leaving the White House. Instead of focusing on Clinton and Lewinsky, JFK Jr. interviewed Gary Hart, another politician brought down by a sex scandal. This issue also provided a profile of Clinton confidant Vernon Jordan, and a column on workplace sexual harassment, something not popular for the time period.

"John had great reluctance to cover the Monica Lewinsky scandal," said Berman. "But if we didn't cover it, we kind of would've been completely irrelevant." Some of the reluctance may have been due to the fact that Kennedy's father had multiple affairs while in the White House. When asked at a press conference covering the launch of 'George' if the magazine would cover the sex lives of politicians, he said, "It would be disingenuous to say I don't have some sensitivity to the seamy side of issues."

JFK Jr. covered the political issues of the day. He never shied away from Presidential stories. All in all, he kept his sense of humor regardless that his magazine was slowly losing advertising revenue. Again, John knew that 'George' was a steppingstone to other ventures. Mayor of New York, Congress, the Presidency? All were possible and not necessarily in that order.

JFK Jr. comedic memo to staff about long hours.

JFK Jr.'s favorite photo of himself.

JFK official portrait in the White House.

The photo on page 326 was JFK Jr.'s favorite of himself. It proves the apple doesn't fall far from the tree.

The world will never know what JFK Jr. would have aspired to become. The only assurance for those who believe in destiny would be that he followed in his family's footsteps, serving others who are less fortunate. When being interviewed about his future, JFK Jr. had the following response. "People often tell me I could be a great man. I'd rather be a good man."

JFK Jr. was a good man. He would've eventually become great, even though his own opinion of himself wouldn't allow him to gloat. His mother and sister raised him to respect others, help others and be his best. The world is a much shallower place without John F. Kennedy Jr. We were callously and heartlessly deprived of perhaps the last chance to rise above those who are determined to subjugate the American public in pursuit of their own interests.

Eighteen

How It Really Happened

July 16, 1999

John picked up Lauren Bessette from work late afternoon on that fateful day. They fought sweltering heat and oppressive traffic, finally arriving at Caldwell around 6:10 p.m. John had sufficient lead time for preflight checks, a legal requirement for all pilots. He obtained a weather briefing, either from a computer or another automated service. Multiple witnesses have confirmed that John made several trips to the phone or was seen using his cell phone repeatedly. Misinformation related to these calls suggest he was calling a 'Manchurian Candidate' flight instructor to accompany him on the trip.

In reality, Carolyn Bessette was getting her nails done at a small boutique in the city. A high-fashioned lady, the color had to match her gown exactly. She was annoyed with the repetitive calls from John and was heard saying, "The more you call the longer it will take." Her chauffeur was circling the block repeatedly, hoping for a timely exit.

John went about the business of preflight preparations, considered his weight and balance, and began loading the airplane. Lauren assisted. Heavy traffic delayed the arrival of Carolyn considerably. She arrived at the airport close to 8:00 p.m. John loaded her bags, and the three boarded the plane and buckled up.

John listened to the ATIS recording, contacted ground control, and taxied to the active runway. He completed his run-up. (A thorough check of flight and engine systems while still on the ground). John contacted the tower, received his clearance for takeoff, taxied onto the runway and applied full power to the meticulously maintained engine. The airplane climbed normally. John retracted the landing gear once clear of the field. The airplane traveled northbound through New York, then eastward tracing the Connecticut and Rhode Island coastlines. So far, the flight was uneventful. John made the crossing to Martha's Vineyard somewhere between Newport and Horseneck Beach. This route provided the additional safety of the Elizabethan Islands in the event of engine failure.

John had listened to the ATIS information at Martha's Vineyard and contacted the tower according to the frequencies programmed into his active communications radio. The call to the tower was confirmed by Steve Lagudi's testimony. He was the radio attendant who heard the call at Republic Airport Long Island.

Lagudi's statement lies in direct conflict with the NTSB's claim that there was no further communication with ATC after John departed Caldwell. Why the lie?

About seven miles Southwest of the Vineyard shoreline nefarious, catastrophic events began to unfold. John was in a standard cruise descent to the Island. Visibility measured at ten miles. John passed through 2,600 feet of altitude when inexplicably his airplane initiated two 'boiler plate' critical flight attitude maneuvers used to train pilots out of control. In fact, to the instructor's eye, John recovered from both appropriately. These two critical attitude procedures and their timing have puzzled author/pilot Ise for many years, despite extensive analysis.

Even more disturbing was their immediate proximity to what appeared to be a stunning, immobilizing, and catastrophic event that caused John's airplane to career out of the sky. It plunged in a nearly perfectly vertical descent at speeds that could only be achieved by severing the tail of the aircraft. The authors have no problem accepting the presence of explosives and their effects on the tail, but two critical attitude recoveries less than two minutes apart seems highly improbable, to this day haunting and terrible.

Very few assassinations are plotted or executed without at least one back-up plan. Most famous assassinations throughout history have always had a back-up in case the initial plot doesn't play out. Why would John's be any different? What if the aneroid bomb hadn't detonated as planned? What if he had reached his destinations and the device was discovered later? What if a huge investigation followed? What if he got to tell the story in 'George' Magazine?

This would have created unwanted, focused attention on murderers who were very clearly trying to remain anonymous. At the very least it would make any clean-up effort quite difficult.

The back-up assassination plan could very easily have been wired into the flight director (autopilot). This would have been a meager task for the electronic wizards of the time. Radio controlled airplanes have been in use for about 75 years, very simple technology in 1999. Alterations or controls could have been introduced through the flight director by remote means or programming. The autopilot would take care of the rest. This would also be timelier and more expeditious than conspicuous installations, including mechanical alterations to the plane.

The altered autopilot would be capable of completely controlling the aircraft. Little would be detected in the shattered remains of the flight director.

As a second benefit supplied by the puzzling critical attitude maneuvers is that they support the official narrative of John entering a death spiral. The plan was flawless. If the bomb doesn't get him, the autopilot can. When the bomb does get him, they could make it look like John got disoriented and crashed into the sea due to pilot incompetence.

Assuming the above scenario correctly sets the state, the last few minutes in John's airplane went like this:

At about 2,600 feet the flight director begins a climbing left turn with bank to approximately 30 degrees. John reacts by turning off the autopilot and leveling the plane, the natural thing a pilot would do at this point, turning it on again to assess the situation. This activity would not be considered a distracting or complicated affair, it's a mere flip of the switch. Considering the excellent visibility, it should have presented no challenge to John's piloting.

We would suggest that John flipped the switch back on and less than two minutes later the airplane experienced a descending right turn with increasing airspeed and rate of descent.

Suddenly, the force of an explosion within the aircraft blew the tail off, rendering its occupants immobile or unconscious. The airplane plunged into the North Atlantic at 4,600 feet per minute in a slightly inverted profile. Crash debris was spread over 120 feet of ocean bottom at a depth of 118 feet. There were no survivors.

John never had time to make a distress call, since everything happened within three minutes. According to diver observations the clothes were partially blown off one of the females. The weaker sides of the fuselage where doors and windows were located were blown clear of the debris field and supposedly never recovered.   A flash in the night sky was observed by several witnesses. Attorney Victor Pribanic heard the explosion while fishing. The FBI report speaks of surveillance radar picking up an outburst from the aircraft at the time of the crash.

There is a plethora of evidence indicating that explosives were responsible for the destruction of John's airplane. Whether the autopilot was rigged also is speculative but makes perfect sense in the sequence of events. The questions concerning who may have been behind the murders remain unanswered.

We pray John and the Bessette women were knocked unconscious by the shockwave and spared the terror and pain of their final moments together on their way to a cherished family celebration.

Nineteen

<u>The Cloak</u>

<u>July 17, 1999, 8:00 a.m.</u>

    Martha's Vineyard was already inundated with investigators, press, FBI, the FAA, and military officials. The search and rescue armada continued to saturate the land and seascape. Televisions everywhere were focused on the missing airplane and its occupants. The airport facility was highly restricted. The FAA was tending to their business regarding Control Tower Records. Oddly, there has never been any mention of CIA presence at the field, but one would imagine they were represented.

CAROLYN BESSETTE KENNEDY
1966-1999

JOHN F. KENNEDY JR.
1960-1999

LAUREN BESSETTE
1964-1999

Carolyn Kennedy, JFK Jr., and Lauren Bessette.

According to Adam Budd, field attendant, a strict hush order had been levied on anyone remotely involved in the unfolding drama. Adam unwittingly spoke with members of the press before receiving the hush order. He told the press of his experience with Air Traffic Control when he reported Kennedy overdue. Adam was immediately reprimanded and feared for his job.

The southwest shoreline buzzed with vehicles from various police agencies. Rescue personnel combed the shore in search of evidence. A good number of boats were already in place for a search and rescue mission. Miles of ocean was closed off to fishing and domestic traffic. Aerial searches commenced from Long Island to the Cape coastline.

During the dark of night, maritime search and rescue authority was snatched away from the Coast Guard and handed to the Air Force. This order required supervisory authority from the Pentagon.

President Bill Clinton.

President Bill Clinton dropped his coffee cup long enough to tell the American public, "No one informed me until 5:00 a.m." Reporters asked, "Why have search efforts been minimal at this point?" In true Ronald Reagan style, Clinton responds, "Well, they better get to work in a hurry, or they won't have jobs."

The aerial searchers were now ordered to focus their efforts at Horton Point, Long Island where a possible Emergency Locator Transmitter signal was received. They continued to search a bogus location for more than twelve hours.

More search and rescue vessels arrived at the island search site. The USS Grasp and NOAA sounding vessel Rude were ordered to the area. Five days later, using sonar sounding matrices and Remotely Operated Vehicles (ROV's) the teams discovered a 120' debris field. Further investigation with the ROV's proved that it was John's airplane.

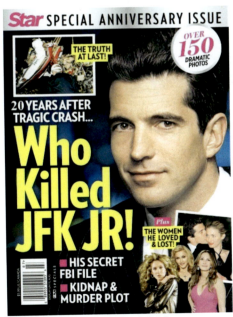

Star Magazine July 2019.

On the 20th anniversary of John's death, an article in Star Magazine described the crime scene. "The grisly discovery of America's favorite son, his wife, Carolyn, and her sister Lauren Bessette fell upon the Navy Salvage Vessel, the USS Grasp. Navy divers found John F. Kennedy Jr.'s body still strapped in his smashed pilot's seat. He was pinned just below the hips by the plane's engine, which had been violently shoved back by the tremendous impact as the aircraft slammed into the water." (1)

Clothed in a light-colored shirt, John's upper body was slumped forward over the control console. His arms swayed gently in the current. Behind him, their faces obscured by wreckage, were the bodies of two women. One of the women had her clothes partially blown off by the shockwave emanating from the explosion.

The roof of the plane above John and the two women had been ripped off. Carolyn and Lauren were buried under a considerable amount of debris. Divers struggled to free their bodies. A high-level decision was made to place the three in body bags before bringing them to the surface.

Sources have said videos of the recovery have been destroyed. No photos are part of any public record. Agencies deny having any visual record of the mission. The bodies were placed in caskets and autopsies lasting forty-five minutes were performed shoreside. The remains were allegedly cremated and subsequently scattered at sea the following day.

MISSING TAPES AND PHOTOS

Many of the tapes and photos recorded aboard the USS Grasp were destroyed. The following excerpts were also sourced in the same issue of Star Magazine mentioned on the previous pages. Admittedly, Star has a tabloid reputation however the cover up article they produced is an excellent example of good investigative reporting.

We quote: "The government released photos of the wreckage but mysteriously omitted material that could have been crucial in a wrongful death claim brought by the Bessette family."

Insiders claim that the disappearance and the ultimate destruction of that evidence was part of a cover-up dictated by Washington. While photos were released showing the remains of the plane on the surface, other photos and video tapes that show the plane in detail lying at the bottom of the Atlantic, including the lifeless bodies were destroyed. Veteran investigator James Brown, a member of the official panel that probed the crash said, "the investigation was dictated by Washington." Indeed, the recovery team had taken underwater photos and videos of the wreckage. These images contained crucial evidence about the crash. They were missing when the NTSB was forced to release a three-inch-thick dossier of photos and documents.

When asked about the missing underwater material in 2001, the Navy responded that they did exist. However, no photographs or videotapes were found at the command site due to the fact these items had been turned over to the NTSB. When asked, NTSB officer Melba Moye said at the time, "We don't have any underwater stills or videos."

In a statement from Captain Keith Arterburn, the Navy finally admitted that four standard VHS tapes were offered to the NTSB but declined. A spokesman for the NTSB says they were declined because they were unnecessary in determining the cause of the crash.

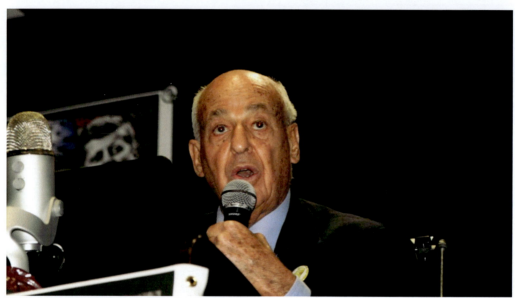

Forensic Pathologist, Dr. Cyril Wecht.

Forensic Pathologist Dr. Cyril Wecht, who has testified in many cases involving crash victims, was mystified at the exclusion of evidence. "It is difficult for me to comprehend why the NTSB would turn down potentially critical evidence," he said. "It's inconceivable."

Incredibly, Captain Arterburn went on to state that under a long-standing practiced procedure, after the NTSB declined the tapes, the Navy destroyed the tapes out of respect for the privacy of the families. He added that still photos had also been sent to the NTSB but only the tapes were returned. The NTSB denied keeping those underwater photos.

Investigator Brown later said that before they were destroyed, the tapes were kept so secret that not even he was allowed to see them. "Only a handful of people, from the NTSB, the FAA, and the military were privy to them." He continued, "It was the first accident I know of that was handled this way, in my opinion, it was dictated from Washington."

What we have here is a totally compartmentalized operation similar to the tactics employed in the tarnished investigation of TWA Flight 800. All the corrupt elements were already in place for the same machine to control the investigation into the crash of John Kennedy Jr. Disappearing and altered evidence, controlled observations made by select individuals, pertinent evidence withheld from legitimate investigators, spin-doctors controlling the media releases and witness intimidation (Adam Budd) are all common elements to both disasters.

The orchestrators of John and his family's demise had a walk in the park compared to TWA Flight 800. According to Hank Hughes, Chief NTSB Investigator for TWA Flight 800. "They made it look like something totally different than what happened. In all my career I never witnessed such a blatant display of procedural violation and disregard for the law."

Meanwhile, back on the Vineyard, searchers gathered washed up remains. A piece of luggage, John's duffle bag and pilot's logbook and a piece of landing gear were all turned over to various officials never to be seen again. The remains of the airplane remained shrouded behind a solid wall at Otis AFB for a short duration. It was then released to insurance officials and promptly shredded.

Every organized assassination has a cleanup plan. Consider the more than 200 witnesses that died very suspiciously after the JFK assassination.

In John's case, the cleaners did a superb job.

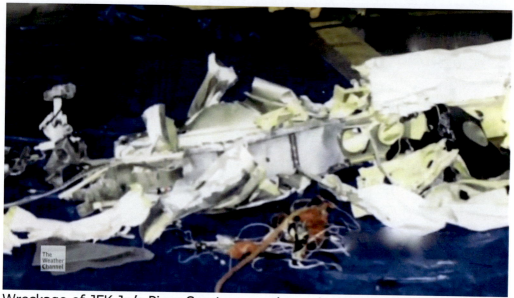

Wreckage of JFK Jr.'s Piper Saratoga as shown by The Weather Channel.

The authors find it interesting that despite overwhelming proof that the murders of President John F. Kennedy, Robert F. Kennedy, and John F. Kennedy, Jr. were all irrefutably the result of conspiracy, that the government of The United States of America continues to ask us to believe in the lies they have contrived and continue to promulgate. They obviously believe that we Americans are ignorant, incapable of discovering the truth and perfectly content to march forward and salute the flag in complete disregard for their heinous criminal activity. For every action there is an equal and opposite reaction. We pray the pendulum has begun to swing back in the right direction!

Footnotes

Growing Up Kennedy

(1) 'It Didn't Start With Watergate' by Victor Lasky, The Dial Press, New York, 1977.
(2) Ibid.
(3) 'The Good Son,' by Christopher Anderson, Gallery Books, New York 2014.
(4) 'The ovine fetal sympathoadrenal response to the maternal administration of methamphetamine,' J. Dickinson, R.L. Andres, and V.M. Parisi.
(5) part 1:1452-57 1994, Am. J. Obstet. GynecoL 170.
(6) 'The Strange Saga of JFK and Dr. Feelgood,' New York Magazine November 22, 2013.
(7) 'One Hell of a Gamble: Khrushchev, Castro, and Kennedy, 1958-1964: The Secret History of the Cuban Missile Crisis,' by Aleksandr Fursenko and Timothy Naftali, W.W. Norton & Company, August 17, 1998.
(8) 'The Good Son,' by Christopher Anderson, Gallery Books, New York, 2014.
(9) 'The Day John Died' by Christopher Anderson, Harper Collins, New York, 2000.
(10) 'Prince Charming: The John F Kennedy Jr. Story,' by Wendy Leigh, New American Library Revised Edition 1999.
(11) 'Jacqueline Bouvier Kennedy Onassis: The Untold Story' by Barbara Leaming, Macmillan, 2014.
(12) 'Prince Charming, The John F Kennedy Jr. Story,' by Wendy Leigh, New American Library Revised Edition 1999.
(13) 'The Day John Died,' by Christopher Anderson, Harper Collins Books, 2000.

(14) Testimony of Sandra Serrano, eyewitness to the assassination of RFK.

(15) 'Prince Charming: The John F Kennedy Story,' by Wendy Leigh, New American Library Revised Edition 1999.

(16) 'Chappaquiddick: The Real Story.' by James E T Lange and Katherine Dewitt, St. Martin's Press March 1993.

(17) Ibid.

(18) St. John Hunt, personal memory of time period.

Becoming His Own Man

(1) 'Prince Charming: The John F Kennedy Story,' by Wendy Leigh, New American Library Revised Edition 1999.

(2) Ibid.

(3) 'The Good Son,' by Christopher Anderson, Gallery Books, New York, 2014.

(4) 'Prince Charming: The John F Kennedy Story,' by Wendy Leigh, New American Library Revised Edition 1999.

(5) 'JFK Jr.' by Stephen Spignesi, Citadel Press Books, 1999.

(6) Ibid.

(7) 'The Good Son,' by Christopher Anderson, Gallery Books, 2014.

(8) Ibid.

(9) 'Prince Charming: The John F Kennedy Story,' by Wendy Leigh, New American Library Revised Edition 1999.

(10) Forever Young, My Friendship With John F Kennedy Jr.' by William Noonan, Penguin Group, 2006.

(11) 'The Good Son,' by Christopher Anderson, Gallery Books, 2014.

(12) Peter Lawford: The Man Who Kept the Secrets,' by James Spada, Bantam, 1991.

(13) 'The Good Son,' by Christopher Anderson, Gallery Books, 2014.

(14) 'Prince Charming, The John F Kennedy Story,' by Wendy Leigh, New American Library Revised Edition 1999.
(15) Ibid.
(16) 'The Good Son,' by Christopher Anderson, Gallery Books, 2014.
(17) 'John F Kennedy Jr.,' by Elaine Landau, Twenty-First Century Books, 2000.
(18) Ibid.
(19) 'The Good Son,' by Christopher Anderson, Gallery Books, 2014.

Headlines in the Tabloids

(1) RFK Jr., Robert Kennedy Jr. and the Dark Side of the Dream,' by Jerry Oppenheimer, St. Martin's Press, 2015.
(2) 'JFK JR.,'by Stephen Spignesi, Citadel Press, 1999.
(3) www.vanityfair.com/magazine/1992/03/dunne199203.
(4) RFK Jr and The Darker Side of the Dream,'by Jerry Oppenheimer, St. Martin's Press, 2015.
(5) People magazine, August 16, 1993.
(6) 'The Day John Died,' by Christopher Anderson, Harper Collins Books, 2000.
(7) 'The Ten Most Fascinating People, Barbara Walters Special, ABC News, 1995.
(8) 'Good House Keeping' magazine, January 1995.
(9) 'American Son, Portrait of John F Kennedy Jr.,' by Richard Blow, Henry Holt and Company, 2002.
(10) Ibid.
(11) from a conversation with David Hunt.
(12) 'JFK Jr.,' by Stephen Spignesi, Citadel Press Books, 1999.
(13) 'Ibid.'

(14) John Kennedy Jr., One Step Ahead of the Pack, Quietly Travels to Cuba,' by Robert D McFadden, New York Times, October 25, 1997.
(15) 'Rabin's Wife Blasts JFK Jr.,' by Richard Sisk, New York Daily News, April 2, 1997.
(16) 'American Son, a Portrait of John F Kennedy Jr.,' by Richard Blow, Henry Holt & Co., 2002.
(17) Ibid.
(18) 'The Day John Died,' by Christopher Anderson, Harper Collins, New York, 2000.
(19) 'American Son, a Portrait of John F. Kennedy Jr.,' by Richard Blow, Henry Holt & Co., 2002.
(20) 'The Day John Died,' by Christopher Anderson, Harper Collins, New York, 2000.
(21) Ibid.

TWA Flight 800 and NTSB

(1) Hank Hughes, Lead Investigator NTSB TWA Flight 800 Video.
(2) Dr. Charles Wetli, Chief Medical Examiner, TWA Flight 800 Video.
(3) Retired Colonel Dr. Dennis F. Shanahan, Senior Consultant Medical Forensics TWA Flight 800 Video.
(4) Hank Hughes, Lead Investigator NTSB TWA Flight 800 Video.
(5) James Hall, Executive Director NTSB TWA Flight 800 Video.
(6) Hank Hughes, Lead Investigator NTSB TWA Flight 800 Video.
(7) Hank Hughes, Lead Investigator NTSB TWA Flight 800 Video.

(8) Hank Hughes, Lead Investigator NTSB TWA Flight 800 Video.

Iranian Air Flight 655

(1) 'The Persian Puzzle-The Conflict Between Iran and America, Kenneth Pollack, Random House, 2004.
(2) 'The Forgotten Story of Iran Air Flight 655, Max Fisher, The Washington Post, October 16, 2013.

John F. Kennedy Jr.—Pilot

(1) 'The Mail Archive,' RA Kris Milligan, July 28, 1999.
(2) 'NTSB Accident Report' ID No NCY99MA178, Full Narrative

July 18, 1999

(1) 'We've become Total Strangers,' New York Post, Jeane Macintosh, 1/7/2003.
(2) UPI Focus, ABC News, July 18, 1999.
(3) UPI Focus, ABC News, July 18, 1999.

(Falsified) Weather Reports

(1) FAA P-8740-30, Good Weather Briefing.
(2) NTSB Accident Report ID No: NCY99MA178, Full Narrative
(3) NTSB Accident Report ID No: NCY99MA178, Full Narrative
(4) NTSB Accident Report ID No: NCY99MA178, Full Narrative
(5) CNN, July 18, 1999
(6) Wikipedia, 2008
(7) AOPA Pilot Protection Services, Landmark Accidents: Vineyard Spiral, Bruce Landsberg, September 1, 2000.

(8)   NTSB Accident Report ID No: NCY99MA178, Full Narrative

Adam Budd Testimony & Final Descent

(1)   Boston Globe, Michael Zuckoff, July 20, 1999.
(2)   Classified FBI Report, Skolnick, 2005.
(3)   Classified FBI Report, Skolnick, 2005.

The Smoking Gun

(1)   UPI Focus, July 18, 1999.
(2)   The Education Forum, Don Jeffries, July 21, 1999.
(3)   The Mail Archive, Kris Millegan, July 27, 1999.
(4)   The Mail Archive, Kris Millegan, reprint Newshawk Inc., John Quinn, July 27, 1999.

Beginnings of a Cover-up

(1)   CNN.com, July 18, 1999.
(2)   NTSB Accident Report, NYC99MA178.
(3)   Hank Hughes, Lead Investigator, NTSB TWA Flight 800 Video.
(4)   Dr. Charles Wetli, Chief Medical Examiner, TWA Flight 800 Video
(5)   Retired Colonel Dr. Dennis F. Shanahan, Senior Medical Forensics, TWA Flight 800 Video.
(6)   Hank Hughes, Lead Investigator, NTSB TWA Flight 800 Video.
(7)   James Hall, Executive Director, NTSB TWA Flight 800 Video.
(8)   Hank Hughes, Lead Investigator, NTSB TWA Flight 800 Video.

(9) Hank Hughes, Lead Investigator, NTSB TWA Flight 800
     Video.

Autopsies and Further Discrepancies

(1) Boston Globe, Joanna Weiss, Matthew Brelis, July 23,
     1999.
(2) CNN.com, July 22, 1999.
(3) The Providence Sunday Journal, "The Last Flight of John
     F. Kennedy Jr.", Gerald M. Carbone, July 25, 1999.
(4) NTSB Accident Report, NYC99MA178.
(5) NTSB Accident Report, NYC99MA178.
(6) NTSB Accident Report, NYC99MA178.
(7) The Providence Sunday Journal, "The Last Flight of John
     F. Kennedy Jr.", Gerald M. Carbone, July 25, 1999.
(8) New York Observer, 'Dr. Bob Arnot's Parting Shot,' Joe
     Hagan, 2/16/2004.
(9) The Providence Sunday Journal, "The Last Flight of John
     F. Kennedy Jr.", Gerald M. Carbone, July 25, 1999.

Motive to Murder JFK Jr.

(1) 'The Inheritance: Poisoned Fruit of JFK's Assassination,
     Christopher Fulton, Trine Day Books, 2018.
(2) Wikipedia
(3) Rense.com, The Reason JFK Jr. Was Murdered, Letters
     from Truly Ott to John Hankey, 9-12-2007.
(4) Galactic Connection, October 29, 2017.

'Delbert' and CIA Division 4

(1) 'The Immaculate Deception—The Bush Crime Family Exposed, Russell S. Bowen, America West Publishers, (pages 31-39), 1991.
(2) 'RFK-Marked For Death—Another Son Sacrificed,' Fannin and Brennan, Cornerstone Publishing, 2023.

The Demise of George

(1) Wikipedia

How It Really Went Down

The Cloak

(1) Star Magazine, July 2019